# 英语语音学

## 第四版

主　编 ◎ 孟宪忠　孟　滢
副主编 ◎ 刘真真
参　编 ◎ 马　洁

A Concise Course of English Phonetics

华东师范大学出版社
·上海·

图书在版编目(CIP)数据

英语语音学/孟宪忠,孟滢主编. —4版. —上海：华东师范大学出版社,2022
ISBN 978 - 7 - 5760 - 3482 - 0

Ⅰ.①英… Ⅱ.①孟…②孟… Ⅲ.①英语—语音学—教材 Ⅳ.①H319.32

中国版本图书馆 CIP 数据核字(2022)第 226863 号

# 英语语音学

主　　编　孟宪忠　孟　滢
责任编辑　陈文帆
责任校对　曹一凡　时东明
装帧设计　庄玉侠

出版发行　华东师范大学出版社
社　　址　上海市中山北路 3663 号　邮编 200062
网　　址　www.ecnupress.com.cn
电　　话　021 - 60821666　行政传真 021 - 62572105
客服电话　021 - 62865537　门市(邮购)电话 021 - 62869887
地　　址　上海市中山北路 3663 号华东师范大学校内先锋路口
网　　店　http://hdsdcbs.tmall.com

印 刷 者　南通印刷总厂有限公司
开　　本　787 毫米×1092 毫米　1/16
印　　张　17.5
字　　数　238 千字
版　　次　2023 年 8 月第 4 版
印　　次　2023 年 8 月第 1 次
书　　号　ISBN 978 - 7 - 5760 - 3482 - 0
定　　价　55.00 元

出 版 人　王　焰

(如发现本版图书有印订质量问题,请寄回本社市场部调换或电话 021 - 62865537 联系)

## 第四版出版说明

在英语交际过程中,语音、语调的正误极大地影响口语交际的效果,也与英语口语的流利程度休戚相关。党的二十大报告针对增强中华文明传播力影响力提出"坚守中华文化立场,提炼展示中华文明的精神标识和文化精髓,加快构建中国话语和中国叙事体系,讲好中国故事、传播好中国声音,展现可信、可爱、可敬的中国形象。加强国际传播能力建设,全面提升国际传播效能,形成同我国综合国力和国际地位相匹配的国际话语权。深化文明交流互鉴,推动中华文化更好走向世界"。英语语音的准确、地道在传播中华文化过程中日显其重要性。本书初版以来,以其道理讲解简明、技能得以强化为特色,赢得广大师生的厚爱。本书历年重印,近年广泛用作高等师范院校教材,也被非师范类院校选作教材,更被列为英语自学考试参考用书。1991年以来,根据教学实际情况的变化,本书作过多次修订,在保持原有特色的基础上,以更为实用、更见实效的内在质量为21世纪的英语教学服务。

此次修订是在2006年出版的《英语语音学》(第三版)的基础上进行的。指导思想仍是语音三要素,并把顺序调整为正常的发音、节奏、语调。修订的主要内容是学习和推广吉姆森语音体系和普通型标准发音。发音要领简明扼要,条理清楚。发音插图元音部分全部改为四边形,直观性强,利于理解吸收。

# 第三版序

在国际交往日益频繁的今天,英语语音教学的重要性怎样强调也不会过分。学语言的、学文学的、学翻译的、学外交外贸的、学信息科学的、学航空飞行的……都不可轻视它。西方学者有句话是专门针对我们英语教师和师范院校学生说的:

A teacher of speech untrained in phonetics is as useless as a doctor untrained in anatomy.

——Gorge Sampson

这样看来,没有受过语音学专门训练的英语老师是没有资格站讲台的啊!

我国大中学校的英语教学,从整体上看,长期固守着琼斯(D. Jones)体系和琼斯音标,80年不变,而没有及时采纳早在20世纪六七十年代就已站稳脚跟的吉姆森(A. C. Gimson)体系和吉姆森音标,造成了我国英语语音教学落后于语言现实几十年的现象。《九年义务教育三年制初级中学英语》(试用修订本)和在全国使用最广的《大学英语》分别于2000年和2001年采取新式音标注音。但我估计许多英语教师对此音标体系的转换不甚理解,可能连新音标的正式名称也叫不上来。知道新旧音标的所谓对应关系者,黑板上见得到,口头上恐怕还是老一套祖母音。这种状况岂不误人子弟?

新音标是由琼斯亲手培养的学术接班人、国际语音学会主席、BBC口语顾问委员会主席、英国伦敦大学语音学教授吉姆森在1962年的一本语音专著中首先使用的。1977年被全面引入琼斯《英语发音词典》第14版,而后风靡全英和国际英语教学界。自那以后,牛津、剑桥、朗文各大出版社的辞书都在使用这套被语音学家们称作吉姆森音标的(the Gimson Transcription)音标体系。琼斯音标是20世纪上半叶保守型标准发音(Conservative RP)的体现,吉姆森音标则是20世纪下半叶至今流行的普通型标准发音

(General RP)的体现。它更注重运用基本元音(Cardinal Vowels)音标来更准确地标注元音音质。后者是前者的继承和发展,能较忠实地反映以 BBC 播音员为代表的、英格兰南部受过中等教育的中青年人口音为基础的普通型标准发音现状,是英国历史上认同度最高、英语世界流行最广泛、描述最详尽的音标体系。我在著名教学法专家张正东教授所著的《中国外语教学法理论与流派》一书中,对吉姆森音标体系的"时代性""精确性""精简性"和"实用性"进行了概括。读者还可以参考拙文《外语教学与研究》1998 年第 2 期《我国英语教学中的语音体系问题》,深入了解吉姆森体系的由来和发展。

吉姆森认为:英语标准发音(RP)应被视为一种在音位体系、音位读音和音位使用诸方面不断发展变化的语音模式。

孟宪忠教授的修订版《英语语音学》参照 2001 年第 6 版《吉姆森英语语音教程》,对英语各个音位进行了更为准确、更为现代化的描述,使音标与内涵更加一致,图表、分类更加符合国际规范,体现了"新世纪高等师范院校教材"的特色。这对培养中学英语师资无疑具有重要意义。

我非常赞成孟教授关于在基本理论指导下进行大量系统实践的主张。"学高为师,身正为范。"对师范生来说,理论与实践同样重要,二者必须携手前行,不可须臾分离。师范院校是培养"教练员"的地方,不能等同于一般的语言学校。目前英语语音教学的落后状况是理论研究不够深入、理论成果不能尽快普及,甚至遭到轻视、蔑视的倾向所造成的。时下实践不算少,就是有点"疯狂"。本书言简意赅,通俗易懂,脉络清晰,三大部分内容能够相互渗透融汇,如意群、节奏、句重音都可以同"语调组"划分、调核的确定、调型的选择结合起来讲。它们密切相关,放到口头交际中便是一家人了。

我衷心地希望使用本书的教师与同学认真培养对语音学理论的兴趣和热情,不同时期代表人物的教材和论文都应注意参考,如周考成、许天福、俞述翰、刘正仪等。还要特别留心英国语音学家们的最新教科书和词典,紧跟他们的描述和注音,便能悟出自己该怎样学,自己该怎样教,语音教学的重点和步骤是什么。

科学的语言理论都渗透着实践的汗水,所以才有神奇的功能。如 19 世纪提出的音位概念把每种语言中纷杂零乱的难以计数的语音归并整理成几十个一套能区别词义的音位;音位变体理论还能使这个比较抽象的语言单位返璞归真、生动鲜活地出现在连贯话语当中。20世纪诞生的区别性特征和对立性理论进一步明确了音位之间的关键区别和内在联系,促成了音系学公式在语音教学中的广泛运用。

我的语调教学经验也能证明理论功效之神奇。从1958年在南开大学求学起,我就爱听、爱模仿《灵格风英语》录音。二十多年的功夫取得了什么结果呢？听过的段落能说得跟录音差不多,未模仿过的新材料,自己读来总是觉得不地道。80年代初接受了当代英语语调理论训练之后,虽已年过四十,但耳朵越来越灵,分辨力越来越强,竟在某日突然发觉:啊,《灵格风英语》中

"唱片放在唱机上。

唱机搁在桌子上。

你正坐在桌子旁。"

这一连串大白话,还饱含着丰富的语调知识哩！如果我们把英国人怎样根据不断变化的语言环境划分语调单位、确定语调核心和选择语调模式的原则讲清楚,那学生也能模仿得惟妙惟肖,甚至举一反三,灵活运用。理论可以使人耳聪目明,提高口头交际能力,对此我深信不疑。

我也赞成编者关于灵活调整发音、节奏和语调讲授顺序的意见。在我国大中学校英语语音教学从琼斯体系向吉姆森体系转换的过程中,大家对普通型标准发音和吉姆森体系还很陌生。再说,近20多年来,英语标准发音又发生了较大变化。形势所迫,我们不得不加强发音教学。在吉姆森或后吉姆森体系中,音位总数减少了,音标式样增加了,音位分类更加科学。音位发音,特别是元音,变化尤其明显:前元音/e, æ/和双元音/eɪ/的起点依次向下移动,后元音/ɒ, ɔː/和/ɪɔ/的起点依次向上移动,后元音/ʊ, uː/向前、向央元音区靠拢,而前元音/iː, ɪ/在某些情况下,也有向前向高移动的趋势。与此同时,央元音/ɜː, ə/和双元音/əʊ/的起点却有所下降。我将此类变化称作"反时针方向元音大转移",看来比较稳妥。今年11月,四川大学出版社聘请四位操标准发音(RP)的南英人士为拙作《英国英语语音学和音系学》和《现代英语标准发音》录制光盘。他们的语音、语调与书中所阐释的理论非常一致,可以听到许多例子来证明这些变化。这让我感到惊喜,同时也让我感到踏实。作为一名英语语音学教师,我愿意和读者一起,通过广播电视、发音词典和理论典籍的帮助,重新审视自己的英语发音。我认为新版教材

如要能够促使学生掌握这些基本变化,还是应把发音部分当作最基础的首要任务。有人在强调语调教学时说:语音是语言的躯体,语调是语言的灵魂。倘若我们换个说法,也同样能够服人:假如躯体不甚健全,那灵魂还能安生吗?再从学生这方面考虑,他们的英语节奏和语调不甚规范,也跟发音不准有关,如短松元音/ɪ, ʊ/过高过紧,央元音太后,又相当忽视连贯话语中的弱式、强式、省音、连音、同化等等。英语语音学是一门系统严密的科学。英语语音学教材在教学目的和要求、内容广度和深度,以及理论体系和编排顺序诸方面,跟旨在教人单学发音的读本之间存在着明显的区别。编者曾有所考虑,待客观条件成熟,还会继续修订。

这本教材沿用英国语调专家罗杰·金顿(Roger Kingdon)体系阐释语调,内容丰富,练习材料充足,不乏名篇名段。可是,该体系符号繁杂,恐怕学生不易掌握。建议教师从中选取少数录音短文和对话进行综合实践。要像分析精读课文那样分析录音课文,标调课文中的语调单位划分、语调核心确定和语调模式选择的原则;再接着根据录音把文字材料转写成吉姆森音标,把录音中实际出现的弱式、强式、省音、连音、同化等也准确地记录下来,以促使本书的基本理论能在口头交际中得以运用。在英语标准发音 RP 理论发祥地——伦敦大学学院语音系,这是一个"保留节目",出现在每年的试题中。我在成都几所大学(包括师范院校)授课时长期使用,师生均有所获,各位不妨试试。

近日偶读李白五言《独坐敬亭山》,对做语音研究似有所悟,现抄赠孟宪忠教授。诗曰:

众鸟高飞尽,孤云独去闲。
相看两不厌,只有敬亭山。

张凤桐
2006年3月于四川大学

# 第三版自序

## 努力学习吉姆森语音体系
## 积极推广普通型标准发音

### （一）

《英语语音学》从1991年出版到现在已经走过了15个年头。本书的修订是1999年出版的，迄今已有七年了。随着改革开放的不断深入和发展，我们国家发生了翻天覆地的变化，新生事物层出不穷，令人目不暇接。学术界也异常活跃，《当代外国语言学与应用语言学文库》的出版和发行就是一个明证。本书已经印刷了近10万册，有时一年就印一两万册，这是我们所始料不及的。

原责任编辑张云皋先生已经病逝，但我们不能忘记他。他是一位勤恳认真负责的好编辑。他生前为《英语语音学》的出版付出了辛勤劳动。此书由张凤桐先生担任主审。张老师一直在本科院校任教，又是专门研究语音的，而且曾赴英国留学伦敦大学学院，师从国际语音协会主席、著名语音学家吉姆森(A. C. Gimson)教授。我们非常高兴由他来主审这部教材。

这次特地修改了英文书名，《英语语音学》(*A Concise Course of English Phonetics*)算是比较理想了。因为我们认为，说话办事都应当简洁明快，不要拖泥带水，这将成为我们教材的特点或特色。

本书编写的指导思想是语音三要素——发音、节奏和语调，简称音、律、调。三要素紧密相连，很难说哪一个更重要。最早提出这一观点的是英国语音学家劳埃德·詹姆斯(Lloyd James)。我们认为，发音是基础，节奏是骨架，语调是灵魂。但是，长期以来，许多人包括教师和学生，只重视发音而忽视节奏和语调，所以本教材为了矫枉过正，破例地把节奏放在了首位。当然，有些学者认为这样做会伤害语音体系的完整性。又考虑到多数教师不熟悉近几十年来的英语语音变化这一事实，先讲发音这个基础部分，有利于我国英语教学的发音模式向吉姆森体系过渡，我们采纳主审人的建议，在第三版把顺序调整了过来。但是，我们希望大家一定要重视节奏和语调的讲授和训练，不要忽视它们，特别是加强它们在语流中训练。不要只重视发音，特别是单独的音位发音，不要再犯把节奏和语调视为不重要的"灰姑娘"的错误。

张凤桐先生在他的《英国英语语音学和音系学》(*British English Phonetics and Phonology*)(第三版)中用英语慢慢地把"音位"等难理解的许多问题给我们讲解清楚了。我们学着同样的办法，用简单的英语也基本上说清楚了。许多学生说他们听懂了。

但是，随着英语辅导报社包天仁先生倡导的三次国际会议的召开，特别是一大批《当代国外语言学与应用语言学文库》图书的引进，我们再也按捺不住已经活跃起来的心情。我们必须把失去的时间补回来。华东师大外语系翁贤青教授说，他曾读到200多封要求为我们编写的教材录音的信件，的确令人感动。国家需要英语语音，人民需要英语语音。我们当教师的没有理由不为老百姓提供学习资料。我们必须把教材编写得简明扼要，我们一定把问题交代得清清楚楚。我们也一定为大家奉献上与教材配套的录音带。

这里，我们不能不提起过去。当许国璋教授的英语教材畅销中国大地的时候，社会上曾流行过48个音标，甚至多到53个音标。一位名叫史延恺的年轻人，当时是复旦大学的研究生，在《外国语》(1982年第1期)发表了《英语48音位说质疑》的文章。我认真考虑了他的意见，慎重选择了国际上通用的44音位的观点。当时的青年人是顶着巨大的压力，鼓足勇气提出质疑的！史延恺先生是我多年的好朋友，我们曾在一个班级任教，住同一个宿舍，又一起经历了文化大革命的洗礼。我完全信赖他，因此我接受了他赞成的44音位的观点，并开始在我主编的教材《实用英语语音教程》(汉语版，1989年，山东教育出版社)和《英语语音学》中使用。

(二)

2004年春季，远在四川大学的张凤桐教授给我寄来了2001年问世的第六版《吉姆森英语语音教程》(*Gimson's Pronunciation of English*)。我们把《教程》对照张凤桐先生的教材认真阅读,的确受益匪浅。吉姆森教程中的元音舌位图对于学习者很有用,直观性强。这一版由英国曼彻斯特大学艾伦·克鲁特登(Alan Crutterden)教授修订,发音要领描述贴近新千年世纪之交的英语现状,简单易懂,条理清楚。这是我们修订教材的重要依据。我们尽了最大努力把文字解释写得简明扼要。我们自我感觉比过去好多了。这是教材修订的重点,也是我们教学和学习的重点,更是我们推行吉姆森普通型标准发音的重点和具体内容。本书引用了书中的许多观点材料,编者特向吉姆森教授和克鲁特登教授表示谢忱。我们要认真学习吉姆森语音体系,积极推广普通型标准发音。只有我们自己学好了,才能教好学生。

英语标准发音体系自19世纪下半叶以来,大体经历了三个时期,每个时期都产生了一名有国际影响的理论权威,不妨以他们的名字来称呼该时期:

亨利·斯威特(Henry Sweet)时期　　　　1877—1917

丹尼尔·琼斯(Daniel Jones)时期　　　　1917—1969

吉姆森(A. C. Gimson)时期　　　　　　1967—至今

英国英语标准发音早在20世纪60年代就进入了吉姆森时期。由于种种原因,我们过去学习得很不够。我们必须认真学习,以求彻底理解,更好地应用,为教学实践服务,并积极推广普通型标准发音。

(三)

我想谈点学习语音的体会。学习理论是非常必要的。张凤桐先生说:"语音理论使成年人耳聪目明,克服早期鹦鹉学舌、盲目练习形成的痼疾。"但是,理论指导下的实践也十分重要。首先,听的训练就十分重要。听,一定要认真听,仔细听,并在听的过程中渐渐用心去领悟、去感知,感悟其中的道理。实际上学什么都要讲究一个悟性。我自己曾在烟台师专张承德老师苦心经营的电教室里度过了许多美好的时光,那里有我学习英语语音和口语岁月的印记。劳埃德·詹姆斯甜美铿锵的嗓音经常萦绕在我的脑际。1965年,我有幸参加了暑期英语培训北外班的学习,聆听了英国专家大卫·克鲁科(David Crook)教授等专家讲座,接受了伊莎白·克鲁科(Isabel

Crook)教授的口语训练。吴千之老师的语音朗读讲座使我受益终生。我要借此机会向大卫·克鲁科夫妇,吴千之老师、钱青、戴显光、杨勋、付封圭老师等南下青岛的北外老师们,表示衷心的感谢和深深的敬意。

我认识张凤桐先生是在20世纪末。1989年,我高兴地读到了发表在《外语教学与研究》上的重要文章《我国英语教学中的语音体系问题》。他在这篇论文中,对英国普通型标准发音的由来和发展做了比较详细的论述。由于业务教学的需要,我向张凤桐先生发出了第一封信。通过多年来的书信往来和电话交谈,我感到张凤桐先生是一位知识渊博而又谦虚谨慎的人。他给我指出了本书开始部分出现的张冠李戴的严重错误,而且给我们找到了与原来我们引用的那段话极其类似的引语。他说:"吉姆森先生是否说过这段话,我不敢妄下断语;但是美国语言学家亨利·艾伦·格里森(H. A. Gleason)的绝妙论述是有现成的根据的。"在此,我们向广大师生表示歉意,并向张凤桐教授表示衷心的感谢。

本书第三版使用的语音图[Fig. 2 选自 Peter Roach 著 *English Phonetics and Phonology*: *A Practical Course*(《英语语音学和音系学实用教程》)除外]全部选自张凤桐的著作《英国英语语音学和音系学》(第三版)(*British English Phonetics and Phonology*)(四川大学出版社2002年版)。特此说明。

时光飞驰,时代在前进,语言在发展、在变化。尽管尽了最大努力,书中肯定仍有不少缺点错误,欢迎专家、学者、广大师生和英语爱好者批评指正。

孟宪忠
2006年7月28日
于潍坊学院心草斋

# 第二版序

忆在80年代中,同教研室的王若瑾老师曾嘱对山东昌潍师专孟宪忠老师主编的《实用英语语音教程》进行审校并为之作序。我以对语音素乏专识,未敢即时答应,后经阅读原稿,认为该书思路新颖,结构自成体系,不因袭旧有套路,而紧扣发音、节奏、语调三要素阐述英语语音的基本理论,并辅以丰富多彩的练习,要言不繁,简明适用,切合新时期师资教学所需,能填补当时英语课本中一大空白,遂勉力为之校毕书稿,并写了简短的序言。现孟老师又以所主编的《英语语音学》见示,嘱为之序。据告知,此书从1991年起已印刷8次,颇受师生及读者欢迎,可谓经受了时间的考验。而全书用简明的英语写成,采用最新的国际通用音标,对音位理论有初步的诠释,凡此皆有利于学习者循序渐进,登堂入室。书中强调在理论指导下进行充分自觉的实践,对节奏、语调与语流从听入手以达于说,给出大量实用的练习,在练习中解决学习者的难点。这些都是符合认知规律的。其中尤以练习及听力范读材料,能有效地解决过去语音教学局限于理论传习、缺少实践场地、以空对空的客观困难。这样教学双方的努力不致成为"半截子"工程。我以为,这是"雪中送炭"的好事,是本书一大优点。

新时期,英语教学从观念上有所突破,在方法上更得到借鉴革新,社会需求导引于前,交流环境推动于侧,其得到重大发展是理所必然,而师资匮缺却更因而突出,尤以地方上各级院校,感之尤深。可虞者,语音教学似已成为最薄弱之一环。历年本科生源在这方面颇难令人满意,入学后虽力求改进,常因积已成习,收效较小。近来更有一种说法,谓中国人说英语,若语音过分"地道",反为彼邦人所藐视,应有明确的"中国口音"方能博得尊重云云。此虽属个别之论,却言之颇能成理。也许在外事往来中,有此情况,亦未可知。但在外语学习中,窃以为不能这样地"以我为主"。语云:"取法乎上,仅得其中。"若取法乎中下,事情就难了。因此,师范专业英语师资的培养,犹木之根本、水之源头,是在大范围中提高英语语音水平的着手点。

　　语音在英语学习中的重要性,编者在本书的修订版前言和导论中言之颇详,也是英语教师通过多年实际探索得到的共识,惜尚未被学者所普遍接受。学习一种外语,实际上是在各种语言要素方面从观念及实践两个角度,对母语的影响不断进行重新检视、扬弃的过程,其有助者要很好地加以利用,其有碍者应及早排除。揆诸语音,更感母语语音(包括方言音)的影响不易摆脱。这不是纠正一两个及至十个二十个"错误"音的问题,而是建立一整套英语或美语的元、辅音体系的问题。而在掌握了单个的音以后,怎样把音连起来成为词,进而连词成句,再进而讲求节奏、停顿、语调、音强、音高、语气、表情等各个方面,也是一个全新体系的建立过程,也要摆脱母语的影响。这是一种无休止的艰苦登攀。所幸的是,如能把狭义的"语音"基础打好,就能初步体会其中奥秘,在奋勉中取得欣悦,逐渐达到"自在"的境界。孟宪忠老师主编的这本教材,为达到这一境界提供了极好的帮助。

　　经过多年的辛勤耕耘,我国外语院校已培养出大量优秀英语师资人才。鉴于师范院校处于"工作母机"的地位,探讨师范外语教学,编印师范外语教材,更具有根本的意义。孟宪忠老师所在的学校以及华东师范大学出版社,能重视这方面的工作,是一大好事,值得祝贺。相形之下,某些人才较多的单位却在师范英语教学及教材方面较少垂顾。若能开展合作,深入探讨师范教学特点,编写出适合师范院校使用的各种科目及类型的英语教材,形成有的放矢、学用结合的局面,如某些其他学科已达到的那样,则英语人才的培养能够真正从基层做起,而我们的英语教学的局面必将逐渐改观。这是我们英语教师的殷切希望。

夏祖煃
1998年7月于北京

# Personal Comment

My overall impression of the book is that it is currently a very good one of its kind. It is the right textbook and reference book for both teachers and students of English at the (esp. normal) college level.

The book is precise and practical, actually quite helpful for readers to acquire the essential knowledge and skills of English phonetics. It provides rich and varied materials for practice and drill. For each phoneme the items of Advice to the Teacher and Students and Spelling and Sound are well designed and necessary.

The book is comprehensive. It includes every aspect and specific item in the entire sphere of English phonetics and endeavors to treat them properly for achieving the goal of the book.

I especially appreciate the fact that the book is written in simple and concise English. This is a worthwhile and gratifying attempt for the Chinese writers in writing English reference books.

It is feasible and beneficial to divide English phonetics into pronunciation, rhythm and intonation for pedagogic purposes (and for academic research too). The order of placing pronunciation after rhythm and intonation or before them is a question open to discussion and demanding verification by practice.

The book would be still better if more comparative studies between English and Chinese were discussed with regard to specific phonetic issues to find the most typical problems of Chinese learners and help them effectively. That will be a strong point of the book.

Yankai Shi (American linguist)

# 前言

高等师范院校英语语音教材《英语语音学》(*English Phonetics，Apply It to Communication Better*)是受国家教委有关部门委托,为适应我国培养中学英语师资的需要而编写的。自1991年初版问世以来,多次重印,受益于本书的人已不限于师范院校学生,熟悉和爱用它的教师也已不限于华东地区。

我们借这次修订的机会,侧重做了如下工作:1.将书中的国际音标全部改用 English Pronouncing Dictionary (14th ed.) 的音标;2.第三部分中,不仅增设了 Phonemes in Combination (Unit 18),多数单元还增设了"正音要领",当然也增加了练习量;3.订正了初版中的疏误。总之,使本书以新的姿态为新的世纪尽其效用。

本书的编写与修订,仍坚持以英语教育专业英语教学大纲为指针,力求科学、准确、简明、实用。然而,它并未沿袭一般英语语音书的套路,而是从实际出发,依据简明实用的编写原则,从语音的三要素(节奏、语调、发音),扼要阐述英语语音学的基本理论,力求重点突出,要言不繁。

本书每一单元之后配有单项和综合的习题。希望学生在教师的指导下,通过"语流"的训练,切实打好语音功底,以达到提高中学英语师资的语音素养,进而提高其英语交际水平的目的。

编写时,考虑到学习语言的客观规律,以及刚入高校的学生的心理因素等方面,我们特将节奏和语调编排在发音的前面,以突出前两者在语音教学中的地位,强调它们的重要性。我们认为,对于已在中学学过几年英语而具有初步语音基础知识和熟巧的学生来说,这种编排是可行的。如果使用本教材的教师习惯于从发音教起,仍可先教发音;本教材不会给教学带来任何困难。

全书除导论和"附言"外,计三大部分,21个单元。对本教材的使用,可作如下安排:导论,1学时;节奏,12学时;语调,15学时;发音,8—10学时;机动,2学时。

教师可根据需要选用习题。凡在正文或习题左方标有 🎤 者,均有录音可资模仿。

参加本书修订工作的是孟宪忠教授和孟滢同志。原编者崔希智教授提出了许多修改建议并提供了许多资料。

我们感到特别欣喜并特此表示感谢的是:承蒙北京外国语大学著名教授夏祖煃先生拨冗为本书欣然作序并审校了新增加部分的书稿;承蒙华东师范大学著名语音学教授翁贤青先生认真审校了本书中的语调符号,并欣然与该校大学外语部张晴老师合作为本书录制了盒式音带。

在编写过程中,我们曾参考了国内外英语语音学专著,并选用了部分内容,恕未逐一注明出处,在此,谨向各位作者表示谢忱。我们水平有限,缺乏经验;书中疏漏不当之处,恳请专家和使用本书者不吝赐教。

编　者

1998年9月

著名英语语音学家、旅美学者史延恺先生与编者就语音、教材编写等问题曾进行过深入的讨论。十分感谢他写下了对本教材的意见和建议,这次重印,我们将他的简评收录在书中。

2002年,我们对教材作了一定修改。除改正印刷错误外,重点把诗歌语音标注作了必要的改动,使其更规范,更符合英语格律诗的要求。我国英诗汉译名家杨德豫编审、河南商邱师范学院许曦明教授都向我们提出了宝贵意见。我们认为,在英诗朗读标注方面下一番功夫是值得的。当然,在实践中究竟如何朗读,请参照录音为好。

孟宪忠　孟滢　重印补记

2002年3月

根据时代发展的需要,我们以吉姆森语音体系为纲对第二版进行了全面修订,并依当前教学实际突出了节奏训练的作用。承蒙四川大学张凤桐教授审校全部书稿并作序,为本书添色,谨致谢忱。

编　者<br>2006 年 9 月

　　为了适应当前的英语教学的需求,第四版修订优化了排版格式,在练习中的听力部分添加二维码,方便广大师生在练习时扫码使用;部分单元新增了一些配套练习及答案,作为教师课堂的补充练习资料;替换了一些过时的单词和例句,并完善更新了第三版中的不足之处。

　　另外,在中国大多数中小学的语音教学中,/ts//dz//tr//dr/通常被归类为破擦音(塞擦音),这对中国人学习英语发音具有重要意义。因此,我们以二维码小贴士的形式介绍了这四个音标(两组),师生都可以扫码了解。

孟　滢<br>2022 年 12 月

# Contents

| | |
|---|---|
| Introduction | 1 |
|     1. English Phonetics | 1 |
|     2. Study Method | 2 |
|     3. The International Phonetic Alphabet | 3 |
|     4. British English and American English | 3 |
|     5. List of Symbols Used | 4 |

## Part One  Pronunciation

| | |
|---|---|
| Unit 1  Organs of Speech | 11 |
| Unit 2  Cardinal Vowels | 12 |
| Unit 3  Classification of English Phonemes | 15 |
|     I. Phonemes and Allophones | 15 |
|     II. Classification of English Phonemes | 16 |
| Unit 4  English Vowels—Pure Vowels | 21 |
|     I. Front Vowels /iː/ and /ɪ/ | 21 |
|     II. Front Vowels /e/ and /æ/ | 25 |
|     III. Central Vowels /ɜː/, /ə/ and /ʌ/ | 29 |
|     IV. Back Vowel /ɑː/ | 36 |
|     V. Back Vowels /ɒ/ and /ɔː/ | 38 |
|     VI. Back Vowels /ʊ/ and /uː/ | 42 |

| | | |
|---|---|---|
| Unit 5 | English Vowels—Diphthongs | 46 |
| | Ⅰ. Closing Diphthongs /eɪ/, /aɪ/ and /ɔɪ/ | 46 |
| | Ⅱ. Closing Diphthongs /əʊ/ and /aʊ/ | 51 |
| | Ⅲ. Centring Diphthongs /ɪə/, /eə/ and /ʊə/ | 55 |
| Unit 6 | English Consonants | 61 |
| | Ⅰ. Plosives /p/, /b/; /t/, /d/; /k/, /g/ | 61 |
| | Ⅱ. Fricatives /f/, /v/; /ʃ/, /ʒ/ | 66 |
| | Ⅲ. Fricatives /s/, /z/; /θ/, /ð/ | 69 |
| | Ⅳ. Fricative /h/; Frictionless Continuant /r/ and the Lateral /l/ | 72 |
| Unit 7 | English Consonants (Continued) | 77 |
| | Ⅴ. Nasals /m/, /n/ and /ŋ/ | 77 |
| | Ⅵ. Affricates /tʃ/ and /dʒ/ | 80 |
| | Ⅶ. Semi-vowels /w/ and /j/ | 83 |
| Unit 8 | Phonemes in Combination | 88 |
| | Ⅰ. The Syllable Theory and Definition | 88 |
| | Ⅱ. The Syllable Structure | 88 |
| | Ⅲ. Open Syllables and Closed Syllables | 89 |
| | Ⅳ. Syllabification | 90 |
| Unit 9 | Consonant Clusters and Incomplete Plosion | 95 |
| | Ⅰ. Consonant Clusters | 95 |
| | Ⅱ. Incomplete Plosion | 95 |
| Unit 10 | Sound Changes in Connected Speech | 99 |
| | Ⅰ. Liaison | 99 |
| | Ⅱ. Strong Forms and Weak Forms | 101 |
| | Ⅲ. Elision | 107 |
| | Ⅳ. Assimilation | 110 |

Ⅴ. Length of a Sound　　　　　　　　　　　　　　114

## Part Two　Rhythm

Unit 11　Word Stress　　　　　　　　　　　　　　123
    Ⅰ. Kinds of Stress　　　　　　　　　　　　　123
    Ⅱ. Stress Placement　　　　　　　　　　　　124
    Ⅲ. Stress Influence on Meaning of Words　　128

Unit 12　Sentence Stress　　　　　　　　　　　　133
    Ⅰ. Sense Stress　　　　　　　　　　　　　　133
    Ⅱ. Logical Stress　　　　　　　　　　　　　138
    Ⅲ. Emotional Stress　　　　　　　　　　　　139

Unit 13　Rhythm and Its Features　　　　　　　　142
    Ⅰ. Rhythm　　　　　　　　　　　　　　　　142
    Ⅱ. Rhythm Group and Its Division　　　　　142
    Ⅲ. Features of English Rhythm　　　　　　　142

Unit 14　Rhythm Patterns　　　　　　　　　　　　151

Unit 15　Sense-groups and Pausing　　　　　　　162
    Ⅰ. Sense-groups and Their Divisions　　　　162
    Ⅱ. Pausing　　　　　　　　　　　　　　　　164

## Part Three　Intonation

Unit 16　A Brief Introduction　　　　　　　　　　171
    Ⅰ. Definition　　　　　　　　　　　　　　　171
    Ⅱ. Function　　　　　　　　　　　　　　　171
    Ⅲ. Illustrating Intonation　　　　　　　　　172

## Unit 17　Basic Tones and Their Training　176

　　Ⅰ. Basic Tones　176
　　Ⅱ. Basic Training of Tones　178

## Unit 18　Tone-groups　183

　　Ⅰ. Tone-groups　183
　　Ⅱ. Tone-group Division　184
　　Ⅲ. Structure of the Tone-group　184
　　Ⅳ. Features of an English Tune　189

## Unit 19　Functions of Tunes and Their Uses　194

　　Ⅰ. Falling Tune　194
　　Ⅱ. Rising Tune　197
　　Ⅲ. Falling-rising Tune　200

## Unit 20　Combined Tunes　205

　　Ⅰ. Fall + Fall　205
　　Ⅱ. Fall + Rise　206
　　Ⅲ. Rise + Fall　207
　　Ⅳ. Rise + Rise　208
　　Ⅴ. Fall + Fall-rise　209
　　Ⅵ. Fall-rise + Fall　210
　　Ⅶ. Fall-rise + Rise　211

## Unit 21　Reading of Long Sentences　215

　　Ⅰ. Tune Broken Upwards (Broken Tune or Accidental Rise)　215
　　Ⅱ. Intonation of Vocatives　216
　　Ⅲ. Intonation of Parenthesis　217
　　Ⅳ. Intonation of Reporting Phrases　218

Additional Remarks: Reading as an Exercise in
Enunciation and Delivery                                    222
    1. Some Basic Points                                222
    2. Models for Appreciation and Imitation            225

Appendix I  Rules of Reading                                236

Appendix II  British English and American English in Comparison  246

Appendix III  Glossary                                      247

Main References                                             252

# Introduction

## 1. English Phonetics

There are three areas we need to know about the study of a language, i.e., phonetics, lexicology and grammar, but phonetics is essential. Phonetics, the study and science of speech sounds, is a branch of linguistic studies. It is closely connected with the study of grammar, lexicology and so on. "Without phonetics there can be no morphology of a spoken language, without intonation no syntax," as Professor Firth declared. H. A. Gleason also noted in *An Introduction to Descriptive Linguistics* "A speaking knowledge of a language, therefore, requires very close to a one hundred percent control of the phonology and control of from fifty to ninety percent of the grammar, while one can frequently do a great deal with one percent or even less of the vocabulary." So we must make great efforts at phonetics first and foremost in order to study English well.

English pronunciation could be held to embrace three component factors, i.e., the sounds, the rhythm and the intonation. But it is difficult to say which of them is more important. However, more and more people, even those who speak English as their mother language, have come to realize that it is far from enough to be able to reproduce accurately all the phonemes in isolation. They have also found that correctly pronounced phonemes cannot ensure a good general pronunciation unless the proper rhythm and intonation are used. Famous Professor A. Lloyd James compared rhythm and intonation to carrier waves of the broadcasting station. He said, "Just as every broadcasting station in the world has its own carrier waves, so every language has its own rhythm and intonation. A receiving station that is tuned to receive a certain carrier wave receives that wave, and all the sound waves carried by it, easily and accurately. Every Englishman is a receiving station tuned to pick up sounds and speech transmitted on the carrier wave of English rhythm and intonation. If these are not normal, then reception, which in this case implies understanding, is made difficult, if not impossible." If we wish to acquire a good English pronunciation, we must do our utmost to break down habits of rhythm that are firmly ingrained, and we must accustom ourselves to using speech melodies that are as foreign to our native ear as they are foreign to our native grammar.

The plenty of excercises in this book will enable the English learners to have a good command of English phonetics only if they have got the correct study method.

## 2. Study Method

This is an intermediate level book of practical English phonetics for college students. The students are expected to do systematically a lot of practice — training and excercises under the guidance of the teacher and the fundamental theory explained in the book.

As we all know, language learning begins with the ear. So in learning English pronunciation, the students are required, first of all, to listen carefully and attentively and to hear accurately phonemes, stresses and tunes. Then they should make every effort to imitate all of them. It is important to realize that imitation is the best and soundest method in learning pronunciation when coupled with an adequate knowledge of phonetic theory. Theory and practice should always go hand in hand. It is imperative to make clear the characteristics of English rhythm, the most striking one of which is that the stressed syllables tend to occur at relatively regular intervals of time. Then the students are led in chanting the exercises on stress patterns while beating the time with their hands. The loud collective reading will leave deep impressions on the minds of the students, cultivating good language habits. It is necessary to study English tunes and their functions. A world of practice will be done on phonemes by the students in learning the first two parts. It is not surprising that they will be able to articulate the phonemes pretty well by the time they finish the book. This is what we often say "Where water flows, a channel is formed." Nevertheless, it is significant and profitable to review and sum up the important points for correctly pronouncing each phoneme. So long as they keep on practising reading aloud every day, the students will have a good command of English pronunciation in time.

## 3. The International Phonetic Alphabet

The International Phonetic Alphabet (IPA for short) is a system of letters and symbols designed by the International Phonetic Association in 1888 to provide a universally understood system to represent pronunciations of all languages in the world. It has proved to be scientific and useful in teaching and research.

There are two types of transcription for English, namely, the Phonemic Broad Transcription and the Phonetic Narrow Transcription. The former is widely used in textbooks and dictionaries whereas the latter, which has additional symbols, is rather complicated and less commonly used. One point worthy of note is that phonemic symbols should be put in two slanting bars / / while phonetic transcriptions in square brackets [ ].

## 4. British English and American English

There are several varieties of English pronunciation, such as British, American, Australian, Canadian, South African, etc. But BrE and AmE are two most influential ones. The type of English pronunciation described and introduced in this textbook is known as British Received Pronunciation (RP for short). It is based on London dialect and generally spoken by the educated in Southern England and it is what was traditionally used by the BBC news readers. It is easily understood in all English-speaking countries. This type of English has been studied, investigated, described and recorded more comprehensively and thoroughly than any other types. In our country RP has always been adopted as a teaching standard in middle schools and colleges for about 80 years. However, in recent years, some people have tried to learn American English. Generally speaking, AmE includes Eastern American, Southern American and General American (GA for short). GA is spoken by the majority of the American people. It is widely used in textbooks, radio and TV programmes in the U.S.A.

The students can learn either BrE or AmE; however, they are advised not to mix them up.

## 5. List of Symbols Used

### Symbols for Phonemes

#### 1. Vowels

(1) /iː/    as in **key** /kiː/

(2) /ɪ/    as in **pit** /pɪt/

(3) /e/    as in **pet** /pet/

(4) /æ/    as in **pat** /pæt/

(5) /ɑː/    as in **car** /kɑː/

(6) /ɒ/    as in **pot** /pɒt/

(7) /ɔː/    as in **score** /skɔː/, **course** /kɔːs/

(8) /ʊ/    as in **put** /pʊt/

(9) /uː/    as in **coo** /kuː/

(10) /ʌ/    as in **bus** /bʌs/, **brother** /ˈbrʌðə/

(11) /ɜː/    as in **cur** /kɜː/

(12) /ə/    as in **about** /əˈbaʊt/, **upper** /ˈʌpə/

(13) /eɪ/ as in b**ay** /beɪ/
(14) /əʊ/ as in g**o** /gəʊ/
(15) /aɪ/ as in b**uy** /baɪ/, b**y** /baɪ/
(16) /aʊ/ as in c**ow** /kaʊ/
(17) /ɔɪ/ as in b**oy** /bɔɪ/
(18) /ɪə/ as in p**eer** /pɪə/
(19) /eə/ as in p**ear** /peə/
(20) /ʊə/ as in p**oor** /pʊə/

## 2. Consonants

(21) /p/ as in **p**ea /piː/, hel**p** /help/
(22) /b/ as in **b**ee /biː/, ru**b** /rʌb/
(23) /t/ as in **t**oe /təʊ/, sea**t** /siːt/
(24) /d/ as in **d**oe /dəʊ/, see**d** /siːd/
(25) /k/ as in **c**ap /kæp/, pa**ck** /pæk/
(26) /g/ as in **g**ap /gæp/, pe**g** /peg/
(27) /f/ as in **f**at /fæt/
(28) /tʃ/ as in **ch**in /tʃɪn/
(29) /dʒ/ as in **g**in /dʒɪn/
(30) /v/ as in **v**at /væt/
(31) /θ/ as in **th**ing /θɪŋ/
(32) /ð/ as in **th**is /ðɪs/
(33) /s/ as in **s**ip /sɪp/
(34) /z/ as in **z**ip /zɪp/
(35) /ʃ/ as in **sh**ip /ʃɪp/
(36) /ʒ/ as in mea**s**ure /ˈmeʒə/
(37) /h/ as in **h**at /hæt/
(38) /m/ as in **m**ap /mæp/
(39) /n/ as in **n**ap /næp/
(40) /ŋ/ as in ha**ng** /hæŋ/

(41) /l/ as in **led** /led/

(42) /r/ as in **red** /red/

(43) /j/ as in **yet** /jet/

(44) /w/ as in **wet** /wet/

3. non-phonemic symbols

/i/      as in **c**i**ty** /ˈsɪti/

/u/      as in **act**u**al** /ˈæktʃuəl/

## Rhythm

### 1. Word Stress

ˈ = primary stress, as in **open** /ˈəʊpən/

ˌ = secondary stress, as in **ice cream** /ˈaɪsˌkriːm/

ˈ-ˈ- = even stress, as in **Chinese** /ˈtʃaɪˈniːz/

### 2. / = rhythm-unit boundary

### 3. | = tone-group boundary

### 4. ‖ = pause

## Intonation

### 1. Tones[①]

**Level Tones**

High Level      ˈM as in ˈNow.

---

① Double marks indicate Emphatic Tones, e.g. ˈˈM Emphatic Level Tones. For details, please refer to Unit 16.

Low Level         ˌM as in ˌNow.

**Falling Tones**

High Fall         ˋM as in ˋTwo.

Low Fall          ˎM as in ˎTwo.

**Rising Tones**

High Rise         ˊM as in ˊNo.

Low Rise          ˏM as in ˏNo.

**Falling-rising Tones**

Fall-rise Undivided:

High Fall-rise Undivided     ˇM as in ˇYes.

Low Fall-rise Undivided      ˬM as in ˬYes.

Fall-rise Divided:

High Fall-rise Divided       ˋM ˏM  as in ˋThat's ˏright.

Low Fall-rise Divided        ˎM ˏM  as in ˎThat's ˏright.

## 2. Tunes

(1) Fall           ˋ   ( ⌢ )

(2) Rise           ˊ   ( ⌣ )

(3) Fall-rise      ˇ   ( ⌵ )

## 3. Combined Tunes

(1) Fall + Fall          ˋ + ˋ          ( ⌢ + ⌢ )

(2) Fall + Rise          ˋ + ˊ          ( ⌢ + ⌣ )

(3) Rise + Fall          ˊ + ˋ          ( ⌣ + ⌢ )

(4) Rise + Rise          ˊ + ˊ          ( ⌣ + ⌣ )

(5) Fall + Fall-rise     ˋ + ˇ          ( ⌢ + ⌵ )

(6) Fall-rise + Fall     ˇ + ˋ          ( ⌵ + ⌢ )

(7) Fall-rise + Rise     ˇ + ˊ          ( ⌵ + ⌣ )

# Part One

# Pronunciation

# Unit 1

# Organs of Speech

The most essential of English pronunciation is the sounds, the focus points of which ought to be the phonemes, the syllable theory and sound changes.

Speech sounds are made with the air stream from the lungs and manipulated by the organs of speech. Therefore, to facilitate the study of English speech sounds, it is necessary for us to have a clear idea of the vocal organs and their functions. Fig. 1 is a diagram showing a side view of the organs of speech.

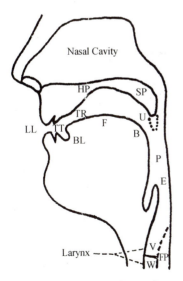

| | | | |
|---|---|---|---|
| LL. | Lips (Labia) | BL. | Blade of tongue, including the tip |
| TT. | Teeth (Dentis) | F. | Front of tongue |
| TR. | Teeth ridge (Alveolus) | B. | Back of tongue |
| HP. | Hard palate (Palatum) | E. | Epiglottis |
| SP. | Soft palate (Velum) | FP. | Food passage |
| U. | Uvula | V. | Vocal folds |
| P. | Pharynx | W. | Windpipe (Trachea) |

Fig. 1  Organs of speech

# Unit 2

## Cardinal Vowels

## Cardinal Vowels

It has become traditional to locate cardinal vowels on a four-sided figure (quadrilateral) of the shape seen in Fig. 2 (the design used here is the one recommended by the International Phonetic Association in 1989). Cardinal vowels don't belong to any language in the world. They are extremes of vowel quality, but they are taken as reference points in describing and classifying the vowels of all languages under the sun. The vowels in Fig. 2 are called Primary Cardinal Vowels.

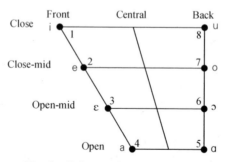

Fig. 2　Primary Cardinal Vowels

### Questions for Discussion

1. What are cardinal vowels?
2. What is the use of them?

To produce a sound, we draw air into the lungs and then release it slowly through the larynx, the pharynx and the mouth. If the soft palate is lowered, the air passes through the nasal cavity. In the larynx are the vocal folds, which can be brought near together or drawn apart. If the vocal folds are brought near together, the compressed air in the lungs has to force its way out and make the vocal folds vibrate, thus producing voiced sounds such as vowels and voiced consonants. If the vocal folds are drawn apart, the air leaves freely. There is no vibration of the vocal folds. The sound, thus made, is voiceless. And the interference with the air passage in various manners and at various places makes the sounds different.

## Questions for Discussion

1. Study the diagram in Fig. 1 and commit to memory the names for different parts of Organs of Speech.
2. How are sounds produced?
3. Write a short essay about the making of
   (1) /t, d/    (2) /s, z/    (3) /n/    (4) /l/

## Exercise P-1

 扫码听音频

 1. Read the following passage after the recording.

### 'Do You 'Speak ﹢English?

I had an a'musing ex﹢perience | 'last ﹨ year. 'After I 'left a 'small ﹨village | in the 'south of ﹢ France, | I 'drove on to the 'next ﹨town. 'On the ﹢ way, | a 'young man ﹨ waved to me. I ﹨ stopped | and he 'asked me for a ﹨ lift. As 'soon as he 'got into the ﹢ car, | I ₁said 'good ﹨ morning to him in ﹨ French | and he re-﹨ plied | in the 'same ﹨ language. A'part from a 'few ﹢ words, | I do 'not ·know any 'French at ﹨ all. ﹨Neither of us ₁spoke during the ﹨ journey. I had 'nearly 'reached the ﹨ town, | when the 'young man

ˈsuddenlyˋsaid, | ˈveryˋslowly, | "ˈDo you ˈspeakˊEnglish?" As I ˈsoonˊlearnt, | he wasˋEnglish himˋˋself!

 2. Read the following famous poem according to the tonetic stress marks.

### Comˈposed upon ˈWestminsterˋBridge

*by William Wordsworth*

Earth ˈhas not ˈanyˈthing to ˈshow moreˋfair:
ˈDull would ˈhe be of ˋsoul who could ˈpassˋby
A ˈsight soˋˋtouching ˈin its ˈmajesˈty:
ˈThisˋCityˊnow doth ˌlike a ˈgarment ˈwear

The ˈbeauty ˈof theˋmorning: ˋsilent, ˋbare,
ˊShips, ˊtowers, ˊdomes, ˊtheatres, and ˈtemplesˊlie
ˈOpen unˈto theˊfields, and to theˋsky;
ˈAll ˈbright and ˈglitterˈing in the ˈsmokelessˋair.

ˈˈNever did ˈsun more ˈbeautiˈfullyˋsteep
In his ˈfirstˋsplendourˊvalley, ˈrock orˋhill;
ˈNe'erˋsaw I, ˈneverˋfelt, a ˈcalm soˋdeep!
The ˈriver ˈglideth ˈat ˈhisˋˋown ˈsweetˋwill:
Dearˊ God! the ˈveryˋhouses ˈseem aˋsleep;
And ˈall that ˈmightyˋheart is ˈlyingˋstill!

# Unit 3

# Classification of English Phonemes

## I. Phonemes and Allophones

In the study of English phonetics it is necessary to distinguish between phonemes and allophones. Many linguists agree that English has 20 vowels and 24 consonants. But in fact each of these can be pronounced in many slightly different ways, so that the total number of sounds actually produced in speech is practically endless. For example:

(1) The /æ/ in **at** is short, and the /æ/ in **add** is long, and the /æ/ in **can** is nasalized, etc.

(2) The /l/ in **let** is clear, and the /l/ in **tell**, **told** and **always** is dark, and the /l/ in **could** is voiceless, etc.

(3) The /k/ in **key**, **kiss** is advanced, the /k/ in **cop**, **cook** is retracted and the /k/ in **cup**, **curl** is normal, neither advanced, nor retracted.

However, the native speakers still hold that English has one /æ/ sound and one only, one /l/ sound and one only, and one /k/ sound and one only. Why? The answer is that they have customarily divided all those slightly different sounds they could possibly produce into a definite number of groups. Only those "sounds" which serve to distinguish one word from another are regarded as belonging to different groups, or to different phonemes in our technical term. Phonemes are distinctive (有区别性的) and contrastive (对比的). So the phoneme is "the smallest contrastive linguistic unit which may bring about a change of meaning", as A.C. Gimson defined. The /æ/ sounds, the /l/ sounds and the /k/ sounds mentioned above are called allophones of the phonemes /æ/, /l/ and /k/ respectively.[①]

The symbols used to represent phonemes are phonemic symbols, which are put between slashes / / instead of in square brackets [ ].

There are 44 basic phonemes in English. They are divided into vowels and consonants.

Vowels are sounds produced without obstruction of the air passage in the mouth but with the vibration of the vocal folds. So all vowels are voiced.

Consonants are sounds produced with a complete or partial obstruction which prevents the air from going freely through the mouth. They are either voiced or voiceless.

## II. Classification of English Phonemes

### 1. English Vowels

There are 20 vowels in English. Twelve pure vowels /iː, ɪ, e, æ, ɜː, ə, ʌ, ɑː, ɒ, ɔː, ʊ, uː/ and eight diphthongs /eɪ, aɪ, ɔɪ, əʊ, aʊ, ɪə, eə, ʊə/.

The pure vowels can be classified according to four different principles.

(1) According to the part of the tongue raised, /iː, ɪ, e, æ/ are called front vowels, /uː, ʊ, ɔː, ɒ, ɑː/ back vowels and /ɜː, ə, ʌ/ central vowels.

(2) According to the length of vowels, they are divided into long vowels and short vowels. The pure vowels in transcription with two dots are long vowels. The diphthongs are also long. The rest are short ones.

(3) According to the shape of the lips, vowels can be divided into rounded vowels and unrounded (spread) vowels. The rounded vowels are /ɒ, ɔː, ʊ, uː/ and the rest are unrounded vowels.

---

[①] Allophones are not distinctive. They are in complementary distribution and phonetically similar while phonemes are in parallel distribution.

(4) According to the degree of tenseness of the muscles, the pure vowels are classified as tense vowels and lax vowels.

All the short vowels are lax vowels because in their production the muscles of speech organs are lax. All the long vowels are tense vowels except /ɑː/ because the muscles are usually tense when they are produced.

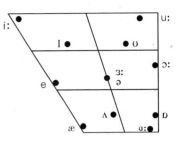

Fig. 3  RP pure vowels

The classification of pure vowels is shown in the diagram (See Fig. 3):

| front | central | back |
| spread | neutral | rounded |

The eight diphthongs (See Fig. 4 and Fig. 5) can be classified as closing diphthongs /eɪ, aɪ, ɔɪ, əʊ, aʊ/ and centring diphthongs /ɪə, eə, ʊə/.

When we pronounce a closing diphthong the tongue moves from an opener position to a closer position. When we produce a centring sound the tongue moves towards the central vowel /ə/.

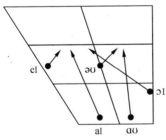

Fig. 4  RP closing vowels

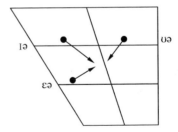

Fig. 5  RP centring diphthongs

## 2. English Consonants

There are 24 consonants in English. They are classified according to three different principles:

(1) the vibration of the vocal folds;

(2) the place of articulation;

(3) the manner of articulation.

N. B. /r/ was regarded as a fricative consonant in the past, now it is taken as a frictionless continuant by the contemporary phoneticians. In some books it is put together with /w/ and /j/ under the same heading as a semi-vowel.

English consonants can be divided into two groups according to the first principle. Those with the vibration of the vocal folds are called voiced consonants. Those without the vibration of the vocal folds are called voiceless or breathed consonants.

Table 1　English Consonants

| place of articulation \ manner of articulation | bilabial | labio-dental | dental | alveolar | post-alveolar | palato-alveolar | palatal | velar | glottal |
|---|---|---|---|---|---|---|---|---|---|
| vibration of the vocal folds | -V. V. | -V. V. | -V. V. | -V. V. | V. | -V. V. | V. | -V. V. | -V. |
| Plosive | p b | | | t d | | | | k g | |
| Affricate | | | | | | tʃ dʒ | | | |
| Fricative | | f v | θ ð | s z | | ʃ ʒ | | | h |
| Nasal | m | | | n | | | | ŋ | |
| Lateral | | | | l | | | | | |
| Frictionless continuant | | | | | r | | | | |
| Semi-vowel | w | | | | | | j | | |

According to the place of articulation, i. e., where the obstruction of the air passage is formed, consonants can be distinguished as bilabial, labio-dental, dental, alveolar, post-alveolar, palato-alveolar, palatal, velar, and glottal consonants.

According to the manner of articulation, they can be distinguished as plosives, fricatives, affricates, nasals, laterals, frictionless continuant and semi-vowels.

The classification of consonants is shown in Table 1.

## Questions for Discussion

1. How are vowels produced?
2. How are consonants produced?
3. Classify vowels in different ways.
4. Classify consonants in different ways.
5. Classify English phonemes.

## Exercise P-2

 扫码听音频

 1. Read the following dialogue after the recording.

### A、Dialogue

*Teacher:* To'day we are re'viewing ˋ prefixes. Will someone 'give me a ˋ word using a ˊ prefix?

*Mary:* Re-ˋ mark. The 'prefix is ˋ re-. It 'means "a ˋ gain". I have to re-'mark the ˋ clothes.

*Teacher:* ˋ Very ˊ good. And ˋ what does the 'word "re'mark" ˋ mean?

*Mary:* It ˊ means | "to 'make a comment".

*Teacher:* 'Can you 'use both 'words in a ˊ sentence?

*Mary:* ˋ Yes. "The 'teacher re ˊ marked | that she had re ˋ marked the ˋ papers."

*Teacher:* ˋ Very ˌgood. ˇ Mary, | 'can you 'give me an'other 'word 'using the "r-e-" ˊ prefix?

*Mary:* ˋ Yes. Re-ˋ lease. It ˊ means | "to 'lease something a ˋ gain". The 'word "re-'lease" 'means "to let ˋ go".

Teacher: ˋFine.

 2. Read the poem after the recording.

## The ˈComing of ˋSpring

I amˋcoming, ˌlittle ˊmaiden,
With the ˈpleasantˋsunshine ˌladen,
With the ˊhoney for the ˊbee,
With theˋblossom for theˋtree.
ˈEvery ˈlittle ˈstream is ˊbright,
ˈAll the ˈorchardˋtrees areˋwhite,
ˈAnd each ˈsmall and ˈwaving ˊshoot,
ˈHas for ˇthee ˈsweetˋflowers or ˋfruit.

# Unit 4

# English Vowels — Pure Vowels

English vowels are divided into two large groups: pure vowels (monophthongs) and diphthongs. Pure vowels are simple vowel sounds. When we utter a pure vowel, the tongue and lips do not move. A diphthong is a glide from one vowel to another within one syllable. When we utter a diphthong, the tongue and lips must move from one position to another. The description of RP[①] vowels in this book lies heavily on *Gimson's Pronunciation of English* (6th edition, 2001). It is important to observe the difference. In English there are 12 pure vowels and 8 diphthongs.

In the pure vowels there are four front vowels: /iː/, /ɪ/, /e/ and /æ/ as in seat, sit, set and sat.

## I. Front Vowels /iː/ and /ɪ/

/iː/

**Brief Descriptions**

a. The front of the tongue is raised to a height slightly below and behind the front close position;

b. The lips are spread;

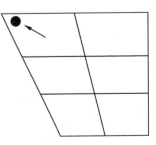

Fig. 6 Variants of RP /iː/

---

① RP: received pronounciation, the accent of stardard southern British English.

c. The tongue is tense;

d. The side rims make a firm contact with the upper molars;

e. It is generally long.

**Spelling and Sound**

e—be, these, evening, complete

ee—see, tree, been, need, cheese, wheel

ea—sea, leaf, reason, east, meat, read

ie—piece, field, belief, yield

ei, ey—seize, receive, key

i—machine, police, magazine, sardine, routine, suite

/ɪ/

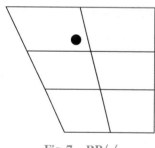

Fig. 7　RP/ɪ/

**Brief Descriptions**

a. The RP vowel /ɪ/ is pronounced with a part of the tongue nearer to the centre than to the front. It is raised just above the close-mid position;

b. The lips are loosely spread;

c. The tongue is lax;

d. The side rims make a light contact with the upper molars;

e. It is generally short.

**Spelling and Sound**

i—it, sit, bit, fifth, with, rich

y—city, pity, rhythm, symbol

e—pretty, wicket, except, English

a—village, language

Unit 4  English Vowels — Pure Vowels  23

### Advice to the Teacher and Students

The /iː/ in English is longer than the 〈i〉 in Chinese. The difference between /iː/ and /ɪ/ is not merely the length of sound. There is also a difference in tongue position or quality. For /iː/, the part of the tongue that is the highest, is the centre of the "front"; for /ɪ/, the highest is the hinder part of the "front". Thus the quality of the two sounds is different.

**Exercise P-3**   扫码听音频

 1. Listen and compare the following two vowels.

| /iː/ | /ɪ/ | /iː/ | /ɪ/ |
|---|---|---|---|
| deep /diːp/ | dip /dɪp/ | wheat /wiːt/ | wit /wɪt/ |
| green /griːn/ | grin /grɪn/ | peak /piːk/ | pick /pɪk/ |
| feel /fiːl/ | fill /fɪl/ | seat /siːt/ | sit /sɪt/ |
| beach /biːtʃ/ | bitch /bɪtʃ/ | deed /diːd/ | did /dɪd/ |

2. Read and repeat the following phrases.

(1)

a ˈkey and a ˋbee / a ˈleaf and a ˋtree/ a ˈteam ˋleader/ˈeat the ˋmeat/ ˈheat the ˋbeef/ ˈeat the ˋbeef/ ˈpeople's po ˋlice

(2)

a ˈbig ˋfish/ a ˈfish and a ˋpig/ a ˈship on the ˋriver/ ˈonly a ˋfish/ ˈtinned ˋchicken/ a ˈbig ˋcity/ ˈlittle ˋLily/ ˈlittle by ˋlittle

3. Read and repeat the following sentences.

(1)

ˈEat the ˋmeat, but ˈdon't ˈeat the ˋbeef, please.
ˈDo you ˈsee the ˈgreen ˈleaves in the ˊtree?
We've ˈbeen in the ˈgreen ˈfields for ˈthree ˋweeks.
ˈThree ˈgeese are ˈeating ˈgreen ˋleaves in the ˈwheat ˋfields.
Please ˈkeep these ˈstreets ˋclean.

The 'teacher re'peated the ˋspeech to 'greet the ˋpeople.
We 'eat ˊ meat, ˊ peas, ˊ beans and ˋcheese for 'three ˋmeals.
'Three ˇcheese ˋsandwiches, 'one ˇmeat ˋsandwich, and 'three ˋteas, please.

(2)

It's a 'little ˋbaby.
Please 'give him 'this ˋticket.
'Little 'Lily 'lives in this 'pretty ˋcity.
'Finish it in a ˋminute | if it is 'not ˋdifficult.
He will 'bring his 'sister with him to the ˋparty.
It's a ˋpity | that it's 'still ˋmisty in this 'city of ˋItaly.
I 'think it's an 'interesting ˋfilm.
'Isn't it a ˋpity | that you 'live in a 'big 'city like ˋthis?
A 'little 'pill can 'cure a 'great ˋill.
Please 'give Tim the 'tickets for the ˋfilm.
It 'isn't 'easy to 'dig a ˊpit with 'only a ˋpick, | ˊis it?
The 'teacher is 'going to 'give Hill a ˋquiz | to 'see if he can 'use "'it" corˋrectly.

## 4. Tick the right word you heard.

(1) The 'best ('sheep, 'ship) 'stayed in the ˋcountry.
(2) He does 'not want to ('live, 'leave) ˋthat way.
(3) He had a 'bad (ˋsleep, ˋslip).
(4) There is a ('beach, 'bitch) in the ˋpicture.
(5) 'Move ('these, 'this) ˋplease.
(6) 'First, you 'must (ˋheat, ˋhit) it.
(7) Those ('hills, 'heels) are 'quite ˋhigh.
(8) We 'need to 'get more (ˋbeads, ˋbids).
(9) I 'asked him to 'take the (ˋlead, ˋlid).
(10) I 'want you to ('feel, 'fill) this ˋdish.

Unit 4   English Vowels — Pure Vowels

5. Read for fun.

(1)

'See the 'breeze 'teasing the ˊ tree,
'Weaving the ˊ leaves | or 'shaking them ˋ free.
'Tossing the 'fleece of ˋ sheep, | that ˊ keep
On 'peacefully ˊ feeding, | 'half a ˋ sleep.

The 'fish in the 'river 'swiftly ˊ swim,
And 'slip through the ˊ weeds | with a 'silver ˋ gleam,
Till they 'flick their 'fins and 'rise with a ˊ swish
To 'nibble the ˊ midges (蚊蚋) | that 'skim the ˋ stream.

(2)

'Silly ˋ Billy! 'Silly ˋ Billy!
'Why is 'Billy ˋ silly?
'Silly 'Billy 'hid a ˋ shilling,
'Isn't 'Billy ˋ silly?

## Ⅱ. Front Vowels /e/ and /æ/

/e/

### Brief Descriptions

a. The front of the tongue is raised between the close-mid and open-mid positions;
b. The lips are loosely spread;
c. The tongue is tenser than for /ɪ/;
d. The side rims make a light contact with the upper molars;
e. It is generally short.

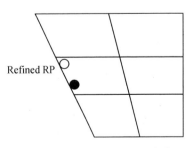

Fig. 8   Variants of RP /e/

### Spelling and Sound

e—egg, send, set, bed, went

ea—head, breath, dead

a—any, many, Thames /temz/

Note: says, said, friend, bury

/æ/

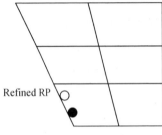

Fig. 9  Variants of RP /æ/

### Brief Descriptions

a. The front of the tongue is raised to just above the open position;

b. The lips are neutrally open;

c. The side rims make a very slight contact with the back upper molars.

### Spelling and Sound

a—at, sat, hand, lamp, rash, manly

ai—plait, plaid

### Advice to the Teacher and Students

Some students cannot distinguish /e/ from /æ/. In their pronunciation, /bæt/ and /bet/ sound alike. They should open their mouths wide (teeth and lips farther apart than for /e/) and keep their tongues lying flat in their mouths almost at the lowest position for front vowels when they make /æ/. Be sure not to round the lips. The teacher is advised to instruct students to start from /e/, then slightly lower the tongue and lengthen the more open /æ/ a little.

### A Brief Summary of the Front Vowels

The front vowels have the following features in common:

a. The front of the tongue is raised to various levels in the direction of the hard palate.

b. The tip of the tongue is usually kept down behind the lower teeth.
c. The lips are spread.

## Questions for Discussion

1. How are /iː/ and /ɪ/ produced? What's the difference between them?
2. How are /e/ and /æ/ pronounced? How are they different from each other?
3. What are the common features of the front vowels?

### Exercise P-4

 扫码听音频

 1. Listen and compare the following three vowels.

| /e/ | /æ/ | /ɪ/ | /e/ |
|---|---|---|---|
| beg /beg/ | bag /bæg/ | bit /bɪt/ | bet /bet/ |
| said /sed/ | sad /sæd/ | lid /lɪd/ | led /led/ |
| pet /pet/ | pat /pæt/ | hill /hɪl/ | hell /hel/ |
| pen /pen/ | pan /pæn/ | tin /tɪn/ | ten /ten/ |

 2. Listen and repeat the following phrases.

(1)

ˈred ˋpens/ ˈred ˋdresses/ ˈset ˋexpressions/ ˈbest ˋfriends/ ˈbest ˋmen/ a ˈletter to a ˋfriend/ ˈget ˋready/ ˈsell ˋeggs

(2)

a ˈblack ˋcat/ a ˈblack ˋhat/ a ˈblack ˋhandbag/ ˈJack and ˋBlack/ ˈstand ˋback/ ˈcatch the ˋrat/ˈclap ˋhands

 3. Listen and repeat the following sentences.

(1)

ˈJenny is ˈgetting ˈbetter and ˋbetter.
ˈDon't forˈget to ˈlet the ˈhens ˋout.
ˈDon't forˈget to ˈtell ˋTed | to ˈget ˈready for the ˋtest.
ˊEast or ˋwest, | ˈhome is ˋbest.

'All is ˊwell | that 'endsˋwell.

'Better to 'do ˊwell than toˋsay ˌwell.

'Birds of a ˊfeather | 'flock toˋgether.

'Ten 'best 'men were 'sent to 'help theirˋfriends. They 'said they 'went at 'ten toˋten, | or was it 'ten to ˋtwelve. They 'don't re'memberˋwhen | they ˌwent, ˊdo you?

(2)

'Harry was 'standing by theˋtaxi.

The 'rabbit 'dashed from the 'sandyˋbank.

'Get a ˊladder | and 'hang 'up theˋbanner.

She had a 'fan in herˋhand.

'Hands 'thanked the 'man for 'bringing 'back his 'blackˋhat.

'Jack's 'black 'cat | is 'catching that 'fatˋrat.

The 'man 'ran·back to 'gather his 'blackˋhandbag.

'Henry 'thanked the 'man with a 'Panamaˊhat | for 'sending his 'moneyˋback.

I'm ˊglad | I am 'not 'married to that 'bad-temperedˋman.

They were 'trapped on the 'sands andˋcaptured.

'Dad at'tacked the 'bad 'man in theˋvan | with aˋhammer.

'Dad 'won't at'tack until he is atˋtacked.

### 🎤 4. Tick the right word you heard.

(1) 'Did you 'see the ('bill, 'bell) on theˊtable?

(2) He 'asked the as'sistant to | 'show him the (ˋpin, ˋpen).

(3) 'Did he 'buy a (ˊpan, ˊpen)?

(4) The (said, sad) 'woman 'died of 'heart diˋsease.

### 🎤 5. Read the following rhymes.

'Good, 'better, ˊbest,

'Never 'let itˋrest;

Till 'good is ˊbetter,

And 'betterˋbest.

'Jack had aˋrat; 'Sam had aˋcat.
'Sam's cat 'ate 'Jack'sˋrat.
'Jack 'asked 'Sam to 'pay for hisˋrat.
'Sam ′ said, | "I'll 'give you my 'cat for yourˋrat.

## Ⅲ. Central Vowels /ɜː/, /ə/ and /ʌ/

The three central vowels in English are /ɜː/, /ə/ and /ʌ/ as in **bird**, **sofa** and **up**.

/ɜː/

### Brief Descriptions

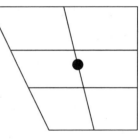

Fig. 10  RP/ɜː/

a. The center of the tongue is raised between the close-mid and open-mid positions;
b. The lips are neutrally open;
c. No contact is made between the tongue and the upper molars;
d. It is generally long.

### Spelling and Sound

er, ear—her, serve, earth, heard

ir—bird, first, girl

ur—turn, church, nurse, purse, suburban

w+or —word, world, work, worse

our—journey, courtesy

### Advice to the Teacher and Students

In making the sound, the tip of the tongue generally touches the base of the lower teeth so as to avoid a back vowel value. The main body of the tongue is rather flat, only the middle of the tongue is somewhat raised.

/ə/

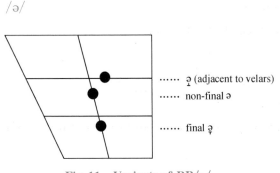

Fig. 11　Variants of RP/ə/

**Brief Descriptions**

a. Its quality is that of a central vowel with a neutral lip position. /ə/ has a very high frequency of occurrence in unstressed syllables;

b. It has in non-final positions a tongue-raising between the open-mid and close-mid positions, e.g. asleep, fatigue;

c. In the vicinity of velar consonants /k, g/ and /ŋ/, however, the tongue will be raised to the close-mid and retracted positions under the influence of the following consonant, e.g. again, long ago;

d. In the final position the vowel is articulated in the open-mid central position or in the most open region of the central area, e.g. mother, over;

e. It is generally short.

**Spelling and Sound**

i—possible, horrible

e—gentlemen, pavement

a—woman, about, breakfast

o—oblige, method, Europe

u—suppose, column

ar—particular, forward

er—father, better, manner

or—doctor, effort

oar—cupboard

ou—famous, spacious

our—colour, neighbour

ure—figure, nature, literature

re—centre, metre, litre

## Advice to the Teacher and Students

English rhythm has much to do with /ə/ because it often occurs in weak forms in unstressed syllables to help acquire the characteristic stress pattern. In nonfinal positions, the tongue position for /ə/ is about the same as that for /ɜː/, but /ə/ is very short in terms of its length. Be sure that the tongue position for /ɜː, ə/ should not be as back as that for Chinese 饿(è).

### Exercise P-5

 扫码听音频

 1. Listen and compare the following vowels.

| /ɜː/ | /ə/ |
|---|---|
| murmur /ˈmɜːmə/ | summer /ˈsʌmə/ |
| first /fɜːst/ | suffer /ˈsʌfə/ |
| sir /sɜː/ | officer /ˈɒfɪsə/ |
| turf /tɜːf/ | litter /ˈlɪtə/ |

| /ɜː/ | /ɔː/ |
|---|---|
| stir /stɜː/ | store /stɔː/ |
| word /wɜːd/ | ward /wɔːd/ |
| year /jɜː/ | your /jɔː/ |
| curse /kɜːs/ | cause /kɔːz/ |

 2. Listen and repeat the following phrases.

(1)

a ˈbird and a ˋworm/ ˈthirty ˈshirts and ˋskirts/ ˈthirty ˋgirls/ ˈlearn a ˋmethod/ ˈturn the ˋcorner/ a ˈworld-ˈfamous ˋexpert/ the ˈearly ˋbird / the ˈbird on the ˋperch/ preˈfer a ˋshirt/ preˈfer a ˋskirt/

(2)

the ˈleader and the ˋteacher/ the ˈteacher and the ˋworker/ ˈbetter and ˋbetter/ ˈover and ˈover aˋgain/ ˈsooner or ˋlater/ about the ˋworker/ aˈround the ˋcorner

## 3. Read and repeat the following sentences.

(1)

'Learn, 'learn and 'learn a ˋgain.

It's the 'early ´bird | that 'catches the ˋworm.

'Work comes ˋfirst.

'First ´come, | 'first ˋserved.

I 'gave her some ˋpearls | for her 'thirty-first ˋbirthday.

I 'urged the 'thirty 'thirsty ˋnurses | to 'drink ˋfirst.

The 'workers 'worked in the 'dirty ˋworkshop.

(2)

'Better 'late than ˋnever.

The 'wonderful 'weather was ˋover.

The 'best 'player was ˋinjured.

I'm a'fraid that the 'colour is 'unsuitable for my ˋmother.

The 'farm ma´chine and the ˋfarmer | were the 'heart of the ˋmatter.

The time of the concert was altered.

## 4. Tick the right word you heard.

(1) He was ('first, 'forced) to ˋdo it.

(2) He 'often 'wears (ˋshorts, ˋshirts).

(3) I'm (ˋworking, ˋwalking).

(4) She is (ˋyearning, ˋyawning).

## 5. Read for fun.

'Worms 'squirm in the 'earth

When 'first is ˋheard

The 'murmur and 'chirp

Of the 'early ˋbird.

You should re'member

To at'tend the ˋlecture.

Who 'says 'better late 'than ˋnever?

You'd 'better be `earlier.

/ʌ/

## Brief Descriptions

a. The centre of the tongue is raised to just above the fully open position;
b. The lips are neutrally open;
c. No contact is made between the tongue and the upper molars;
d. It is generally short.

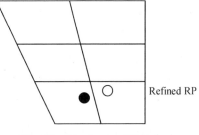

Fig. 12   Variants of RP /ʌ/

## Spelling and Sound

u—up, sun, cut, dull, mum

o—son, come, one, among, done, month, colour, monkey, mother, nothing, Monday, London

ou—country, enough, young, southern

oo—blood, flood

oe—does

## Advice to the Teacher and Students

Some Chinese learners tend to use lip-rounding for /ʌ/. In their pronunciation, bus /bʌs/ sounds too much like boss /bɒs/, cup /kʌp/ too much like cop /kɒp/. This mistake may be corrected by spreading the lips.

Some students often confuse /ʌ/ with /æ/. In their making of /ʌ/, luck /lʌk/ sounds like lack /læk/. To avoid this mispronunciation, they should take care not to move the tongue too forward. Remember /ʌ/ is a central vowel while /æ/ is a front vowel.

## A Brief Summary of the English Central Vowels

a. The main body of the tongue is rather flat, only the centre of the tongue is somewhat raised in the direction of the junction between the hard palate and the soft palate.

b. The tongue-tip is drawn away from the lower teeth.

c. The lips are spread.

## Questions for Discussion

1. How is the central vowel /ɜː/ produced?
2. How is the central vowel /ə/ pronounced?
3. What's the difference between the two phonemes /ɜː/ and /ə/?
4. How is the central vowel /ʌ/ made?
5. What are the common features of the central vowels?

## Exercise P-6

 扫码听音频

 1. Listen and compare the following vowels.

| /ʌ/ | /æ/ |
|---|---|
| cut /kʌt/ | cat /kæt/ |
| much /mʌtʃ/ | match /mætʃ/ |
| bug /bʌg/ | bag /bæg/ |
| cup /kʌp/ | cap /kæp/ |
| /ʌ/ | /ɒ/ |
| but /bʌt/ | boss /bɒs/ |
| duck /dʌk/ | dock /dɒk/ |
| tun /tʌn/ | Tom /tɒm/ |
| colour /ˈkʌlə/ | collar /ˈkɒlə/ |
| luck /lʌk/ | lock /lɒk/ |

Unit 4  English Vowels — Pure Vowels

 2. Listen and repeat the following phrases.

'much ˋ love/ a 'lovely ˋ couple/ a 'lovely ˋ cousin/ a 'cup and some ˋ nuts/ a 'cup of ˋ honey/ 'shut ˋ up/ 'just ˋ once/ an'other 'cup of ˋ punch/ a 'wonderful ˋ sunset/ 'blood for ˋ blood/'honey on the ˋ bun

 3. Listen and repeat the following sentences.

'Hurry ˋ up! The 'sun has 'come ˋ up.
It's 'fun to 'run and 'jump in the ˋ sun.
I 'love 'buns and 'butter for ˋ supper.
The 'summer 'sun 'covers the 'huts in the 'southern ˋ countries.
'Ask 'mother if the 'mutton is e'nough for ˋ supper.
'Well be'gun is 'half ˋ done.
'Every 'country has its ˋ customs.
'Money is ˋ something, | but 'not ˋ everything.
'Does this 'bus 'come from the 'Summer ʹPalace?
'Let us 'help pull out the 'truck stuck in the ˋ mud.

4. Tick the right word you heard.

(1) — Do you 'know how he ʹ did it?
    — He 'used a (ˋ pun, ˋ pan).
(2) 'Everyone 'envied him his 'new (ˋ hut, ˋ hat).
(3) The ('gnat, 'nut) an ˋ noyed her.
(4) Mr. ('Barton, 'Button) is a ˋ barber.

5. Read for fun.

'Hurry ˋ up! 'Hurry ˋ up!
There 'comes the ˋ bus.
'Don't ˋ worry, | I'm 'always ˋ lucky.
I 'surely can 'catch the ˋ bus.

# IV. Back Vowel /ɑː/

The five back vowels in English are /ɑː, ɒ, ɔː, ʊ, uː/ as in **d**ar**k**, **d**o**ck**, **d**oo**r**, **w**ou**l**d and **d**o.

/ɑː/

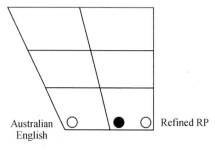

Fig. 13　Variants of RP /ɑː/

**Brief Descriptions**

a. The part of the tongue raised is between the centre and back in the fully open position;
b. The lips are neutrally open;
c. No contact is made between the side rims and upper molars;
d. It is generally long.

**Spelling and Sound**

a—after, staff, past, path

ar—car, star, part, march, dark, garden (when final or followed by a consonant)

al—calm, palm, half (l is silent)

**Advice to the Teacher and Students**

Many students confuse /ɑː/ with /ʌ/, so that their cart /kɑːt/ sounds much like cut /kʌt/. To avoid this mistake, they should pay attention to the differences in the formation of the two vowels. For /ɑː/, the tongue almost lies flat in the mouth. The tip of the tongue does not touch the lower teeth. The lips are neutrally open. As for /ʌ/, the part of the tongue that is raised is the centre of the tongue. The tip of the tongue touches the base of the lower teeth. The lips are widely open but not as wide as that for /ɑː/. Remember /ɑː/ is a back truly open vowel while /ʌ/ is a central vowel.

### Exercise P-7

 扫码听音频

1. Listen and compare the following two groups of vowels.

| /ɑː/ | /ʌ/ | /ɑː/ | /æ/ |
|---|---|---|---|
| lark /lɑːk/ | luck /lʌk/ | bark /bɑːk/ | back /bæk/ |
| calm /kɑːm/ | come /kʌm/ | part /pɑːt/ | pat /pæt/ |
| march /mɑːtʃ/ | much /mʌtʃ/ | barn /bɑːn/ | ban /bæn/ |
| heart /hɑːt/ | hut /hʌt/ | barge /bɑːdʒ/ | badge /bædʒ/ |

2. Listen and repeat the following phrases.

a ˈfast ˋcar/ a ˈmarvelous guiˋtar/ ˈheart-to-ˋheart/ ˈMargaret and ˋGarth/ a ˈlarge ˋshark/ a ˈstarved ˋartist/ a ˈstarry ˋMarch ˌnight

3. Listen and repeat the following sentences.

He ˈlaughs ˊbest who ˈlaughs ˋlast.
A ˈlarge ˈarmy ˈmarched past the ˋgrassland.
ˈBarbara and ˈCharles are ˈdancing in a ˈlarge ˋgarden.
The ˈcar was ˈparked in the ˋfarmyard.
ˈHalf the ˈclass have ˋpassed.
ˈMargaret's ˈaunt is ˈfar ˈsmarter than her ˋfather.
A ˈbargain is a ˋbargain.
ˈMartin's ˈaunt is ˈtaking a ˈsun-bath in the ˈafterˋnoon.
ˈFather's ˈcar ˈruns ˈveryˋfast.
The ˈdance ˈparty in the ˇfarmyard ˈlasted ˈfar into theˋnight.
ˈArnold ˈcan't ˈtell a ˈbarber from aˋcarpenter.

4. Tick the right word you heard.

(1) ˈDid he ˈbuy a (ˊcart, ˊcat)?

(2) I 'see it's a (`hat,`hut).

(3) There is a (`bun,`barn) there.

(4) He 'likes her (`form,`farm).

## 5. Read for fun.

You can 'drive a ´car,

'Running on the 'road`fast.

I can 'drive a ´star,

'Flying in the`dark.

The 'best I´laugh,

I ˌlaugh the`last.

## V. Back Vowels /ɒ/ and /ɔː/

/ɒ/

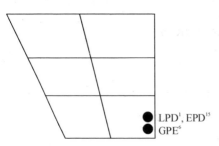

Fig. 14  Variants of RP /ɒ/

### Brief Descriptions

a. The back of the tongue is slightly above the fully open position with wide open jaws and slightly open lip rounding;

b. No contact is made between the side rims and the upper molars;

c. It is generally short.

### Spelling and Sound

o—on, dock, dog, sorry, holiday, gone

a—was, what, watch, want, quality

ou, ow—cough, trough, knowledge

au—because, sausage, Austria, Australia

/ɔː/

### Brief Descriptions

a. The back of the tongue is raised between the open-mid and close-mid positions with medium lip rounding;
b. No contact is made between the side rims and the upper molars;
c. It is generally long.

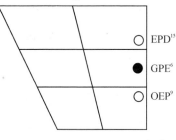

Fig. 15 Variants of RP /ɔː/

### Spelling and Sound

or—horse, cord, born, sword

aw—saw, jaw, law, yawn

ou, au—ought, bought, daughter, fault, cause

a—all, talk, salt, war, water

ore, oor, oar, our—before, more, door, floor, oar, board, court, four

### Advice to the Teacher and Students

At present the tongue position is often as close as that of RP/ʊ/. Many students substitute /ɒ/ for /ɔː/. In their pronunciation, spot /spɒt/ and sport /spɔːt/ sound alike. To avoid such a mistake, they should open the lower jaw less wide (about two thirds of the jaw-opening for /ɒ/) and raise the back of the tongue higher.

Some students confuse /ɒ/ with /ɑː/. In their pronunciation, pot /pɒt/ sounds like part /pɑːt/. This mistake may be corrected if they round their lips a little.

### Exercise P-8

 扫码听音频

 1. Listen and compare the following two groups of vowels.

/ɒ/         /ɔː/         /ɒ/         /ɑː/
cock /kɒk/  cork /kɔːk/  dock /dɒk/  dark /dɑːk/

shot /ʃɒt/    short /ʃɔːt/    god /gɒd/    guard /gɑːd/
Bonn /bɒn/    born /bɔːn/    shop /ʃɒp/    sharp /ʃɑːp/
chock /tʃɒk/    chalk /tʃɔːk/    hot /hɒt/    heart /hɑːt/

## 2. Read and repeat the following phrases.

(1)

a ˈlongˋ job/ ˈpopular ˋsongs/ ˈlots of ˈclocks and ˋwatches/ ˈsocks and ˋstockings/ a ˈbox of ˋsocks/ ˈJohn and ˋBonn/ ˈwatch the ˋswan/ resˈpond to the ˋsong/ ˈcost a ˋlot

(2)

ˈfour ˋscore/ ˈforty ˋhorses/ ˈshort ˋstories/ ˈsports reˋports from ˈchannel ˋfour/ ˈwalk across the ˋlawn/ ˈmorning ˈnews reˋport/ ˈforty reˋporters/ ˈPaul ˊShort and ˈGeorge ˋBall/ to ˈtalk a ˋlot/ a ˈpopular ˋsport/ ˈhot ˋwater/ ˈnot at ˋall/ ˈFoggy ˋBottom/ ˈport of ˋcall/ to ˈflog a ˈdead ˋhorse/ to ˈmake a ˈlong ˈstory ˋshort

## 3. Read and repeat the following sentences.

(1)

ˈJohn is ˋstrong. ˈOliver is ˋnot.

ˈJohn is a ˋdoctor. ˈOliver is a ˋshopper.

ˈOliver ˈwatches ˈJohn ˈload a ˈstrong ˋbox | at the ˋdocks.

They ˈwashed the ˈsocks on the ˋrocks.

ˈJohn has ˈgot a ˈpot of ˈhot ˋwater.

ˈTom's ˈgot a lot of ˋdots | on his ˋsocks.

ˈLots and ˈlots of ˈclocks and ˊwatches | have ˈgone ˋwrong.

The ˈdoctor has a ˈstock of ˈbottles in his ˋoffice.

(2)

ˈMaud is ˋshort. ˈPaul is ˋtall.

ˈMaud is ˈwalking on the ˋlawn. ˈPaul is ˈcrawling along the ˋwall.

Your ˈfour ˈdaughters are ˈallˈvery ˋtall.

'All the 'four were 'born aˇ broad.
The 'tallest of the 'four is 'walking to the ˋ door.
'Paul 'brought 'straw for the ˊ horse | and 'bought 'salt ˇ pork.
'Forty 'horses were 'walking across the ˋ lawn.
The 'robbers were 'caught on the ˊspot by the ˋ cops.
The 'ball 'rolled aˈcross the ˊ lawn | into the ˋ pond.
'Bob 'quarrelled with his ˊ boss | and 'lost his ˇ job.
She 'mops the 'floor 'every ˊ morning | at 'four o'ˋ clock.
You 'ought to 'do what the 'doctor ˋ ordered.

### 4. Tick the right word you heard.

(1) The 'man was ('shot,ˋ short).
(2) The ('clerk, 'clock) is ˋ slow.
(3) The ('cock, 'cork) is 'nowhere to be ˇ found.
(4) It's a 'good ˋ coat, but I 'don't 'like the (ˇ colour,ˇ collar).
(5) She 'wanted to 'find a (ˋ potter,ˋ porter).

### 5. Read for fun.

'Froggy-'boggy 'sat on a ˊ rock,
'Froggy-'boggy had a 'great ˋ shock!
'Froggy-'boggy 'fell off the ˊ top,
'Into the 'pond he 'fell with a ˇ plop!


Good 'morning to 'all who ˊ walk,
Good 'morning to 'all who ˇ crawl;
Good 'morning to 'all who ˊ soar,
Or 'swim, good 'morning, I ˇ call.
To 'broad and to ˋ small, to 'short and to ˇ tall;
Good 'morning, good 'morning to ˋ all.

# VI. Back Vowels /ʊ/ and /uː/

/ʊ/

**Brief Descriptions**

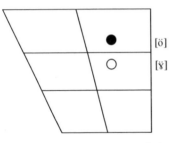

Fig. 16  Variants of RP /ʊ/

a. The part of the tongue raised is nearer to the centre than to the back. It is raised to just above the close-mid position;

b. The lips are closely but loosely rounded;

c. The tongue is lax;

d. No firm contact is made between the tongue and the upper molars;

e. It is generally short.

**Spelling and Sound**

u—put, full, sugar, bull, push, butch, Muslim

o—wolf, woman, bosom

oo—before *t* and *d* in the words: good, foot, hood, soot, stood, wood; before *k* in the words: book, cook, hook, look, rook, brook, took, shook (but: spook /spuːk/)

ou—could, should, would

**Advice to the Teacher and Students**

The students should be made aware of the qualitative difference between /ʊ/ and /uː/. Neither the lips nor the tongue should be tensely held because /ʊ/ is a lax vowel, a vowel with only slight rounded lips. Many Chinese students make this sound too much like /uː/. In their pronunciation, full /fʊl/ sounds too much like fool /fuːl/.

/uː/

### Brief Descriptions

a. The back of the tongue raised is just below the closest position and it is somewhat centralized from true back;
b. The lips are loosely rounded;
c. The tongue is tense;
d. No firm contact is made between the side rims and the upper molars;
e. It is generally long.

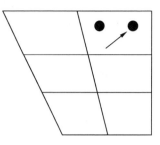

Fig. 17   Variants of RP /uː/

### Spelling and Sound

oo—too, food, soon, moon, spoon

o—do, who, move, lose

ou—you, group, soup, wound (*n*.), through

u—June, rude, Susan

ew, ue, ui, oe—chew, blue, juice, shoe

### Advice to the Teacher and Students

Remember in English /uː/ is somewhat relaxed though it is a long vowel. In the pronunciation of /uː/, the lips are more rounded and closed than for /ʊ/. The back of the tongue is raised higher, too. There is a tendency in recent years for /ʊ/ and /uː/ to move towards the central vowel area.

### A Brief Summary of Back Vowels in English

Back vowels in English have the following features in common:

a. The tongue is retracted, and the back part is raised to various levels in the direction of the soft palate.
b. The tip of the tongue is slightly drawn away from the lower teeth.

c. For /ɒ, ɔː, ʊ, uː/ the lips are rounded, but for /ɑː/ the lips are not.

## Questions for Discussion

1. How are the back vowels /ɑː, ɒ, ɔː, ʊ, uː/ pronounced respectively?
2. What are the common features of back vowels in English?

## Exercise P-9

 扫码听音频

 1. Listen and compare the following back vowels.

| /ʊ/ | /uː/ |
|---|---|
| full /fʊl/ | fool /fuːl/ |
| could /kʊd/ | cooed /kuːd/ |
| /uː/ | /ɔː/ |
| tool /tuːl/ | tall /tɔːl/ |
| boot /buːt/ | bought /bɔːt/ |
| moon /muːn/ | morn /mɔːn/ |

2. Read and repeat the following phrases.

(1)

a ˈgoodˋbook/ a ˈgoodˋcook/ a ˈgoodˋhook/ ˈgoodˋwood/ a ˈgood-lookingˋwoman/ ˈput theˋbook/ ˈtook theˋbook/ ˈpull andˋpull/ ˈshook andˋshook

(2)

ˈfood andˋsoup/ ˈSue andˋPrue/ ˈtwoˋshoes/ at ˈnoon inˋJune/ ˈblueˋboots/ ˈshoes andˋboots/ to ˈchoose a ˈgoodˋschool/ ˈonce in a ˈblueˋmoon/ a ˈgood-lookingˋman/ ˈfruitˋpudding/ to ˈcook theˋfood

3. Read and repeat the following sentences.

(1)

He had a ˈgoodˋlook | at the ˈcookeryˋbook.
The ˈwoman ˈpushed theˋbook | with herˋfoot.

'Put the 'firewood by the ˋ bushes.

Mr. 'Wood 'looks like a 'good ˋ cook.

The 'cook under'stood the 'sugar was 'no ˋ good.

He 'took a 'book to the ˊ wood and had a 'good ˋ look at it.

(2)

Please 'choose either ˊ boots or ˋ shoes.

Who 'said the 'soup was 'too ˋ cool?

You may 'use the 'blue ˋ boots | and 'don't ˙ move the 'new ˋ shoes.

'Hugh's 'tooth is ˋ loose.

'Hugh 'shoots a ˋ goose | and 'loses his 'loose ˋ tooth.

As a ˊ rule, | Sue is 'foolish and 'stupid at ˋ school.

The 'bush was 'full of 'good ˋ wood.

ˋ Look, the 'screw has 'got ˋ loose.

It was ˊ true that Mr. 'Luke 'killed the ˊ wolf and 'saved the 'woman from the 'cruel ˋ beast.

She should 'go to her 'dentist at 'two o''clock in the after ˊ noon to 'get the 'bad tooth 'pulled ˋ out.

## 4. Read for fun.

'Look, 'look, ˋ look,

The 'good 'old ˋ cook,

'Took out a ˋ pudding!

'Look! 'Look! ˋ Look!

At 'noon 'I 'took a ˊ book

And 'sat by the 'pool in the ˋ wood.

I 'soon 'took off my ˊ shoe

And 'put my 'foot in the ˋ pool.

ˋ Oh! How ˋ cool! How ˋ cool!

# Unit 5

# English Vowels—Diphthongs

A diphthong is a glide from one vowel to another. When we make a diphthong the position of the tongue and that of the lips are changed to some extent, yet the position of the second vowel is usually not reached. The first element is strong, clear and distinct whereas the second element is rather weak, short and unclear. Diphthongs may be said to be the union of the two vowel sounds blending into one. So it is of great importance to pay good attention at the same time to both the change from one vowel to another and the union of the two vowels.

There are eight diphthongs: five closing diphthongs and three centring diphthongs.

The five closing diphthongs are /eɪ, aɪ, ɔɪ, əʊ, aʊ/ as in b**ay**, b**uy**, b**oy**, kn**ow**, n**ow**.

## I. Closing Diphthongs /eɪ/, /aɪ/ and /ɔɪ/

/eɪ/

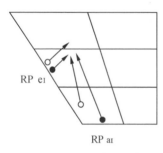

Fig. 18  RP /eɪ, aɪ/

**Brief Descriptions**

a. The glide begins from slightly below the close-mid front position and moves in the direction of RP /ɪ/, there being a slight closing movement of the jaw;

b. The lips are spread;

c. The starting point is somewhat closer than RP

/e/ of bet.

## Spelling and Sound

a—a, face, lady, male, ape, late, waste, ache, apricot, cradle

ai, ay—rain, aim, waist, day, may, pay

ei, ey—eight, rein, veil, weigh, they, obey, survey

ea—great, break, steak

## Advice to the Teacher and Students

Say it as the standard Chinese ⟨ei⟩. Giving sufficient length to the first element. The second element of the diphthong can only be touched on.

/aɪ/

## Brief Descriptions

a. It begins at a point slightly behind the front open position and then moves in the direction of /ɪ/;

b. The closing movement of the low jaw is obvious;

c. The lips change from a neutral to a loosely spread position.

## Spelling and Sound

i, y—I, time, write, bite, climb, by, cry, dry, try

igh, eigh—high, light, fight, might, height

ie, ye—die, lie, pie, tried, dye, good-bye

ei, ai—either, aisle

Note: eye, buy

## Advice to the Teacher and Students

In the making of /aɪ/, the front of the tongue is the highest, the diphthong begins at a front vowel, slightly more open than for /æ/, and immediately moves in the direction of /ɪ/. To pronounce /aɪ/ correctly, it is not necessary that /ɪ/ should be actually reached.

/ɔɪ/

### Brief Descriptions

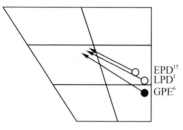

Fig. 19　Variants of RP /ɔɪ/

a. The tongue glide begins at a point between the open-mid and open back positions and moves in the direction of /ɪ/;
b. The tongue movement extends from the back to centralized front;
c. The lips are open-rounded for the first element;
d. The lips change from rounded to spread for the second.

### Spelling and Sound

oi—oil, voice, boil, point, noise
oy—boy, toy, employ, oyster

### Advice to the Teacher and Students

Diphthong /ɔɪ/ glides from a position between /ɒ/ and /ɔː/ to /ɪ/. In the pronunciation of the sound the lips change from rounded to spread while the lower jaw moves upward. If students can pronounce the pure vowels very well, they will find it less difficult in producing a diphthong.

**Exercise P-10**  扫码听音频

 1. Listen and compare the following diphthongs.

|  /eɪ/ | /aɪ/ | /ɔɪ/ |
| --- | --- | --- |
| bay /beɪ/ | buy /baɪ/ | boy /bɔɪ/ |

say /seɪ/         sigh /saɪ/        soy /sɔɪ/
mail /meɪl/       mile /maɪl/       moil /mɔɪl/
nail /neɪl/       Nile /naɪl/       noil /nɔɪl/
/aɪ/              /æ/               /ɑː/
bite /baɪt/       bat /bæt/         bar /bɑː/
fight /faɪt/      fat /fæt/         far /fɑː/
bike /baɪk/       back /bæk/        bark /bɑːk/
type /taɪp/       tap /tæp/         tar /tɑː/

## 2. Read and repeat the following phrases.

(1)

'April ˋ8th/ 'May 'eighˋteenth/ 'eighty-ˋeight/ the 'late ˋtrain/ 'make a misˋtake/ the 'same ˋway/ a 'rainy ˋday/ the 'same misˋtake/ 'eight ˋcakes/ 'bake ˋcakes/ Mayˋ Day/ a 'greatˋ change/ a ˋrailway ˌstation/

(2)

a 'nice ˋkite/ 'five ˋkites/ 'high in the ˋsky/ a 'nice ˋchild/ a 'white ˋknife/ 'five 'iceˋcreams/ a 'lightˋ bike/ 'ninety-ˋnine/ˋtypewriter/ 'flyˋhigh/ 'Fridayˋ night/ 'by andˋ by/ a 'rise in theˋ price/ my 'short-'sighted ˋeyes/ 'time andˋ tide/ a 'niceˋ tie

(3)

ˌthe 'voice of ˋjoy/ the 'boy's ˋtoy/ a 'toy and a ˋcoin/ 'Roy's ˋoyster/ 'spoil theˋ joy/ 'spoil theˋ boy/ the 'noise of theˋ boys/ the 'noise of theˋ toys/ anˈnoy theˋ boys/ 'spoil theˋ toys/ 'toil and 'moil on theˋ soil

## 3. Read and repeat the following sentences.

(1)

'Jane 'came on a 'grey, 'rainy ˋday.
They 'came on the 'same ˊday | by the 'same ˋtrain.
Please 'take the 'paper a ˋway.
'Don't 'make the 'same misˋtake.
'Turn to 'page 'eighty-ˋeight.

They ˈsay they may ˈplay the ˈsame ˎgame.
The ˈtrain is ˈwaiting at the ˋrailway ˌstation.
ˈJane may ˈstay aˊway | and ˈplay with ˎKate.
ˈJames ˈplays with his ˊtrains | and ˎplanes.
ˈJames ˈtakes a ˊcake | from ˈJane's ˎplate.
They ˈsay the ˈtrain ˈcame ˈevery ˈeightˊdays | in ˎMay.

(2)

ˈFive ˈtimes ˊfive | is ˈtwenty-ˎfive.
ˈStrike while the ˈiron is ˎhot.
ˈGreat ˈminds ˈthink aˎlike.
ˈClive ˈclimbs ˈhigh ˈspires at ˎnight.
ˈDinah /ˈdainə/ is ˈquiteˋnice | but ˈfrightfully ˎshy.
ˈClive deˈcides to inˈvite ˈDinah to ˎdine.
ˈDinah deˈcides to arˈrive onˎtime.
The ˈchild with a ˈwide ˊsmile | is ˈriding on my ˎbike.
A ˈwhite ˊkite | is ˈflying ˈhigh in the ˎsky.
She has a ˈfly in her ˈright ˎeye, | and that's ˈwhy she's ˎcrying.
The ˈchild ˈtried ˈnineˋtimes for the ˋwriting ˌprize.
My ˈeyes are ˋtired | because I ˈtried to ˈread in the ˈpoor ˎlight.
My ˈchild is ˈquiteˋtired | ˈcrying by my ˎside.
He'd ˈdrive ˈfive ˈmiles onˋFriday ˌnight | to a ˎfight.
Mr. ˈWhite ˈtried andˋtried | but he ˈcouldn't ˈclimb ˎhigher.
You might ˈbuy aˋbike | for your ˎwife.

(3)

I'll ˈleave the ˈchoice of the ˈtoy to my ˎboy.
Please aˈvoid ˈpouringˋoil | on the ˎsoil.
The ˈspoiled ˈboy deˈstroyed the ˎtoys.
He has a ˈnoisyˋvoice | and ˈspoils our enˋjoyment.
Their ˈhands wereˋoily | and ˈsoiled by their ˎtoil.
The ˈboy was overˋjoyed | with his ˈnoisy ˎtoys.
The ˈboy ˈRoy was anˈnoyed about the ˎnoise.

It's a 'joy to 'watch 'Roy 'playing with his ˎtoys.
'Don't 'spoil the ˋboy | by 'giving him 'too many ˎtoys.

### 4. Tick the right word you heard.

(1) He is 'making a (ˋcart, ˋkite).
(2) It's 'getting (ˋlight, ˋlate).
(3) The ('coin, 'corn) was 'found in the ˋcellar.
(4) She 'took 'cover in a (ˋshed, ˋshade).
(5) The deˈtective ('taped, 'tapped) the ˋtelephone ˌcalls.

### 5. Read for fun.

'Rain, 'rain, 'go aˋway!
'Tom and 'Mary 'want to ˋplay.
'Rain, 'rain, 'go aˋway!
'Come aˈgain anˈother ˋday.


'Joyce, ˋJoyce,
'Shouting at the 'top of his ˋvoice,
'Making such a ˋnoise,
ˋOh, 'Joyce! ˋJoyce!


I 'asked my 'mother for 'five ˋcents,
To 'see the 'elephant 'jump the ˋfence.
He 'jumped so ˊhigh, | he 'touched the ˇsky,
And 'never 'came ˊback | till the 'fourth of Juˋly.

## II. Closing Diphthongs /əʊ/ and /aʊ/

/əʊ/

### Brief Descriptions

a. It begins at a central point between the close-mid and open-mid positions,

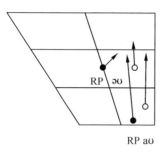

Fig. 20  RP /əʊ, aʊ/

and then moves in the direction of RP /ʊ/;

b. There is a slight closing movement of the lower jaw;

c. The lips are neutral for the first element but have a tendency to round on the second element;

d. The starting point may have a tongue position similar to that described for /ɜː/;

e. The lips change from neutral to lightly rounded.

**Spelling and Sound**

o—so, old, home, both, folk

oa—road, soap, oak, toast

oe—toe, doe, sloe, foe, hoe

ou, ow—soul, though, shoulder, know, blow

**Advice to the Teacher and Students**

Be sure to make the first element more prominent than the second. Students should take care not to confuse /əʊ/ with /ɔː/, /ɜː/ or /uː/.

/aʊ/

**Brief Descriptions**

a. It begins at a point between the back and front open positions, slightly more fronted than the position for RP /ɑː/, and moves in the direction of RP /ʊ/;

b. The lips change from a neutrally open to a weakly rounded position.

**Spelling and Sound**

ou, ow—out, brow, house, sound, cow, town, allow, fountain

Unit 5 English Vowels — Diphthongs

## Advice to the Teacher and Students

Pay great attention to the glide from one sound to the other. The second element /ʊ/ is not actually reached.

### Exercise P-11  扫码听音频

 1. Listen and compare the following three groups of vowels.

| /əʊ/ | /aʊ/ |
|---|---|
| know /nəʊ/ | now /naʊ/ |
| oat /əʊt/ | out /aʊt/ |
| tone /təʊn/ | town /taʊn/ |
| load /ləʊd/ | loud /laʊd/ |
| coat /kəʊt/ | doubt /daʊt/ |
| /əʊ/ | /uː/ |
| nose /nəʊz/ | lose /luːz/ |
| boat /bəʊt/ | boot /buːt/ |
| dome /dəʊm/ | doom /duːm/ |
| pole /pəʊl/ | pool /puːl/ |
| /aʊ/ | /ɔː/ |
| loud /laʊd/ | lord /lɔːd/ |
| down /daʊn/ | dawn /dɔːn/ |
| now /naʊ/ | nor /nɔː/ |
| cow /kaʊ/ | core /kɔː/ |

2. Read and repeat the following phrases.

(1)

a ˈnarrowˋroad/ ˈoldˋcombs/ ˈoldˋfolks/ ˈhold theˋcoat/ ˈgoˋhome/ ˈshoulder toˋshoulder/ ˈgrowˋold/ ˈrow aˋboat/ a ˈslowˋboat/ the ˈlowˋroad/ ˈsoldˋgold/ ˈoldˋbowl/ ˈhold theˋbowl/ ˈonly aˋshow/ ˈthrowˋsnow/ ˈwindowˋenvelope/ ˈhold one's ˈnose to the ˈgrind-ˋstone

(2)

a ˈloudˋ sound/ ˈround theˋ house/ ˈthousands uponˋ thousands/ ˋdown ˈtown/ ˈcrowds before theˋ house/ ˈshouts of theˋ crowds/ ˈoutside theˋ town/ ˈsouth of theˋ town/ ˈbrownˋ houses

### 3. Read and repeat the following sentences.

(1)

ˈJoan is ˈcombing her ˈgoldenˋ hair.

ˈJoe has a ˈnoble, ˈRomanˋ nose.

ˈJoan and ˈJoe ˈgo for aˋ stroll.

ˈJoe ˈshows ˈJoan hisˋ roses.

ˈJoan ˈwon't ˈgo ˙home aˋ lone.

ˈSo ˈJoe ˈgoes ˙home withˋ Joan.

ˈJoe and ˈJoan ˈrowed the ˊboat | along theˋ coast.

ˈDon't ˈthrowˋ stones.

He ˈwon't postˈpone theˋ show.

ˈDon't ˈgo ˙home aˋ lone. You ˈdon't ˈknow how ˈlonely theˋ road is.

(2)

Mr. ˈBrown ˈfound a ˈmouse in theˋ house.

Mr. ˈBrown ˈlives in a ˈround ˈhouse near theˋ town.

ˈNoˋ doubt | he ˈheard the ˈloud ˈshouts of theˋ crowd.

The ˊcrowd, | which aˈmounted to aˋ thousand, | surˈrounded the ˊhouse, | which ˈfaced the ˈsouth of the ˈcountry ˋtown.

ˈNow I have ˈnoˋ doubt | he can proˈnounce the ˈword "aˋ mount".

"ˈMouse", "ˈmound" and "ˈmouth" areˋ nouns.

### 4. Tick the right word you heard.

(1) The (ˈcost, ˈcoast) ˈdidn't ˈchange veryˋ much.

(2) I ˊhope | we ˈwon't be (ˈcalled, ˈcold) in theˋ morning.

(3) We ˈaren't ˈusing the (ˈhall, ˈwhole) ˋcloset.

(4) He (ˈphoned, ˈfound) Missˋ Barr.

(5) 'Where is the (` cow, ` core)?

## 5. Read for fun.

I 'know the 'film is on ` show.
The 'name is ´ Roses | on the ` Road.
My ` fellows, | will you ´ go?
Some say "´ Yes", | some say "` No".

` Cow, |` cow,
'Friendly and ` brown,
'Let down your ´ milk,
'For the 'mighty ` town.

## Ⅲ. Centring Diphthongs /ɪə/, /eə/ and /ʊə/

The three centring diphthongs are /ɪə, eə, ʊə/ as in **peer**, **pare**, **poor**.

/ɪə/

### Brief Descriptions

a. It begins with /ɪ/ or a point somewhat closer than /ɪ/ and then glides smoothly to /ə/;
b. Its first element is more prominent than the second;
c. The lips are neutral throughout, with a slight movement from spread to open.

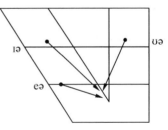

Fig. 21  Final /ɪə, eə, ʊə/

### Spelling and Sound

ear, eer, ere—ear, dear, fear, tear, deer, here
eir, ier —weird, fierce
ea, io, eu, eo—idea, violion, museum, theory

### Advice to the Teacher and Students

Some students often confuse /ɪə/ with /ɪl/. In their pronunciation, *hear* /hɪə/ and *hill* /hɪl/ sound alike. This mistake can be corrected if the tongue is not curled up when it moves from /ɪ/ to /ə/.

/eə/

### Brief Descriptions

a. It begins with /e/ and then glides smoothly to /ə/;
b. Its first element is more prominent than the second;
c. The lips are neutrally open throughout.

### Spelling and Sound

are—care, rare, share, mare

air—air, fair, chair, chairman

ear—bear, pear, wear

### Advice to the Teacher and Students

Students should take care not to pronounce /eə/ as /el/ or /eɒ/.

/ʊə/

### Brief Descriptions

a. It begins with /ʊ/ and then glides smoothly to /ə/;
b. Its first element is more prominent than the second;
c. The lips are weakly rounded at the beginning of the glide and become neutrally spread as the glide progresses.

### Spelling and Sound

oor—poor, moor

ure—sure

our—tour, dour, gourd

### Advice to the Teacher and Students

The tongue moves towards /ə/ as the sound is made. If the sound is final and before a pause, the second part of the diphthong is a little lower than the usual /ə/. In fact it is nearly as low as /ʌ/. So is the case with /ɪə/ and /eə/.

**Exercise P-12**  扫码听音频

 **1. Listen and compare the following sounds.**

|  | /ɪə/ | /eə/ | /ʊə/ | /ɪə/ | /ɪl/ | /eə/ | /el/ |
|---|---|---|---|---|---|---|---|
| (1) | peer | pear | poor | hear | hill | hair | hell |
|  | /pɪə/ | /peə/ | /pʊə/ | /hɪə/ | /hɪl/ | /heə/ | /hel/ |
| (2) | tear | tare | tour | fear | fill | bare | bell |
|  | /tɪə/ | /teə/ | /tʊə/ | /fɪə/ | /fɪl/ | /beə/ | /bel/ |
| (3) | mere | mare | moor | peer | pill | fair | fell |
|  | /mɪə/ | /meə/ | /mʊə/ | /pɪə/ | /pɪl/ | /feə/ | /fel/ |
| (4) | sheer | share | sure | near | nill | wear | well |
|  | /ʃɪə/ | /ʃeə/ | /ʃʊə/ | /nɪə/ | /nɪl/ | /weə/ | /wel/ |

**2. Read and repeat the following phrases.**

(1)

ˈnear ˋhere/ a ˈclear iˋdea/ ˈnear the ˋpier/ ˈcheer and ˋcheer/ ˈcheer Mr. ˋLear/ ˈhear my iˋdea/ ˈeasier and ˋeasier/ a ˈdear ˈYoung Pioˋneer/ ˈhere and ˋthere / ˈsneer at the iˋdea/ ˈnear the ˈhero's ˋear

(2)

a ˈbear with a ˋpear/ a ˈmare at the ˋsquare/ a ˈmayor in the ˋarmchair/ a ˈpair of ˋchairs/ the ˈbear near the ˋchair/ ˈupstairs or ˋdownstairs/ ˈwear the ˈnew ˋpair/ ˈcareful or ˋcareless/ ˈsomewhere ˋdownstairs/ ˈpears and 'pears ˋeverywhere/ 'wear and ˋtear/ 'air ˋwarfare/ reˈpair the ˋchair

(3)

'tour the ˋmoor/ 'get 'poorer and ˋpoorer/ 'tour ˋEurope/ a 'tourist from ˋEurope/ a 'casual ˋtourist/ 'cruel to the ˋpoor

### 3. Read and repeat the following sentences.

(1)

ˋHear! ˋHear! What a 'good i ˋdea!

My ˋdear, | can I 'see the 'deer ˋclearly here | when it ap ˊpears?

The 'girl with the 'fair ˊhair | 'dared 'Tom to 'kill the 'bear with his ˋbare ˌhands.

The 'mayor de ˊclared | that their 'town with the 'vast ˊsquare | is 'beautiful beyond com ˋparison in the ˌarea.

(2)

Mr. 'Lear will be 'here this ˋyear.

Mr. 'Lear's 'beard has disapˋpeared.

The 'atmosphere 'here is 'very ˋclear.

His 'beard has 'nearly disap'peared into his ˋbeer.

ˋCheers! Here's to the 'bearded mountaiˋneer!

It's a 'good iˋdea | to have some ˋbeer ˋhere, ˌdear.

'Come ˋnearer | and 'sit ˋhere.

It's ˋclear | that the 'man with a 'heavy 'beard is from Ko ˋrea.

He 'suddenly ap ˋpeared near ˌhere | with a 'glass of ˋbeer.

A 'man 'can't ˋhear | without his ˋears.

(3)

Mr. 'Claire is 'having his ˋhaircut, | 'sitting in an ˋarmchair.

I have 'looked ˋeverywhere, | ˊupstairs and ˋdownstairs, | but they 'aren't ˋanywhere.

The 'pear is over 'there on the ˋchair.

'Take ˋcare, | there's a 'chair at the 'foot of the ˋstair.

The 'boy was ˋscared | because there were a 'pair of ˋbears over ˌthere.

'Where will you 'have the 'chairs re˅paired?

The 'girl with 'golden ˊ hair | is com'paring the re'sults with 'great ˋ care.

(4)

I'm ˋ sure | he is 'very ˋcruel.

'Are you 'sure the 'poor 'steward is inˊ sured?

The 'tourist 'toured the 'moor inˋ February.

'Fewer 'tourists 'visit the 'rural aˋreas.

The 'poor 'man was asˋ sured | that his 'child could be ˋ cured.

The 'poor 'man 'found a 'curious ˋjewel | when he col'lected maˋ nure.

I'm ˋ sure | this is 'newer and ˋpurer.

The 'doctor 'wasn'tˊ sure | that he could 'cure the 'poorˋ tourist.

### 4. Tick the right word you heard.

(1) The ('bill, 'beer) is ˋhere, Mr.ˋ Pierre.
(2) I 'can't (ˋ spare, ˋ spell) it.
(3) She 'doesn't 'like the (ˋ wooer, ˋ wool).
(4) A ('quill, 'queer) ˋ driver, | ˋ isn't he?

### 5. Read for fun.

"ˋ Gill, ˋ Gill, my ˌdear, | 'where is my ˋ beer?"

"ˋ Oh, | I'm ˋ sorry | I've 'no iˋdea.

I re'member 'putting it 'right ˅ here.

'Why should it ˌdisapˋpear?"

 6. Read the following dialogue after the recording.

### Aˋ Dialogue

*Mr. Johnson:* ˊ Bill, | we'd 'like you to 'come toˋ dinner next ˌweek.

*Mr. White:* ˋ Thank you, ˌFred. I'dˋ like to.

*Mr. Johnson:* Would ˌnextˋ Wednesday be all ˊright?

*Mr. White:* ˋ Fine. 'Whatˋ time?

*Mr. Johnson:* ˋ Six o'ˌclock.

*Mr. White*: I'd 'better 'write that ˋdown. That's 'six o'ˊclock, | ˊWednesday, | 'February the 'sixˋteenth.

*Mr. Johnson*: ˋRight. 'Do you 'know where we ˊlive?

*Mr. White*: ˋNo, | not exˇactly.

*Mr. Johnson*: The ad'dress is 'three-four'teen 'Maple ˋAvenue. You ˏknow how to ˋget there, | ˊdon't you?

*Mr. White*: ˋYes. It's 'just off ˋThird Street, | ˋisn't it?

*Mr. Johnson*: ˋThat's ˊright. ˋVery ˊwell. We'll 'see you next ˋWednesday.

*Mr. White*: ˋFine. ˋThank you.

# Unit 6

# English Consonants

There are 24 phonemes in RP consonant system. They may be classified according to the manner of articulation as follows:

6 plosives: /p, b; t, d; k, g/ as in **p**in, **b**in; **t**in, **d**in; **c**ome, **g**um

2 affricates: /tʃ, dʒ/ as in **ch**ain, **J**ane

9 fricatives: /f, v; θ, ð; s, z; ʃ, ʒ; h/ as in **f**ine, **v**ine; **th**ink, **th**is; **s**eal, **z**eal; **sh**eep, mea**s**ure; **h**ow

3 nasals: /m, n, ŋ/ as in su**m**, su**n**, su**ng**

1 lateral: /l/ as in **l**ight

1 frictionless continuant: /r/ as in **r**ight

2 semi-vowels: /w, j/ as in **w**est, **y**es

N. B. /r/ was regarded as a fricative consonant in the past according to Jones, now it is taken as a frictionless continuant by the contemporary phoneticians, such as Gimson, J. C. Wells and Peter Roach. In some books it is put together with /w/ and /j/ under the same heading.

## I. Plosives /p/, /b/; /t/, /d/; /k/, /g/

/p/, /b/

### Brief Descriptions

/p/ is a voiceless, bilabial plosive consonant（双唇爆破清辅音）.

a. Raise the soft palate so that the nasal cavity is closed;

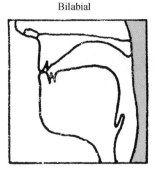

Fig. 22 Tongue position for /p/ and /b/

b. Breathe in the air and close the lips;
c. Hold the air behind the closure;
d. Part the lips open suddenly so that the air comes out of the mouth with a plosive sound;
e. Do not vibrate the vocal folds.

/b/ is a voiced bilabial plosive consonant（双唇爆破浊辅音）.

The organic formation for /b/ is exactly the same as that for /p/ except that the air comes out of the mouth less forcefully and that the vocal folds vibrate.

**Spelling and Sound**

/p/

p—pen, post, price, stop, cheap, open, computer, price
pp—happen, appeal, happy, apple, slipper

/b/

b—big, bag, table, habit, grab, crab
bb—robber, rubber, lobby, rabbit

/t/, /d/

**Brief Descriptions**

/t/ is a voiceless alveolar plosive consonant（齿龈爆破清辅音）.
a. Raise the soft palate so that the nasal cavity is closed;
b. Put the tip and blade of the tongue against the upper teeth ridge so that a closure is formed;
c. Hold the air behind the closure;
d. Release the closure and blade suddenly so that

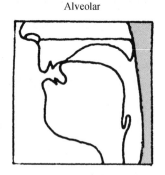

Fig. 23 Tongue position for /t/ and /d/

the air escapes with a plosive sound;
e. Do not vibrate the vocal folds.

   /d/ is a voiced alveolar plosive consonant（齿龈爆破浊辅音）. The organic formation for /d/ is the same as that for /t/ except that the air is released less strongly and that the vocal folds vibrate.

Spelling and Sound

/t/

t—tea, time, Peter, item, best, next
tt—butter, kitty, bottle, litter


/d/

d—day, dog, dance, reader, radio, guard
dd—addition, riddle, daddy, sudden


/k/, /g/

Brief Descriptions

   /k/ is a voiceless velar plosive consonant（软腭爆破清辅音）.
a. Raise the soft palate so that the nasal cavity is closed;
b. Lift the back of the tongue to touch the soft palate so that a closure is formed;
c. Stop the air stream behind the closure;
d. Break the closure and the plosive sound is heard;
e. Be careful not to vibrate the vocal folds.

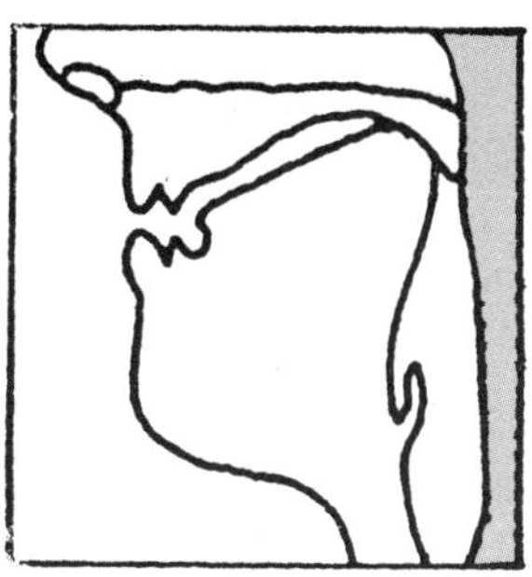

Fig. 24　Tongue position for /k/ and /g/

   /g/ is a voiced velar plosive consonant（软腭爆破浊辅音）. The organic formation for /g/ is the same as that for /k/ except that the vocal folds vibrate when the air is released.

## Spelling and Sound

/k/

c—catch, can, exclaim, cry, cool

k—keep, kind, baker, skip

ck—back, duck, luck, clock

/g/

g—gas, get, again, sugar, big, pig

gg—egg, piggy, foggy, digger

gh—ghost, Ghana

gu—guide, guy, guest, guess

## Question for Discussion

How are the plosives produced?

## Exercise P-13

 扫码听音频

 1. Listen and compare the following three pairs of plosive consonants.

| /p/ | /b/ |
| --- | --- |
| pan /pæn/ | ban /bæn/ |
| pet /pet/ | bet /bet/ |
| pox /pɒks/ | box /bɒks/ |
| cap /kæp/ | cab /kæb/ |
| /t/ | /d/ |
| tab /tæb/ | dab /dæb/ |
| ten /ten/ | den /den/ |
| tick /tɪk/ | dick /dɪk/ |
| butter /ˈbʌtə/ | rudder /ˈrʌdə/ |
| /k/ | /g/ |
| class /klɑːs/ | glass /glɑːs/ |

Unit 6  English Consonants

kick /kɪk/         gig /gɪg/
excuse /ɪksˈkjuːz/  exam /ɪgˈzæm/
peck /pek/         peg /peg/

## 2. Read the following phrases and sentences.

ˈstep by ˋstep/ a ˈpiece of ˋpaper/ a ˋblood ˌbank/
ˈbread and ˋbutter/ ˈtwist and ˋturn/ ˈtit for ˋtat/
a ˈdead ˋduck/ ˈkeep the ˋkey/ ˈgain ˋground/ a ˈbag of ˋeggs
The ˈpupils ˈput on the ˈplay *A Poˈtato* ˋPlot in the ˌpark.
ˈBruce ˈbeat ˊBill ˈblack and ˋblue beˈcause ˈBill ˈbullied his ˋbrother.
ˈTed went to ˈtell ˊTom that their ˈteacher would ˈgive them a ˋtest toˌmorrow.
ˈCasey's ˈcousin ˊKarl is the ˋcarpenter ˈKate ˈhired to ˈmake the ˊdesk and the ˋbook-case.
ˈGay's ˈgrandpa ˈgot some ˈgas from the ˋgarage to ˈget the ˈgrease off his ˋbag.

 3. Tick the right word you heard.

(1) ˈTommy is a (ˋpiggy, ˋpicky) ˌeater.
(2) I ˈfound my ˈkeys in the (ˋbag, ˋback).
(3) ˈDid the ˈdoctor ˈgive you a (ˊpill, ˊbill)?
(4) ˈLet's ˈtake a (ˈcap, ˈcab) to the ˋairport.
(5) ˈLend me your (ˋrope, ˋrobe). I ˈcan't find ˋmine.
(6) He (ˈhid, ˈhit) his ˈlittle ˋbrother.
(7) Please (ˈtry, ˈdry) ˈthis ˋdish.
(8) The ˈchildren ˈleft their (ˈcarts, ˈcards) in the ˋyard.

 4. Listen to the recording and learn the proverbs and sayings by heart.

A ˈman's as ˋold as he ˊfeels, | and a ˈwoman's as ˈold as she ˋlooks.
An ˈexpert's ˋone who knows ˈmore and ˊmore about ˈless and ˋless.
Who ˈchatters ˇ to you will | ˈchatter ˋof you.
If a ˈman deˋceives me ˊonce, | ˋshame on him; | if he deˈceives me
   ˇtwice, | ˈshame on ˋme.
ˇTwo ˈthings a ˈman should | ˋnever be ˌangry at: | what he ˊcan

ˋhelp ǀ and what heˋcan't ˌhelp.

ˊOld menˋ go to ˌdeath, ǀ but ˈdeathˋcomes to ˇyoung men.

## Ⅱ. Fricatives /f/, /v/; /ʃ/, /ʒ/

### Brief Descriptions

/f/, /v/

/f/ is a voiceless labio-dental fricative consonant（唇齿清擦音）.

a. Raise the soft palate so that the nasal cavity is closed;
b. Cause the air to pass in a continuous stream between the lip and the teeth with friction;
c. Press the lower lip against the upper teeth;
d. Do not vibrate the vocal folds.

/v/ is a voiced labio-dental fricative consonant（唇齿浊擦音）.

The organic formation for /v/ is the same as that for /f/ except that the vocal folds vibrate.

### Spelling and Sound

/f/

f—face, fall, sofa, careful, leaf, half

ff—off, office, coffee, affair

ph—photograph, phone

gh—cough, enough, laugh, rough

/v/

v—vague, very, level, avoid, stove, alive

/ʃ/, /ʒ/

### Brief Descriptions

/ʃ/ is a voiceless palato-alveolar fricative sound（腭龈清擦音）.

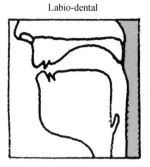
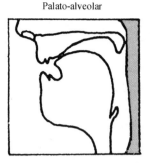

Labio-dental    Palato-alveolar

Fig. 25  Tongue position for /f/ and /v/    Fig. 26  Tongue position for /ʃ/ and /ʒ/

a. Raise the soft palate so that the nasal cavity is closed;
b. Raise the tip and blade of the tongue towards the hard palate, narrowing the air passage;
c. Cause a broad current of air to pass over the blade of the tongue with friction;
d. Do not vibrate the vocal folds.

/ʒ/ is a voiced palato-alveolar fricative consonant (腭龈浊擦音).

The organic formation for /ʒ/ is the same as that for /ʃ/ except that the vocal folds vibrate.

### Spelling and Sound

/ʃ/

ch—chef, chalet, machine
sh—fish, dish, shark

/ʒ/

sion—vision, explosion, television
ge—garage, mirage, massage

### Question for Discussion

How are the fricatives /f/, /v/; /ʃ/, /ʒ/ pronounced?

### Exercise P-14

 扫码听音频

**1. Listen and compare the following two pairs of fricative consonants.**

| /f/ | /v/ |
|---|---|
| fail /feɪl/ | veil /veɪl/ |
| serf /sɜːf/ | serve /sɜːv/ |
| proof /pruːf/ | prove /pruːv/ |
| refuse /rɪˈfjuːz/ | review /rɪˈvjuː/ |

| /ʃ/ | /ʒ/ |
|---|---|
| plash /plæʃ/ | pleasure /ˈpleʒə/ |
| nation /ˈneɪʃən/ | leisure /ˈleʒə/ |
| rush /rʌʃ/ | rouge /ruːʒ/ |
| wishing /ˈwɪʃɪŋ/ | vision /ˈvɪʒən/ |

**2. Read the following phrases and sentences.**

ˈvery ˋfunny / a ˈfresh ˋeffort / a ˋfish ˌfarm / for ˋever

ˈvery ˋvain / ˈvelvet ˌglove / a ˈshort ˋshirt / ˈshoulder to ˋshoulder / ˈmeasure for ˋmeasure

The ˈfarmers forˈgot their ˋfear | and ˈtreated the ˈfighters to ˋfruits ˈfresh from their ˋfarm.

ˈHave you ˈever ˈvisited Virˊginia?

She ˈwishes to ˈbrush up her ˊEnglish | and ˋRussian.

ˇUsually | he ˈtakes ˈpleasure in ˈcleaning the ˊgarage | at his ˋleisure.

**3. Tick the right word you heard.**

(1) Toˇmorrow | I'm going to ˈbuy a ˈnew (ˋfan, ˋvan).

(2) The (ˈservice, ˈsurface) at the ˈworkers' ˊclub has ˈgotten ˈreally ˋpoor.

(3) I am ˈsurprised at your (ˋfail, ˋveil).

(4) ˈThat's a (ˈvocal, ˈfocal) ˈpoint | in his ˋargument.

## 4. Read and memorize the following proverbs.

(1) 'Fine 'feathers 'make fine ˋbirds.

(2) 'Birds of a 'feather 'flock toˋgether.

(3) For'bidden 'fruit is the ˋsweetest.

(4) 'Foolsˋ rush ˊ in | where 'angels 'fear to ˋ tread.

 5. Listen to the recording and try to learn it by heart.

'You can ˌfool 'some of the 'people ˊ all the ˌtime, | 'all the 'people ˋsome of the ˌtime, | but you 'can't fool ˇ all the people | ˋ all the ˌtime.

## Ⅲ. Fricatives /s/, /z/; /θ/, /ð/

/s/, /z/

### Brief Descriptions

/s/ is a voiceless blade-alveolar fricative sound (舌尖齿龈清擦音).

a. Raise the soft palate so that the nasal cavity is closed;

b. This consonant is made between the blade of the tongue and the upper teeth ridge. The blade is near, but not touching the teeth ridge. Shape a groove along the central line of the tongue;

c. Force the air out through the narrow channel with friction;

d. Do not vibrate the vocal cords.

Fig. 27  Tongue position for /s/ and /z/

/z/ is a voiced blade-alveolar fricative consonant (舌尖齿龈浊擦音). The organic formation for the sound is exactly the same as that for /s/ except that the vocal cords vibrate when the air is forced out of the narrow channel.

### Spelling and Sound

/s/

s—see, say, sow, science, house, horse, case

ss—essay, cross, miss, glass

c—city, cease, celebrate

ce—face, glance, rice, space, juice

/z/

s—as, his, is, easy

z—zoo, zone, zero

ss—possess

zz—fuzzy

/θ/, /ð/

### Brief Descriptions

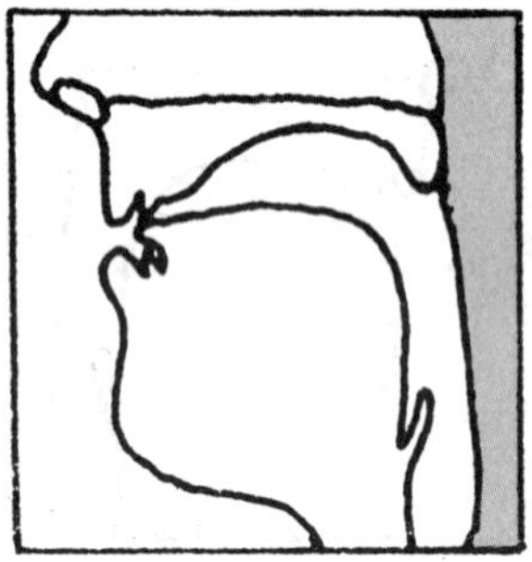

/θ/ is a voiceless dental fricative sound（清齿擦音）.

a. Raise soft palate so that the nasal cavity is closed;
b. Place the tip of the tongue close to the upper teeth;
c. Breathe out the air through the narrow passage, making a fricative sound;
d. Do not vibrate the vocal folds.

/ð/ is a voiced dental fricative consonant（浊齿擦音）. The organic formation for /ð/ is about the same as that for /θ/ except that the vocal folds vibrate.

Fig. 28　Tongue position for /θ/ and /ð/

### Spelling and Sound

/θ/

th—thin, thaw, healthy, truthful, sooth, faith

/ð/

th—the, than, another, further, lathe, smooth

## Question for Discussion

What are the differences between /θ, ð/ and /s, z/?

## Exercise P-15

 扫码听音频

🎙 1. Listen and compare the following fricative consonants.

| | /s/ | /z/ | /θ/ | /ð/ | /s/ | /θ/ |
|---|---|---|---|---|---|---|
| (1) | said | z | mouth | mouths | sick | thick |
| | /sed/ | /zed/ | /maʊθ/ | /maʊðz/ | /sɪk/ | /θɪk/ |
| (2) | rice | rise | thigh | thy | face | faith |
| | /raɪs/ | /raɪz/ | /θaɪ/ | /ðaɪ/ | /feɪs/ | /feɪθ/ |
| (3) | hiss | his | ether | either | seem | theme |
| | /hɪs/ | /hɪz/ | /ˈiːθə/ | /ˈaɪðə/ | /siːm/ | /θiːm/ |
| (4) | price | prize | bath | bathe | mouse | mouth |
| | /praɪs/ | /praɪz/ | /bɑːθ/ | /beɪð/ | /maʊs/ | /maʊθ/ |

| | /z/ | /ð/ | /s/ | /ʃ/ |
|---|---|---|---|---|
| (1) | closing | clothing | sake | shake |
| | /ˈkləʊzɪŋ/ | /ˈkləʊðɪŋ/ | /seɪk/ | /ʃeɪk/ |
| (2) | breeze | breathe | sew | show |
| | /briːz/ | /briːð/ | /səʊ/ | /ʃəʊ/ |
| (3) | bays | bathe | sock | shock |
| | /beɪz/ | /beɪð/ | /sɒk/ | /ʃɒk/ |
| (4) | zoos | those | fasten | fashion |
| | /zuːz/ | /ðəʊz/ | /ˈfɑːsn/ | /ˈfæʃn/ |

2. Read the following phrases and sentences.

(1) ˈsetˋsail/ ˈsafetyˋrazor/ ˈsail under ˈfalseˋcolors
(2) ˈsave one'sˋskin/ zip andˋzeal/ ˈsink orˋswim

(3) through ˈthick and ˋthin

(4) ˈthen and ˋthere

(5) ˈSam isˋ so ˊsilly | andˋ so ˌself-imˊportant | that ˈSally ˈhates to be hisˋ deskmate.

(6) ˈRuth ˈdoesn't ˊthink | that "ˈhealth is ˈwealth" is aˋ truth.

(7) ˈNeither myˊ father | nor myˋ mother would withˈdraw theirˋ promises.

(8) They ˈdon'tˋ know | whether the ˈweather perˋ mits | though they are ˈplanning to ˈhold a get-toˋ gether.

## 3. Tick the right word you heard.

(1) Do you ˈknow what the (ˈprice, ˈprize) ˊis?

(2) He had ˈthree (ˈpens, ˈpence) in hisˋ pocket.

(3) She (ˈsewed, ˈshowed) theˋ jacket.

(4) He has a ˈbig (ˋmouse, ˋmouth).

(5) ˈDo you ˈlike (ˊzoos, ˊthose)?

## 4. Read for fun.

Aˈmidst the ˊmists | and the ˈcoldestˋ frosts,

With ˈbare ˊwrists | and ˈstoutestˋ boasts,

He ˈthrusts his ˊfists | aˈgainst theˋ posts,

And ˈstill he inˊ sists | he ˈsees theˋghosts.

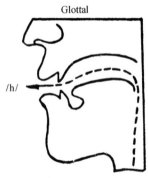

Fig. 29　Tongue position for /h/

## Ⅳ. Fricative /h/; Frictionless Continuant /r/ and the lateral /l/

/h/

**Brief Descriptions**

/h/ is a voiceless glottal fricative consonant (清喉摩擦音).

a. Raise the soft palate but do not vibrate the vocal cords;

b. Keep the tongue in position for the immediately following vowel;

c. Allow the air stream to pass through the wide-open glottis producing audible friction.

### Spelling and Sound

h—help, high, hill, habit

wh—who, whom, whose

/r/

### Brief Descriptions

/r/ is a voiced post-alveolar frictionless continuant or approximant (后齿龈无摩擦延续音).

a. Raise the soft palate so that the nasal cavity is closed;

b. The tip of the tongue is held in a position near to, but not touching the back part of the teeth ridge;

c. Allow the air stream to pass freely, without friction, over the central part of the tongue;

d. The vocal folds are in vibration;

e. The shape of the lips is determined largely by that of the following vowels, e.g. read /riːd/, rude /ruːd/.

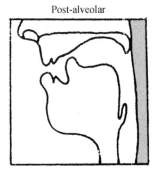

Fig. 30　Tongue position for RP post-alveolar approximant /r/

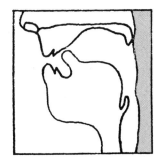

Fig. 31　Tongue position of RP voiced

## Spelling and Sound

r—right, rice, red, really

rr—mirror, arrow, arrive

wr—write, wrong, wrap

/l/

## Brief Descriptions

/l/ is a voiced alveolar lateral consonant (齿龈浊边音). It has two allophonic variants: clear /l/ and dark /ɫ/. Clear /l/ occurs before a vowel and before /j/ while dark /l/ occurs elsewhere, i.e. before a consonant or at the end of an utterance (before a pause) in Standard British English.

a. Close the nasal cavity by raising the soft palate;

b. Put the tip of the tongue against the upper front teeth-ridge for clear /l/, the front of the tongue being somewhat depressed;

c. Put the tip of the tongue against the upper front teeth-ridge and raise the back of the tongue towards the soft palate for dark /ɫ/;

d. Hold the air in the middle of the mouth;

e. Force the air out over both sides or one side of the tongue, making a lateral voiced sound.

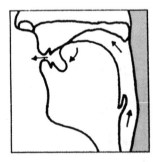 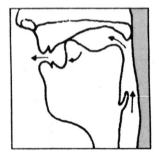

Fig. 32  Tongue position for the clear /l/    Fig. 33  Tongue position for the dark /ɫ/

## Spelling and Sound

l—look, little, low, feeling

ll—really

l—girl

ll—sell, hill, full

## Advice to the Teacher and Students

Some students tend to confuse /r/ with /l/. The mistake may be corrected if they remember not to let their tongue-tip touch the hard palate when they pronounce /r/.

## Questions for Discussion

1. What's the organic formation for /r/?
2. Please tell the difference between the clear /l/ and the dark /ł/.

## Exercise P-16

 扫码听音频

 1. Listen and compare the following two consonants.

| /r/ | /l/ |
| --- | --- |
| read /riːd/ | lead /liːd/ |
| road /rəʊd/ | load /ləʊd/ |
| room /ruːm/ | loom /luːm/ |
| berry /ˈberɪ/ | belly /ˈbelɪ/ |

2. Read the following phrases and sentences.

ˈsleep like a ˋlog/ ˈlook aˋlive/ ˈrack and ˋruin/ ˈrun aˈlong the ˋrailroad

He has ˈhurt hisˋhand with a ˈheavyˋhammer.

ˈHogg ˈran ˈhand in ˈhand with ˈHall down the ˋhill.

ˈRobert has ˈwon a ˈgloriousˋvictory over ˈRodgers in an enˈdurance ˋrace.

ˈRainey is ˈreading Rosˈsetti's ˈrhymes in the ˋreading-room.

A ˈlittle ˈpill may ˈwell ˈcure a ˈgreat ˋill.

## 3. Tick the right word you heard.

(1) ˈDry (ˈhair, ˈair) has ˈalways been a ˈgreat ˋproblem for ˌRuth.

(2) ˈDid you (colˈlect, corˈrect) the ˊpapers?

(3) We've ˈmade a misˋtake; | ˈthis is the ˈwrong (ˋload, ˋroad).

(4) ˈTom ˈlikes his ˈwhite (ˋhat, ˋrat).

## 4. Memorize these English proverbs.

(1) ˈLook beˈfore you ˋleap.

(2) ˈLive and ˋlearn.

(3) Let ˈsleeping ˈdogs ˋlie.

(4) ˈAll ˈroads ˈlead to ˋRome.

(5) A ˈcreaking ˈgate ˈhangs ˋlong.

# Unit 7

# English Consonants (Continued)

## V. Nasals /m/, /n/ and /ŋ/

/m/

### Brief Descriptions

/m/ is a voiced bilabial nasal consonant（双唇鼻音）.

a. Lower the soft palate so that the air can pass through the nose;
b. Close the lips to hold the air in the mouth;
c. Breathe in through the nose and keep the tongue still;
d. Vibrate the vocal cords as the air comes out of the nose.

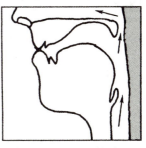

Fig. 34  RP /m/

### Spelling and Sound

m—my, many, Amy, jam, worm, map
mm—summer, immigrant, swimmer
mb—lamb, climb, tomb, bomb

/n/

### Brief Descriptions

/n/ is a voiced alveolar nasal consonant（齿龈鼻音）.

a. Lower the soft palate to release the air through the nose;

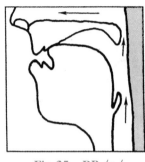

Fig. 35  RP /n/

b. Put the tip of the tongue against the upper front teeth-ridge and upper side teeth;
c. Keep the teeth slightly parted;
d. Vibrate the vocal cords.

**Spelling and Sound**

n—no, now, island, person, kitchen, fan

nn—manner, dinner, tunnel, granny

kn—know, knock, knit, knife

/ŋ/

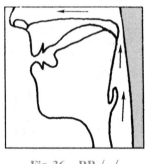

Fig. 36  RP /ŋ/

**Brief Descriptions**

/ŋ/ is a voiced velar nasal consonant（软腭鼻音）.

a. Lower the soft palate so that the air can pass only through the nose;
b. Raise the back of the tongue against the soft palate to stop the air behind the closure;
c. Vibrate the vocal cords.

**Spelling and Sound**

ng—wing, long, thing, song, sing

n—angry, pink, drink, bank, sink

**Advice to the Teacher and Students**

Some students often use /n/ in place of /ŋ/ and thus make /sɪn/ and /sɪŋ/ sound alike. This mispronunciation may be corrected if they take care to raise the back of the tongue firmly when they pronounce words with /ŋ/.

## Questions for Discussion

1. What are the common features of the nasal consonants?
2. Do they have any influence upon their adjacent vowels as in <u>moon</u>, <u>noon</u> and <u>sing</u>?

### Exercise P-17  扫码听音频

 1. Listen and compare the following sounds.

| /m/ | /n/ | /n/ | /ŋ/ |
|---|---|---|---|
| bomb /bɒm/ | Bonn /bɒn/ | thin /θɪn/ | thing /θɪŋ/ |
| gum /gʌm/ | gun /gʌn/ | sin /sɪn/ | sing /sɪŋ/ |
| map /mæp/ | nap /næp/ | ban /bæn/ | bang /bæŋ/ |
| more /mɔː/ | nor /nɔː/ | tun /tʌn/ | tongue /tʌŋ/ |
| | /n/ | | /l/ |
| knife /naɪf/ | knot /nɒt/ | life /laɪf/ | lot /lɒt/ |
| night /naɪt/ | nine /naɪn/ | light /laɪt/ | line /laɪn/ |

2. Read the following phrases and sentences.

ˈarm in ˋarm / ˈmiss the ˋmark

ˈnatural ˋnumber / ˈnext to ˋnone

ˈking of ˈall ˋkings / ˈsing a ˋsong

ˈTom's ˈmanager beˊlieves | that ˈmoney ˈmakes the ˈmareˋgo.

ˈMartin ˈlent his ˇmotorcar | to ˋMary | who must ˈmeet her ˈmum toˈmorrow ˋmorning.

A ˈfriend in ˊneed | is a ˈfriend inˋdeed.

ˈNell's ˇneighbour | ˈnever ˈknew ˈNell'sˋnickname.

A ˈlittle ˇlearning | is a ˋdangerous ˌthing.

 3. Tick the right word you heard.

(1) ˈTom is ˈquite a (ˋswimmer, ˋswinger), ˋisn't he?

(2) I ˈpicked up the (ˋ mail, ˋ nail).

(3) ˈDid you ˈsee the ˈfamous (ˈmime, ˈmine) ˊ last week?

(4) ˈDo you ˈknow what ˈhappened to his (ˊ life, ˊ knife)?

## 4. Read this moving poem.

**To My ˋ Mother**

*by Robert Louis Stevenson*

You ˋ too, | my ˋ mother, | ˈread my ˋ rhymes
For ˈlove of unforˈgotten ˋ times,
And you may ˈchance to ˈhear once ˊ more
The ˈlittle ˊ feet | aˈlong the ˋ floor.

## Ⅵ. Affricates /tʃ/ and /dʒ/

/tʃ/, /dʒ/

### Brief Descriptions

/tʃ/ is a voiceless palato-alveolar affricate consonant (腭龈塞擦清音).

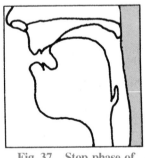

Fig. 37  Stop phase of /tʃ, dʒ/

a. Raise the soft palate to stop the air passage and put up the tip of the tongue to touch the back part of the teeth-ridge to form a retracted /tʃ/ closure;

b. The main part of the tongue is in position for /ʃ/;

c. Release the closure slowly, and the air escapes all over the central part of the tongue with friction;

d. The lips are usually somewhat protruded;

e. The vocal cords are not made to vibrate.

/dʒ/ is a voiced palato-alveolar affricate consonant (腭龈塞擦浊音). The affricate /dʒ/ is formed like /tʃ/ except that the breath force is

Unit 7  English Consonants (Continued)

weaker and the vocal cords are made to vibrate.

**Spelling and Sound**

/tʃ/

ch—bench, catch, coach, March

tch—watch, kitchen, litchi, match

/dʒ/

g—general, geography, gentle, urgent

j—jump, jewel, just, enjoy

dge—bridge, edge, judge

/ts/ /dz/ /tr/ /dr/ are usually classified as fricatives in phonetic teaching in most primary and secondary schools in China, although there is no theoretical support from IPA system. Which, nevertheless, has a big significance for Chinese people to learn English pronunciation. So we have produced exercises for these four sounds (two groups) and you can have them by scanning the code.

（扫码学习/ts/ /dz/ /tr/ /dr/）

## Questions for Discussion

1. How do you make the affricates /tʃ/ and /dʒ/?
2. Can we start from the /t/ proper when pronouncing /tʃ/?

### Exercise P-18

扫码听音频

 1. Listen and compare the following consonants.

| /tʃ/ | /dʒ/ | /tʃ/ | /ʃ/ |
|---|---|---|---|
| chin /tʃɪn/ | gin /dʒɪn/ | chair /tʃeə/ | share /ʃeə/ |
| cheap /tʃiːp/ | jeep /dʒiːp/ | chock /tʃɒk/ | shock /ʃɒk/ |

choke /tʃəʊk/   joke /dʒəʊk/   catch /kætʃ/   cash /kæʃ/
rich /rɪtʃ/      ridge /rɪdʒ/   which /wɪtʃ/   wish /wɪʃ/

## 2. Read the following phrases and sentences.

ˈwatch a ˋmatch/ ˈsearch the ˋchurch
ˈJune and Juˋly/ a ˈjust ˋjudge
a ˈtrue ˋtragedy/ a ˈlarge ˋcage
ˈChildren ˈlike ´peaches, ´cherries and ˋchestnuts ˈvery ˋmuch.
The ˈteacher ˈwatched the ˈdumb ˋchildren ˈmaking ˋgestures to each other.
ˈGeorge's ´jeep | ˈran into a ˈgipsy's ˋcarriage near a ˌbridge.
ˈJane ˈasked ´James | to ˈsend a ˋmessage | to the ˌaged engiˋneer in that ˌvillage.

## 3. Tick the right word you heard.

(1) Is she (´joking, ´choking)?
(2) (ˈMarge, ˈMarch) has been ˈvery ˋpleasant.
(3) The ˈcrowd let ˈout a ˈmighty (ˋcheer, ˋjeer).
(4) ˈShow us your (ˋchin, ˋgin), please.

## 4. Listen to the recording, make the passage with tonetic stress marks and try to read it.

### Comparisons

   Now let's compare our sitting-room with the Bakers'. The Bakers are friends of ours. They live next door to us. Our room is a little larger than theirs and it has more furniture in it. As you see, there's no wireless set in Mr. Baker's room. There isn't a bookcase, either. Mine is in my sitting-room, but his is in his study.

   My wife keeps her music in the music-stool, but Mrs. Baker keeps hers in a separate cabinet near the piano. You can also see that theirs is a grand piano, whereas ours is an upright. Both my wife and Mrs. Baker are very fond of music and both play the piano very well. But my wife doesn't play as well as Mrs. Baker. Mrs. Baker not only plays much better than my wife does, but she's the best pianist in the district. I don't play the piano, but I play the violin.

There's no settee in the Bakers' sitting-room, and there are no small chairs. However, they have three easy chairs whereas we have only two. In their room they have an electric fire, but we, like most English people, have a coal fire. Sometimes we burn logs of wood instead of coal. The Bakers have two vases on their mantelpiece, as well as a clock, and over the mantelpiece they've got a beautiful picture, painted by a famous artist.

## Ⅶ. Semi-vowels /w/ and /j/

/w/

### Brief Descriptions

a. The soft palate is raised so that the nasal resonator is shut off;
b. Raise the back of the tongue up toward the soft palate, assuming the position for a back close-mid to close vowel (depending upon the degree of openness of the following sound) and moving away immediately to the position of the following sound;
c. The lips are rounded more closely when followed by /uː, ʊ/ or /ɔː/ than when preceding a more open or front vowel;
d. The vocal folds should vibrate generally.

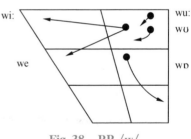

Fig. 38  RP /w/

### Spelling and Sound

w—twin, always, we, swim

wh—whether, white, why

/j/

**Brief Descriptions**

a. The soft palate is raised so that the nasal resonator is shut off;
b. Press the sides of your tongue against the upper back teeth;
c. The tongue assumes the position for a close-mid to close front vowel (depending on the degree of openness of the following sound) and moves away immediately to the position of the following sound;
d. The lips are generally shaped according to the vowel following it. For example, in *yes*, the lips are spread, but in *you*, the lips are rounded;
e. The vocal folds should vibrate generally.

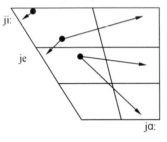

Fig. 39　RP /j/

**Spelling and Sound**

y—yellow, yes, yard, year

**A Brief Summary of Semi-vowels**

The semi-vowels have both the features of vowels and consonants. The following three points ought to be borne in mind.
a. They are extremely short.
b. Once they are produced they will glide to the following sound.
c. There is generally no friction in the making of the semi-vowels.

**Question for Discussion**

Why are /w/ and /j/ called semi-vowels?

## Exercise P-19  扫码听音频

### 1. Read and compare.

| /w/ | /j/ |
|---|---|
| wet /wet/ | yet /jet/ |
| woke /wəʊk/ | yoke /jəʊk/ |
| well /wel/ | yell /jel/ |

| /w/ | /v/ |
|---|---|
| west /west/ | vest /vest/ |
| wine /waɪn/ | vine /vaɪn/ |
| while /waɪl/ | vile /vaɪl/ |

### 2. Read the following phrases and sentences.

ˈwear aˈway/ ˈshare ˈweal and ˋwoe/ ˈtwelve ˋtwins/ ˈyear by ˋyear a ˈyoungˋpianist/ˈyesterday'sˋnewspaper

ˈWilliam ˊwished | to ˈwork his ˈway throughˋcollege | as aˋdish-washer.

ˈWilly ˈwondered | where the ˈwhite womanˋwent.

ˈDid you ˈread ˈyesterday's ˊnewspaper?

ˊYoung, | a ˈstudent of ˈYale Uniˊversity, | is ˈyearning to ˈsee the ˈYellowˋRiver.

ˈWhere there is a ˊwill, | there is aˋway.

ˈEverywhere ˈeveryone ˈworks ˈveryˋwell.

### 3. Tick the right word you heard.

(1) Some of the ˈpilots ˈhaven't ˈtried his (ˋvet, ˋjet).

(2) The (ˈoak, ˈyoke) we ˊsaw | is a hisˈtoricˋitem. It's over ˈ500 years ˋold.

(3) Did you ˈbuy that (ˈaxe, ˈwax) at the ˈhardware ˊstore?

(4) Their (ˈvine, ˈwine) ˈisn't asˋgood ˌthis year.

(5) The (ˈwheat, ˈheat) isˋterrible.

4. Read the following story after the recording.

### The ˈPride of a ˋFather

ˈTwo ˈIrishmen were disˈcussing their ˋfamilies. ˈOne was ˈboasting about his ˈsevenˋsons, | ˌsaying that he had ˈnever had any ˋtrouble with them.

"ˋYes, inˋdeed," he ˌsaid, "they are ˈjust about the ˋfinest ˌboys in the ˌworld. And would you beˋlieve it, | I ˈnever ˈlaid ˈviolent ˈhands on any ˋone of them | exˈcept in ˈself-deˋfence."

 5. Read English phonemes with key words.

(1) Vowels

| | | | |
|---|---|---|---|
| /iː/ | key, these, east | /ɒ/ | dog, nod, pot |
| /ɪ/ | pit, this, sit | /ɑː/ | car, ask, father |
| /e/ | pet, head, next | /eɪ/ | bay, they, name |
| /æ/ | pat, had, hand | /aɪ/ | by, my, sky |
| /ɜː/ | cur, bird, early | /ɔɪ/ | boy, noise, oil |
| /ə/ | about, upper, leader | /əʊ/ | go, those, over |
| /ʌ/ | bus, come, mother | /aʊ/ | cow, now, house |
| /uː/ | coo, do, food | /ɪə/ | hear, near, beard |
| /ʊ/ | put, foot, look | /eə/ | air, hair, therefore |
| /ɔː/ | course, horse, score | /ʊə/ | poor, sure, gourd |

(2) Consonants

| | | | |
|---|---|---|---|
| /p/ | pea, pen, paper | /θ/ | think, both, nothing |
| /b/ | bee, club, baby | /ð/ | this, with, rather |
| /t/ | tea, toe, water | /s/ | sun, pass, sister |
| /d/ | day, bed, order | /z/ | z, zip, lazy |
| /k/ | cap, clock, picnic | /ʃ/ | she, wash, fashion |
| /g/ | go, bag, sugar | /ʒ/ | measure, usual, division |
| /f/ | fat, off, different | /h/ | hat, heard, behind |
| /v/ | vat, five, river | /tʃ/ | cheap, check, picture |

/dʒ/ jeep, bridge, enjoy         /n/ know, son, dinner
/r/  red, fruit, story           /ŋ/ ring, ink, longer
/l/  led, seller, table          /w/ we, wet, away
/m/  map, home, common           /j/ yes, yet, beauty

# Unit 8

# Phonemes in Combination

## I. The Syllable Theory and Definition

Vowel and consonant phonemes are combined into larger units of speech, namely, syllables or portions of words.

They are phonological units that are larger than the phonemes but smaller than words. They are also necessary units in the production of any spoken language.

There is no satisfactory definition for such a unit of speech.

Many linguists have attempted to define the syllable, yet none of them has ever succeeded. But we can imagine there should be a unit between the phoneme and the word, which ought to be called syllable. We are not in a position to give a definition to syllables. However, we may as well quote the following as a definition.

"Syllables may be defined as the smallest sound-groups into which our speech organs and our ear naturally divide the sentence. It is an intermediate level of phonological organization between phonemes and words."

## II. The Syllable Structure

English words are composed of one or more syllables. Syllables then are composed of one or more phonemes. Every syllable has a nucleus (or peak), which is usually a vowel. The nucleus of the syllable may be preceded by one or more consonant phonemes called the <u>onset</u> and followed by one or more consonant phonemes called coda.

In poems, certain English words rhyme. In rhyming words, the nucleus and the coda of the final syllable of both words are identical, as in:

The woods are lovely, dark and deep,

But I have promises to keep,

And miles to go before I sleep,

And miles to go before I sleep.

In the analysis of syllable structure, we call the nucleus+coda a rime of the syllable. The structure of the monosyllabic words "sprints" can be shown as follows:

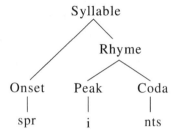

In British RP the maximal number of onset consonants is three, and the maximal number of coda is four. There are some rules concerning the occurrence of English consonants in the onset and the coda.

## III. Open Syllables and Closed Syllables

In British English there are two types of syllables: Open syllables and closed syllables. Closed syllables are those that have one or more consonants at the end. All of the vowels can appear in these circumstances. Examples: eat, seat, art, heart, ought, fought, ooze, goose, hurt, aid, maid, ride, pride, boys, goes, cows, appeared, repaired; sit, sits, let, let's, hat, hats, hut, huts, hot, hots, good, goods.

Open syllables are those without any consonant at the end. In British RP only a restricted set of vowels can occur. Examples: bee, ah, awe, boo, bay, buy, bough, bear, I, tour.

Please notice that none of the short lax vowel /ɪ, e, æ, ʌ, ɒ, ʊ/ can appear in stressed open syllables. This is a principle that can never be violated in syllabification.

## Ⅳ. Syllabification

Descriptions of stress and rhythm are usually made on the basis of syllables. The realization of a vowel or consonant can vary a great deal in different positions in the syllable. We think it quite helpful in learning English pronunciation to break up polysyllabic words into proper syllables. Many Chinese learners prefer, erroneously on many occasions, the CV-type syllable structure in reading and speaking English. A syllabified transcription can be an effective aid in acquiring the specific characteristics of General RP syllables or the language as a whole.

Here are some rules guiding syllable divisions.

(1) Words should not be divided in a way that creates illegal English syllable structure. For example, stressed syllables must not end with a short lax vowel such as /ɪ/, /e/, /æ/, /ʌ/, /ɒ/ or /ʊ/, that is, they should be followed by a consonant in the stressed syllable.

Examples:

*city*     /ˈsɪt.ɪ/
*better*   /ˈbet.ə/
*ladder*   /ˈlæd.ə/
*butter*   /ˈbʌt.ə/
*bottle*   /ˈbɒt.l/
*woman*    /ˈwʊm.ən/

/e/, /æ/, /ʌ/ and /ɒ/ are also prevented from closing unstrssed syllables.

/ɪ/ and /ʊ/ like /ə/ are permitted to close an unstressed syllable when a consonant begins a following syllable.

Examples:

*develop*    /dɪˈvel.əp/

*July* /dʒʊˈlaɪ/

*ability* /əˈbɪl. ə. tɪ/

(2) When a number of consonants are sandwiched between two vowels, no consonant cluster should in any way violate the combination rules of English. Thus the word *sculpture* is divided as /ˈskʌlp. tʃə/, and the word *central* is divided as /ˈsen. trᵊl/ while /ˈskʌl. ptʃə/, /ˈsentr. ᵊl/ should be avoided.

(3) In a compound of two or three words, the original word boundaries are generally preserved. For example, *handwritten* could in theory be divided as /ˌhænˈdrɪt. ᵊn/ but we would prefer /ˌhændˈrɪt. ᵊn/.

Why should the English words be syllabified?

A syllabified transcription has the following advantages:

- The learner can predict the pre-fortis clipping of especially the short, lax vowels. If the Chinese students do not make the short lax vowels unduly long and tense their English rhythm or stress patterns can be vastly improved.

## Questions for Discussion

1. What is a syllable?
2. Please explain "open syllables" and "closed syllables".
3. How do you understand syllabification?

## Exercise P-20

 扫码听音频

 1. Listen to the following rhymes and consolidate what you have previously learned.

(1)

Thirty days has September,

April, June and November;
February has twenty-eight alone;
All the rest have thirty-one
Excepting leap-year, that's the time
When February's days are twenty-nine.

(2)

I like to go out in the garden;
I like to get up on the wall;
I like to do anything really;
But I hate to do nothing at all.

(3)

In winter I get up at night,
And dress by yellow candle light.
In summer quite the other way.
I have to go to bed by day.

(4)

Jack and Jill went up the hill
To fetch a pail of water.
Jack fell down and broke his crown
And Jill came tumbling after.

(5)

When people call the Elephant to mind,
They marvel more and more
At such a little tail behind
So large a trunk before.

**2. Tick the right word you heard.**

(1) His mother told him not to (sleep, slip) on the floor.

(2) I'm not sure whether the (pen, pan) leaks or not.

(3) They lost the (battle, bottle) two weeks ago.

(4) It was one of the elephant's (tasks, tusks).

(5) We need more (paper, pepper).

(6) I (wander, wonder) where he'll (wander, wonder) next.

(7) Don't get too close to the (bee, bay).

(8) Only officials can go on that (base, bus).

(9) All the (fares, furs) are more expensive than before.

(10) Do you like this kind of (soup, soap)?

(11) We heard the man (shouting, shooting).

(12) He was (really, rarely) aware of the danger.

(13) John's just bought six (tires, ties) for $9.00.

(14) I saw the (rock, wreck).

(15) Was it a large (fine, fan)?

(16) They made the (plan, plane).

(17) The dog is in the (pound, pond).

(18) The (trucks, tracks) are here.

(19) The (towel, tile) was long.

(20) We need a new (curtain, carton).

### 3. Tick the word you heard.

(1) I found a long (rope, robe) in the closet.

(2) She's torn her (shirt, skirt) on a cactus thorn.

(3) This (team, theme) will probably seem familiar to you.

(4) How did he get the (gash, cash) he has in his hand?

(5) (They've, Dave) solved the problem.

(6) He has (cheered, jeered) by the large crowd which assembled at the station.

(7) They'll send him to (Yale, jail), won't they?

(8) The papers were lost in the (fire, file).

(9) I'd like to make a (collect, correct) call to 328-749-9301.

(10) The company offered him a good (price, prize).

(11) At the moment he appears to be (sinking, thinking).

(12) Would you show me a blue (jacket, packet)?

(13) There was a (lock, knock) on the door.

(14) She (let, led) him into the house.

(15) She stopped (sinking, singing) now.

(16) There were many different (sorts, swords).

(17) Is it the (rate, weight)?

(18) Did you manage to get the (train, chain)?

(19) I want my (share, chair).

(20) Don't speak to the (drudge, judge) in that way.

## 4. Tick the word you heard.

(1) Have you (found, phoned) her yet?

(2) The car is on the (curve, curb).

(3) Let's look at the (loan, lawn).

(4) He was (steering, staring) absent-mindedly towards the shore.

(5) The (thief, thieves) moved stealthily along the corridor.

(6) Have you ever seen a (fairy, ferry)?

(7) His job is making (breeches, bridges) for the army.

(8) We found this (spoor, spur) quite by chance.

(9) The (dish, ditch) is very deep.

(10) The black (sort, suit) should be removed from the show window.

(11) The (mayor, major) looked at the map.

(12) Do you have the (money, many) ready?

(13) Please (cash, catch) that check for me.

(14) The (peel, pill) doesn't taste good.

(15) The (theme, scene) of that play would have been interesting ten years ago.

(16) They always (hide, had) it.

(17) Look at the big (locks, logs).

(18) It's a little (dark, duck).

(19) The baby is (teasing, teething).

(20) She gave him a (bush, push).

# Unit 9

## Consonant Clusters and Incomplete Plosion

### I. Consonant Clusters

When two or more consonants come immediately one after another (without any vowels inserted between them), they are called consonant clusters. Words like desks /desks/, spring /sprɪŋ/, stew /stjuː/, screen /skriːn/, throw /θrəʊ/, fly /flaɪ/ and tests /tests/ are such examples.

In Chinese there is no such phenomenon and the Chinese students often find it hard to pronounce consonant clusters correctly. As a rule, it may be helpful for the Chinese learners of English to remember two things when they are trying to pronounce them:

(1) Do not insert any vowel between the consonants. For instance, blue /bluː/, not /bəluː/; lamp /læmp/, not /læməp/.
(2) The first consonant must be said softly and quickly, the second is very often formed while the first one is being pronounced. As in /kw/, the vocal organs are almost ready for /w/ except that the back of the tongue is raised to block the air passage before one starts for /k/. So the effect is a sound of mingled rounded /k/ and /w/.

There are three kinds of consonant clusters: initial (struggle), medial (deskmate), and final clusters (twelfth), etc.

### II. Incomplete Plosion

When the release stage of a plosive sound is missing or delayed, it is known as incomplete plosion. It takes place in a word when a plosive is followed immediately by another plosive, or a fricative, or an affricate. It may also take place at the junction of words (unless they are separated by a pause).

For example:

(1) Incomplete plosion at the junction of words:

a*t t*able, bla*ck c*offee, bla*ck sh*irt, ben*d d*own

(2) Plosive + plosive:

baske*tb*all, perfe*ct*, goo*db*ye, lo*gb*ook
a goo*d g*irl, a bi*g p*otato, sto*p t*alking
What a ba*d b*oy!
I can never forget the day when the bi*g t*op burnt.

(3) Plosive + fricative:

ri*cksh*aw, bes*ts*eller, nee*df*ul, a re*d s*kirt
a to*p s*tudent, a goo*d r*est
I like po*p s*ongs.
Have you visite*d V*ienna?

(4) Plosive + affricate:

a bi*g ch*ance, a goo*d j*ob, ri*pe ch*erries
a bla*ck j*eep

## Questions for Discussion

1. What is meant by consonant clusters?
2. What is called incomplete plosion?

Unit 9  Consonant Clusters and Incomplete Plosion    97

### Exercise P-21

 扫码听音频

1. Read the following words, taking care not to insert any vowel sound in the consonant clusters.

(1) Initial clusters

spill    stuff    score    smog    snap    slim

sprain   split    square   sphere

(2) Medial clusters

succeed    expression    abroad    extreme    exhaust

reflect    antarctic    completely

(3) Final clusters

grasp    chest    cast    text    dusk    film

select   soft    belt    width    length    twelve

2. Read the following words and phrases, paying attention to incomplete plosion.

ˈold-boy    ˋnitpick    a ˋdrug-store    a ˈpink ˋvase

ˈone ˈhundred ˋpounds    ˈweak point

an ˈabsent-ˈminded proˋfessor

 3. Read the following passage after the recording.

**Christmas**

ˈOne of the ˈbiggest ˈholidays of the year is ˋChristmas Day, Deˌcember ˌ2 ˋ5. It is the ˈday ˈChristians ˈcelebrate the ˈbirthday of ˈJesus ˋChrist. The ˈholiday ˈhas ˈmore than just reˈligious sigˋnificance, howˇever. It is traˈditionally a ˈtime of ˈpeace and ˈharmony aˈmong ˋpeople. ˈHouses and ˈstores are ˈdecorated with ˈbright ˊlights and the traˈditional ˈsymbols of the ˈholiday and ˇwinter: ˊpine trees, ˊholly, ˈgold and ˈsilver ˊstars, etˋc. A ˈcommon ˈsight at ˊChristmastime is a ˋsnowman, a ˌlarge ˌfigure of a ˈman made of ˋsnow. The ˈChristmas ˊseason is a ˈtime to ˈvisit ˈfriends and ˊneighbors and to enˈjoy ˊcookies, ˊcandy, and ˋother ˌfood with them. ˈSanta ˊClaus, a ˋlegendary ˌfigure in ˌred with a ˌlong ˌwhite ˊbeard, ˈbrings ˈchildren ˊpresents on ˈChristmas ˋEve, Deˌcember ˌ2ˋ4.

（请朗读数遍后，再划分语调组）

# Unit 10

# Sound Changes in Connected Speech

## I. Liaison

Liaison means the linking of sounds or words. In connected speech, English words belonging to the same sense group (意群) should be said in a united manner rather than pronounced separately as if they were isolated. Only in this way can the sequences of words (sounds) be said smoothly and rapidly.

The main types of liaison (sound-linking) are:

(1) Consonant (except r) + vowel    The final consonant of the preceding word is united to the initial vowel of the next word in the same sense group.

    e.g. give it up             half an hour
    a place of interest      pick up an orange
    sit in the open air

(2) -r or -re + vowel    When a word ending with the letter "-r" or "-re" is followed by a word beginning with a vowel, the sound /r/ is usually inserted in the pronunciation.

    e.g. after all /ˌɑːftərˈɔːl/      far and wide
    over and over again        a letter-opener
    a country of their own     the centre of the city

(3) Vowel + vowel    When a word ending in a vowel is followed by another word beginning with a vowel, a short /j/ glide is inserted after /iː/, /ɪ/, /eɪ/, /aɪ/ and /ɔɪ/, or a /w/ glide after /uː/, /ʊ/, /əʊ/, and /aʊ/.

e.g. at the end           /ət ðɪ ˈjend/
hurry up                  /ˌhʌrɪ jʌp/
try again                 /ˌtraɪ jəˈgeɪn/
row away                  /ˌrəʊ wəˈweɪ/
How old are you?          /haʊ ˈwəʊld ə juː/

## Questions for Discussion

1. When do we have liaison?
2. Is it of any help for us to speak English fluently?

## Exercise P-22

 扫码听音频

1. Read the following expressions, paying attention to sound linking.

(1) ˈnot at ˋall              let us ˈthink it ˋover
(2) ˈput it ˋon              ˈwait a ˋminute
(3) ˈfirst of ˋall            ˈtake up an ˋapple

2. Read the following phrases, paying attention to the union of two vowels.

(1) ˈsee ˈeye to ˋeye with     ˈhigh up in the ˋair
(2) by ˋaccident               ˈdo aˈway with
(3) how ˋold                   to inˈvite one to a ˋparty

3. Listen to the passage, and then put tonetic stress marks according to the recording.

### Thomas Jefferson

Many of the leaders who helped to found the United States were highly cultured; yet even among them Thomas Jefferson stood out for his learning and his talents. He was learned in Greek philosophy and in ancient literature; he was a successful lawyer; and as a gifted architect, he designed his own beautiful home in Virginia as well as the buildings of the University of Virginia. He was also a musician and a clever inventor, who originated many useful devices including folding doors, revolving chairs, and an improved plow.

Jefferson's most outstanding achievement was as chief author of the Declaration of Independence. This document has inspired people who believe in freedom all over the world and all through the years. Jefferson also drew up the constitution for his state, Virginia, and served as its governor. He was sent to France as the foreign minister of the U.S. and afterward was President Washington's Secretary of State. A few years later he became the country's third president, serving in the position for two terms. After 40 years of brilliant public service Jefferson left political life. In his remaining years he founded the University of Virginia, and acted as its administrator, which he considered as his most important work, above all his political achievements.

## II. Strong Forms and Weak Forms

Some structural/grammar words have both strong forms and weak forms. Whether strong forms or weak forms should be used depends on:

(1) the position of a word in a sentence;

(2) the degree of stress of a word;

(3) other factors.

When they bear stress, no change in sound quality takes place and so the strong forms are used. Otherwise, weak forms are used. A weak form of a word may be noted by:

(1) a shortening in the length of a vowel, e.g.

/iː/ becomes /ɪ/ as in we, he, been

/uː/ becomes /ʊ/ as in to, who, you

/ɜː/ becomes /ə/ as in sir, were, per

(2) a change in the vowel sound, e.g.

was /wɒz/ —— /wəz/

us /ʌs/ —— /əs/

by /baɪ/ —— /bə, bɪ/

(3) the absence of a sound, e.g.

and /ænd/ —— /ənd, nd, ən, n/

them /ðem/ —— /ðm/

her /hɜː/ —— /ɜː, ə/

Only structural words have weak forms. Here is a list of them:

| Special Verbs | Strong forms | Weak Forms |
| --- | --- | --- |
| be | /biː/ | /bɪ/ |
| am | /æm/ | /əm, m/ |
| is | /ɪz/ | /z, s/ |
| are | /ɑː/ | /ə/ |
| was | /wɒz/ | /wəz/ |
| were | /wɜː/ | /wɒ/ |
| have | /hæv/ | /həv, əv, v/ |
| has | /hæz/ | /həz, əz, z/ |
| had | /hæd/ | /həd, əd, d/ |
| do | /duː/ | /dʊ, də, d/ |
| does | /dʌz/ | /dəz, dz/ |
| shall | /ʃæl/ | /ʃəl, ʃl/ |
| should | /ʃʊd/ | /ʃəd, ʃd, ʃt/ |
| will | /wɪl/ | /l/ |
| would | /wʊd/ | /wəd, d/ |
| can | /kæn/ | /kən, kn, kŋ/ |
| could | /kʊd/ | /kəd, kd, kt/ |
| must | /mʌst/ | /məst, məs/ |
| **Pronouns** | **Strong Forms** | **Weak Forms** |
| you | /juː/ | /ju, jə/ |

| | | |
|---|---|---|
| he | /hiː/ | /hɪ, iː, ɪ/ |
| she | /ʃiː/ | /ʃɪ/ |
| we | /wiː/ | /wɪ/ |
| me | /miː/ | /mɪ/ |
| him | /hɪm/ | /ɪm/ |
| her | /hɜː/ | /ɜː, hə, ə/ |
| us | /ʌs/ | /əs, s/ |
| them | /ðem/ | /ðəm, ðm/ |
| his | /hɪz/ | /ɪz, z/ |
| my | /maɪ/ | /mɪ/ = non-RP |
| your | /jɔː/ | /jɒ, jə/ |
| myself | /maɪˈself/ | /məˈself/ |
| yourself | /jɔːˈself/ | /jəˈself/ |
| himself | /hɪmˈself/ | /ɪmˈself/ |
| herself | /hɜːˈself/ | /həˈself, əˈself/ |
| yourselves | /jɔːˈselvz/ | /jəˈselvz/ |
| themselves | /ðəmˈselvz/ | /ðmˈselvz/ |
| that | /ðæt/ | /ðət/ |
| some | /sʌm/ | /səm, sm/ |
| who | /huː/ | /hʊ/ |
| whom | /huːm/ | /hʊm/ |
| **Prepositions** | **Strong Forms** | **Weak Forms** |
| at | /æt/ | /ət/ |
| by | /baɪ/ | /bə, bɪ/ |
| for | /fɔː/ | /fə, fər/ |
| from | /frɒm/ | /frəm, frm/ |
| into | /ˈɪntuː/ | /ˈɪntu, ˈɪntə/ |
| to | /tuː/ | /tu, tə/ |
| of | /ɒv/ | /əv, əf, f/ |
| upon | /əˈpɒn/ | /əpən/ |

| Conjunctions | Strong Forms | Weak Fomrs |
|---|---|---|
| and | /ænd/ | /ənd, ən, n/ |
| as | /æz/ | /əz/ |
| but | /bʌt/ | /bət, bt/ |
| nor | /nɔː/ | /nə, nɔ/ |
| than | /ðæn/ | /ðən, ðn/ |
| or | /ɔː/ | /ə/ |
| till | /tɪl/ | /tl/ |
| until | /ʌnˈtɪl/ | /ənˈtɪl/ |

| Other Parts of speech | Strong Forms | Weak Forms |
|---|---|---|
| a | /eɪ/ | /ə/ |
| an | /æn/ | /ən/ |
| the | /ðiː/ | /ðɪ, ðə/ |
| there | /ðeə/ | /ðə/ |
| many | /ˈmenɪ/ | /mənɪ, mnɪ/ |
| sir | /sɜː/ | /sə/ |
| so | /səʊ/ | /sə/ |
| such | /sʌtʃ/ | /sətʃ/ |
| saint | /seɪnt/ | /sənt, snt, sən, sn/ |

It is very important for English learners to know how to use strong forms and weak forms because it will help them in production (speaking) and comprehension (understanding). Here are some rules about the uses of strong and weak forms:

(1) Strong forms are used when structual words occur at the end of a sentence. e.g.

I'm ˈfond of ˋmusic.

/aɪm ˈfɒnd əf ˋmjuːzɪk/

ˈMusic is ˈwhat I'm ˋfond of.

/ˈmjuːzɪk s ˈwɒt aɪm ˋfɒnd ɒv/

## Unit 10  Sound Changes in Connected Speech

(2) Strong forms are to be used when such words are in contrast. e.g.

I have a ˈletter ˋ for him, not ˋ from him.

/aɪ həv ə ˈletə ˋ fɔː hɪm, nɒt ˋ frɒm hɪm/

(3) Strong forms are used when words are used for emphasis. e.g.

I ˌthink ˌmaybe ˋˋ you ˌknow it.

/aɪ ˌθɪŋk ˌmeɪbɪ ˋˋ juː ˌnəʊ ɪt/

(4) Strong forms are used when they are being used as nouns.

e.g. ˈDid you say "ˊ he"?

/ˈdɪdʒʊ seɪ ˊhiː/

"ˈA", "ˈan" and "ˈthe" are ˋ articles.

/ˈeɪ, ˈæn ənd ˈðiː ər ˋ ɑːtɪklz/

Note: Negative contractions do not take weak forms, such as won't, haven't, can't, etc.

## Questions for Discussion

Is it important to know and to be able to use the weak forms and strong forms of certain words? Why?

## Exercise P-23

 扫码听音频

 1. Read the following everyday sentences, paying attention to strong forms and weak forms.

(1) It's ˈvery ˋ kind of you.

　/ɪts ˈverɪ ˋ kaɪnd əv jʊ/

(2) ˈHow do you ˋ do?

　/ˈhaʊ dʒʊ ˋ duː/

(3) Could you ˈtell me the corˈrect ˊ time?

　/kədʒʊ ˈtel mɪ ðə kəˈrekt ˊ taɪm/

(4) ˈWhere are you ˋgoing?

/ˈweə rə jʊ ˋgəʊɪŋ/

(5) ˈHow are you ˋfeeling toˌday?

/ˈhaʊ wə jʊ ˋfiːlɪŋ təˌdeɪ/

## 2. Read the following sentences, paying attention to the strong forms and weak forms of special verbs.

(1) ˈHave you ˈever been ˊthere?

/ˈhæv jʊ ˈevə bɪn ˊðeə/

— ˈDoes he ˊwant it?

/ˈdʌz hɪ ˊwɒnt ɪt/

— ˋYes, heˋdoes.

/ˋjes hɪ ˋdʌz/

I ˈdon't ˈthink I ˋcould.

/aɪ ˈdəʊnt ˈθɪŋk aɪ ˋkʊd/

(2) The ˈplace has ˋchanged.

/ðə ˈpleɪs həz ˋtʃeɪndʒd/

The ˈstudents have ˋgone.

/ðə ˈstjuːdənts əv ˋgɒn/

You can ˈgo ˋnow.

/juː kŋ ˈgəʊ ˋnaʊ/

## 3. Read the following sentences, paying attention to the strong forms and weak forms of the prepositions.

(1) ˈWhat are you ˋlooking at?

/ˈwɒt ə jʊ ˋlʊkɪŋ æt/

ˈWhat's that ˋfor?

/ˈwɒts ðæt ˋfɔː/

ˈWhere did you ˈcome from ˋyesterday?

/ˈweə dɪd jʊ ˈkʌm frəm ˋjestədeɪ/

(2) ˈCome for a ˊmeal?

/ˈkʌm fər ə ˈmiːl/

I ˈsent it from ˋLondon.

/aɪ ˈsent ɪt frəm ˋlʌndən/

He's ˈgot into ˋdifficulties.

/hiːz ˈgɒt ɪntə ˋdɪfɪkəltɪz/

 4. Read the following sentences, paying attention to the strong forms and weak forms of the conjunctions and articles.

(1) "ˈAnd" is a conˋjunction.

/ˈænd ɪz ə kənˋdʒʌŋkʃən/

You ˈdon't ˋlike it. ˈNor doˋI.

/juː ˈdəʊnt ˋlaɪk ɪt ˈnɔː dʊ ˋaɪ/

"ˈThe" is a ˈdefinite ˋarticle.

/ˈðiː ɪz ə ˈdefɪnɪt ˋɑːtɪkl/

(2) I ˈwrote the ˈletter and ˈtook it to the ˋpost.

/aɪ ˈrəʊt ðə ˈletə ən ˈtʊk ɪt tə ðə ˋpəʊst/

I'll ˈdo it as ˈsoon as I ˋcan.

/aɪl ˈduː ɪt əs ˈsuːn əz aɪ ˋkæn/

ˈHave an ˋapple.

/ˈhæv ən ˋæpl/

## III. Elision

Elision means the omission of a sound or sounds, either within the body of a word or at the junction of words.

A sound may be dropped in the course of the development of the language, that is, a sound which existed in an earlier form of a word is omitted in a later form. This is called historical elision. A sound may also be dropped in rapid casual speech but may exist when said slowly or in isolation. This is called contextual elision. For example:

### 1. Historical Elision

| | | |
|---|---|---|
| victory /ˈvɪktərɪ/ | —— | /ˈvɪktrɪ/ |
| knight /knaɪt/ | —— | /naɪt/ |
| cotton /ˈkɒtən/ | —— | /ˈkɒtn/ |
| sandwich /ˈsændwɪdʒ/ | —— | /ˈsænwɪdʒ/ |
| talk /tɔːlk/ | —— | /tɔːk/ |
| medicine /ˈmedɪsən/ | —— | /ˈmedsn/ |

### 2. Contextual Elision

| | | |
|---|---|---|
| next stop /ˈnekst ˈstɒp/ | —— | /ˈneks ˈstɒp/ |
| a great deal /ə ˈgreɪt ˈdiːl/ | —— | /ə ˈgreɪ ˈdiːl/ |
| not tall /ˈnɒt ˈtɔːl/ | —— | /ˈnɒ ˈtɔːl/ |
| last month /ˈlɑːstˌmʌnθ/ | —— | /ˈlɑːsˈmʌnθ/ |

The vowels that are often omitted are /ə/ and /ɪ/ in unstressed syllables of disyllabic or polysyllabic words. The consonants that are often omitted are mostly plosives, nasals, laterals, and some fricatives. e.g.

/n/ column /l/ calm
/p/ cupboard /h/ ghost
/k/ blackboard /d/ handsome

### Questions for Discussion

What is elision? How many kinds of elision are there in British RP?

### Exercise P-24

扫码听音频

1. Read the following words, paying attention to the omission of vowels.

history /ˈhɪst(ə)rɪ/          victory /ˈvɪkt(ə)rɪ/
dictionary /ˈdɪkʃən(ə)rɪ/     dictation /dɪkˈteɪʃ(ə)n/

London /ˈlʌnd(ə)n/    separate /ˈsep(ə)rɪt/
different /ˈdɪf(ə)rənt/    ordinary /ˈɔːd(ə)n(ə)rɪ/

2. Read the following words, phrases and sentences, paying attention to the omission of consonants.

(1) waistcoat /ˈweɪs(t)kəʊt/    workshop /ˈwɜː(k)ʃɒp/
   sandwich /ˈsæn(d)wɪdʒ/    wildcat /ˈwaɪl(d)kæt/
(2) ˋused to /ˆjuːs(t) tuː/    ˋblood test /ˆblʌ(d) test/
   ˈgetˋhold of /ˈge(t)ˋhəʊld əv/
   ˈfindˋfault with /ˈfaɪn(d)ˋfɔːl(t) wɪð/
   ˈbigˋnoise /ˈbɪ(ɡ)ˋnɔɪz/
(3) They ˈhaven'tˋpaid me. /ðeɪ ˈhævn(t)ˋpeɪ(d) mi/
   Would ˈbiscuits and ˈcheese be eˆnough for him?
   /wʊd ˈbɪskɪts ən(d) ˈtʃiːz bɪ ɪˈnʌ(f) fɔːr (h)ɪm? / (or /fɔːhɪm/)
   ˈWouldn't you ˈlike to ˆhelp me?
   /ˈwʊdn tʃʊ ˈlaɪ(k) tə ˆhelp miː/

3. Read the following words, paying attention to historical elision.

(1) /b/ climb, lamb, bomb
(2) /b/ debt, doubt, subtle
(3) /k/ muscle
(4) /d/ handsome, Wednesday, sandwich
(5) /g/ sign, resign, design
(6) /h/ honest, hour, honor
(7) /k/ knight, knife, knock
(8) /l/ calm, half, talk
(9) /n/ autumn, column, solemn
(10) /p/ cupboard, psycology, pneumonia
(11) /s/ island, corps
(12) /t/ castle, fasten, listen
(13) /w/ sword, write, answer, whole

4. Read the following sentence according to the tonectic stress marks.

ˈFooling the ˋPeople

ˈYou can ˌfool ˈsome of the ˈpeople ˊall theˑtime， | ˈall the ˈpeople ˋsome of the ˌtime， | but you ˈcan't fool ˇall theˑpeople | ˋall the ˌtime.

## Ⅳ. Assimilation

In connected speech a sound may be made more similar to a neighboring sound, and the two sounds often influence each other in such a way that the articulation of one sound becomes similar to or even identical with the articulation of the other one. Sometimes two neighbouring sounds influence each other and are replaced by a new sound which is different from either of the two original sounds. This process is called assimilation. The cause of the process is to save effort and to make the pronunciation of two different sounds easier since the change of manner of pronunciation and the shift of position of the speech organs can hardly take place in an instant in fast reading or speaking.

Assimilation is very common in colloquial and dialectal English. The sounds that are often assimilated are consonants. Three types of assimilation can be distinguished:1. Progressive; 2. Regressive; and 3. Reciprocal.

### 1. Progressive Assimilation

The assimilated sounds are influenced by the preceding sounds.

e. g. worked /wɜːkt/
   cabs /kæbz/
   dogs /dɒgz/
   legs /legz/

## 2. Regressive Assimilation

The sound is influenced by the following sounds. When separate, *news* and *paper* are read as /njuːz/ and /ˈpeɪpə/ respectively. But when in the compound word, *newspaper* is read as /ˈnjuːspeɪpə/ because /z/ is influenced by the voiceless consonant /p/.

e.g. this shop /ðɪs ʃɒp/ —— /ðɪʃ ʃɒp/
width /wɪdθ/ —— /wɪtθ/
this year /ðɪs jɪə(r)/ —— /ðɪʃjɜː/
sad boys /sæd bɔɪz/ —— /sæbbɔɪz/
these young /ðiːz jʌŋ/ —— /ðiːʒjʌŋ/
quite good /kwaɪt ɡʊd/ —— /kwaɪkɡʊd/
light brown /laɪt braʊn/ —— /laɪpbraʊn/

## 3. Reciprocal Assimilation

Two neighbouring sounds influence each other and become a new sound.

e.g. this year /ˈðɪs ˈjɪə/ —— /ˈðɪʃˈʃjɪɜː/
education /ˌedjuˈkeɪʃən/ —— /ˌedʒuˈkeɪʃn/
Don't you do it! /ˈdəʊnt juˋduː ɪt/ —— /ˌˈdəʊn tʃuˋduːɪt/

### Question for Discussion

How do you explain assimilation?

### Exercise P-25

 扫码听音频

 1. Read the following words, phrases and sentences, paying attention to progressive assimilation.

(1) /d/ —— /t/
reached /riːtʃt/  helped /helpt/
(2) /s/ —— /z/
bags /bæɡz/  songs /sɒŋz/

cows /kaʊz/

(3) /z/ —— /s/

What is this?     What's this?

/ˈwɒt ɪz ˋðɪs/ —— /ˈwɒts ˋðɪs/

(4) /n/ —— /m/

happen /ˈhæpn/ —— /ˈhæpm/

open /ˈəʊpn/ —— /ˈəʊpm/

2. Read the following words, phrases or sentences, paying attention to regressive assimilation.

(1) /v/ —— /f/

of ˋcourse /əv ˋkɔːs/ —— /əf ˋkɔːs/

dovetail /ˈdʌvteɪl/ —— /ˈdʌfteɪl/

ˈWhen did he ˈleave Shangˋhai?

/ˈwen dɪd hɪ ˈliːf ʃæŋ ˋhaɪ/

I shall ˈprove to you that ˊhe is unreˋliable.

/aɪ ʃəl ˈprəʊf tə jʊ ðə(t) hɪ ɪz ʌnrɪ ˋlaɪəbl/

(2) /s/ —— /ʃ/

issue /ˈɪsjuː/ —— /ˈɪʃuː/

space shuttle /ˈspeɪs ˈʃʌtl/ —— /ˈspeɪʃ ˈʃʌtl/

Miss Sharp /mɪs ˈʃɑːp/ —— /mɪʃ ˈʃɑːp/

ˈWho's ˈrunning this ˋshow?

/ˈhuːz ˈrʌnɪŋ ðɪʃ ˋʃəʊ/

Of ˈcourse she ˋknows.

/əf ˈkɔːs ʃiː ˋnəʊz/ —— /əf ˈkɔːʃ ʃiː ˋnəʊz/

(3) /z/ —— /s/

hisˋfarm /hɪz ˋfɑːm/ —— /hɪs ˋfɑːm/

He has ˈsix ˋbrothers.

/hɪ həs ˈsɪks ˋbrʌðəz/

ˈRun as ˈfast as youˋcan.

/ˈrʌn əs ˈfɑːst æz jʊ ˋkæn/

(4) /z/ —— /ʒ/

'these ˋshops /'ðiːz ˋʃɒps/ —— /'ðiːʒ ˋʃɒps/

'Tom's ˋshirt /'tɒmz ˋʃɜːt/ —— /'tɒmʒ ˋʃɜːt/

'What does she ˋstudy?

/'wɒt dʌʒ ʃɪ ˋstʌdɪ/

He was ˋshocked.

/hi wəʒ ˋʃɒkt/

(5) /n/ —— /ŋ/

engulf /ɪn'gʌlf/ —— /ɪŋ'gʌlf/

inquest /'ɪnkwest/ —— /'ɪŋkwest/

'This is a ˋgun car.

/'ðɪs ɪz ə ˋgʌŋ kɑː/

'Who can ˋget it for me?

/'huː kəŋ ˋget ɪt fə mɪ/

(6) /n/ —— /m/

sunburnt /'sʌnbɜːnt/ —— /'sʌmbɜːnt/

in ˋpart /ɪn ˋpɑːt/ —— /ɪm ˋpɑːt/

in 'memory of /ɪn'memərɪ əv/ —— /ɪm'memərɪ əv/

'One 'man's 'meat is an'other 'man's ˋpoison.

/'wʌm 'mænz 'miːt ɪz ən'ʌðə 'mænz ˋpɔɪzn/

'What he ʹsays is in 'bad ˋtaste.

/'wɒt hiː ʹsez ɪz ɪm 'bæt ˋteɪst/

(7) /θ/ —— /ð/

| north | —— | northen | /nɔːθ/ | —— | /'nɔːðən/ |
| south | —— | southen | /saʊθ/ | —— | /'sʌðən/ |
| worth | —— | worthy | /wɜːθ/ | —— | /'wɜːðɪ/ |
| mouth | —— | mouths | /maʊθ/ | —— | /maʊðz/ |

### 3. Read the following words, phrases and sentences, paying attention to reciprocal assimilation.

(1) /d/＋/j/＝/dʒ/

graduate /ˈgrædjʊɪt/ —— /ˈgrædʒʊət/

Did you ˈhave a ˈgood ˊ journey?

/dɪdʒʊ ˈhæv ə ˈgʊ(d) ˊ dʒɜːnɪ/

She is ˋ foolish, and yet ˈpeople ˋ like her.

/ʃiːɪs ˋ fuːlɪʃ ən dʒet ˈpiːpl ˋ laɪk hɜː/

(2) /t/＋/j/＝/tʃ/

natural /ˈnætjurəl/ —— /ˈnætʃərəl/

courtyard /ˈkɔːtjɑːd/ —— /ˈkɔːtʃɑːd/

ˈCan't you ˊ see it?

/ˈkɑːn tʃʊ ˊ siːɪt/

I'm ˈglad to ˋ meet you.

/aɪm ˈglæ(d) tə ˋ miːtʃʊ/

(3) /z/＋/j/＝/ʒ/

azure /ˈæzjʊə/ —— /ˈæʒə/

pleasure /ˈplezjə/ —— /ˈpleʒə/

invasion /ɪnˈveɪzjən/ —— /ɪnˈveɪʒən/

usual /ˈjuːzjʊəl/ —— /ˈjuːʒʊəl/

I ˈcan't underˈstand these ˈyoung ˈpeople ˋ nowadays.

/aɪ ˈkɑːnt ʌndəˈstænd ðiːʒ jʌŋ ˈpiːpl ˋ naʊədeɪz/

ˈWhere's ˈyesterday's ˋ newspaper?

/ˈweəʒ jestədeɪz ˋ njuːspeɪpə/

# V. Length of a Sound

The length of sounds is important because it has much to do with the rhythm of English speech.

The length of a sound refers to the length of time during which a sound is held on continuously in a given word or phrase.

The length of a sound is relative. Generally speaking, compared with consonants, vowels are longer. Compared with short vowels, long vowels and diphthongs are longer.

The length of vowels observes the following laws:

(1) The long vowels /iː/, /ɑː/, /ɔː/, /uː/, /ɜː/, and all the diphthongs are longer than the other vowels in similar phonetic context, i.e., when surrounded by the same sounds and pronounced with the same degree of stress.

e.g. /siːt/ —— /sɪt/   /bɑːk/ —— /bæk/
/spɔːt/ —— /spɒt/   /fuːl/ —— /fʊl/
/taɪt/ —— /tɪt/   /geɪt/ —— /get/

(2) The long vowels (and diphthongs) are shorter when followed by a voiceless consonant than when followed by a voiced consonant or when final.

e.g. /biːd/ —— /biːt/   /kɑːd/ —— /kɑːt/
/kəʊd/ —— /kəʊt/   /straɪv/ —— /straɪf/
/tiː/ —— /tiːs/   /meɪ/ —— /meɪk/

(3) The long vowels (and diphthongs) are shorter before a nasal consonant followed in turn by a voiceless consonant.

e.g. /freɪnd/ —— /feɪnt/
/dɑːnd/ —— /dɑːns/
/peɪn/ —— /peɪnt/

(4) The long vowels (and diphthongs), when followed by unstressed syllables, are shorter than those in monosyllables.

e.g. /faɪn/ —— /ˈfaɪnə/   /wɔː/ —— /ˈwɔːtə/
/tʃiːp/ —— /ˈtʃiːpə/   /ɜːn/ —— /ˈɜːnɪst/

(5) The long vowels (and diphthongs) are shorter in unstressed syllables than in stressed syllables.

e.g. /reɪt/ —— /ˈselɪbreɪt/
/fəʊn/ —— /ˈtelɪfəʊn/

/geɪt/ —— /ˈnævɪgeɪt/

(6) The long vowels (and diphthongs) are shorter in falling tones than in rising tones, within a sentence than within a nuclear syllable at the end of a sentence.

e.g. — ˈDo you ´know?
— ˋYes, I ˋknow.

— ˈWhat do you ˋsee?
— I ˈsee a ˋhorse.

The length of the short vowels follows the same laws.

The length of consonants has the following laws:

(1) Final consonants (not including the plosives) are longer when there is a short vowel before it than when there is a long vowel before it.

e.g. /siːn/ —— /sɪn/
/liːv/ —— /lɪv/
/fuːl/ —— /fʊl/

(2) Nasals and /l/ are longer when followed by voiced consonants than when followed by voiceless consonants.

e.g. /fiːld/ —— /felt/
/faɪnd/—— /feɪnt/   /bend/ —— /bent/

(3) Final consonants (not including the plosives) are longer than those followed by an unstressed syllable.

e.g. /mɪs/ —— /ˈmɪstɪ/     /njuːz/ —— /ˈnjuːzriːl/
/peɪn/—— /ˈpeɪnfʊl/

## Question for Discussion

Why is the length of sounds important?

## Exercise P-26

 扫码听音频

 1. Read the following words, paying attention to the length of vowels.

| | | |
|---|---|---|
| hoe /həʊ/ | hoed /həʊd/ | |
| hope /həʊp/ | hoping /ˈhəʊpɪŋ/ | |
| were /wɜː/ | word /wɜːd/ | |
| wert /wɜːt/ | worker /ˈwɜːkə/ | |
| core /kɔː/ | cord /kɔːd/ | |
| court /kɔːt/ | corner /ˈkɔːnə/ | |
| rue /ruː/ | rude /ruːd/ | |
| root /ruːt/ | ruler /ˈruːlə/ | |
| said /sed/ | set /set/ | setter /ˈsetə/ |
| bid /bɪd/ | bit /bɪt/ | bitter /ˈbɪtə/ |
| cab /kæb/ | cap /kæp/ | captain /ˈkæptɪn/ |

 2. Read the following sentences, paying attention to the length of vowels in the same word in different positions and tones.

I ˈlost my ˋk*ey* ˌyesterday.
I ˈdidn't reˈmember where I had ˈput my ˋk*ey*.
ˈHave you ˈseen my ´k*ey*?

ˈMust you ´g*o*?
ˋYes, I must ˋg*o*.
I must ˋg*o* now.

ˈDid you ´see h*i*m?
ˈWhere did you ˋsee h*i*m?
I ˈsaw h*i*m in the ˋpark.

### 3. Read the following words, paying attention to the length of consonants.

| | |
|---|---|
| pool /puːl/ | pull /pʊl/ |
| base /beɪs/ | bus /bʌs/ |
| build /bɪld/ | built /bɪlt/ |
| always /ˈɔːlwəz/ | all /ɔːl/ |
| reach /riːtʃ/ | rich /rɪtʃ/ |
| send /send/ | sent /sent/ |
| selves /ˈselvz/ | self /self/ |
| moonless /ˈmuːnlɪs/ | moon /muːn/ |

### 4. Read the following stories after the recording.

#### ˈMarital ˋProblems

ˈTwo young ˊmen, | ˈeach married about a ˊyear, were disˈcussing ˈvarious ˈmarital ˋproblems.

"I'm the ˈhead of my ˋhouse," ₁said ₁one. "And I ˈthink I ˋshould be, | after ˋall, | I ˈearn the ˋmoney."

"ˇWell," ·said the ·other, "my ˈwife and I have a ˈperfect aˋgreement. I deˈcide all the ˋˋmajor ₁matters | and ˇshe ˈtakes care of all ˋˋminor ₁matters."

"And ˈhow is that ˈworking ˋout?"

With some emˇbarrassment, | the ˈother repˊlied, | "ˇWell, | ˈso ˊfar, ˋˋno ˋmajor ₁matters have ₁come ˋup."

#### The ˈSecret of His Sucˋcess

The ˈself-made millionˊaire | was ˈboasting about the ˈsecret of his sucˋcess.

"I've ˈalways had theˇtheory | that the ˈˈsalary is the ·least imˋportant ₁part of the ₁job," he said.

"ˈDoing ˈthings ˋˋwholeheartedly | to the ˈbest of your aˇbility | ˈbrings you ˈgreater satisˋfaction | than ˋmoney."

"And you be'came ˋrich | after you con'vinced your ˋself | that 'this was ˇtrue?" ˌasked the reˌporter.

"ˋˋNo. 'After I con ˋˋvinced the ˌpeople | whoˋworked for me."

### The 'Arrow and the ˋSong

*by H. W. Longfellow*

I 'shot an 'arrow 'into the ˊair,
It 'fell to 'earth, I 'knew not ˋwhere;
For, 'so 'swiftly it ˊflew, the 'sight
ˑCould 'notˋfollow it 'in its ˋflight.

I 'breathed aˋsong ˌinto the ˌair,
It 'fell toˋearth, I 'knew notˋwhere;
For 'who has 'sight so 'keen and ˊstrong,
That 'it can 'follow the 'flight ofˋsong?

'Long, long 'afterward, 'in an ˊoak,
I 'found the 'arrow, 'still unˋbroke;
'And the 'song, from be'ginning to ˊend,
I 'found aˈgain in the 'heart of a ˋfriend.

# Part Two

# Rhythm

# Unit 11

## Word Stress

Stress is the foundation of rhythm. In this part, we are going to deal with word stress, sentence stress, rhythm and its features, rhythm patterns, sense-groups and pausing. What is more, we will provide you with plenty of exercises so that you will have a thorough understanding of the English rhythm, not only in theory, but also in practice.

Stress may be defined as the degree of force or loudness with which a sound or syllable is articulated. Stress can be classified into word stress and sentence stress. In this unit we only deal with stress within a word.

According to how many syllable (s) a word may contain, we can divide English words into three types: monosyllables（单音节词）, disyllables（双音节词）and polysyllables（多音节词）. In every English word of two or more syllables at least one syllable should be articulated with more force or loudness than the rest, and we call this phenomenon word stress.

## Ⅰ. Kinds of Stress

It is possible to distinguish many levels of stress, but from the practical point of view, it is sufficient to distinguish three principal kinds:

(1) Primary stress（主重音）— heavily stressed, usually marked with a vertical stroke (ˈ) on the upper left-hand corner of a syllable carrying the stress, as in beˈgin.

(2) Secondary stress（次重音）— stressed but subordinate to the primary stress, ususally marked with a vertical stroke (ˌ) on the lower left-hand

corner of a syllable concerned, as in ˌcontriˈbution.

(3) Certain English words have double stress (双重音) or even stress (均重音). Double stress can be marked by a high vertical stroke before each of the stressed syllables, as in /ˌfɪfˈtiːn/, /ˈbɜːˈlɪn/, etc.

## Ⅱ. Stress Placement

Every English word has a definite place for the stress and we are not allowed to change it. If we stress the wrong syllable, it spoils the shape of the word for an English hearer and he may have difficulty in recognizing the word. Although stress placement in English words is very complicated, we still can find some rules to observe:

### 1. General rules of stress placement for simple words

(1) For most English words of two syllables, the stress usually falls on the first syllable.

e.g. ˈcommon, ˈnation, ˈopen, ˈstudy, ˈsorry, ˈany

(2) For words of three or more syllables, the stress usually falls on the third syllable from the end.

e.g. ˈuniverse, ˈrelative, ˈarticle

deˈmocracy, eˈconomy, techˈnology

### 2. General rules of stress placement for complex words (derivatives and compound words)

(1) For words of two or three syllables with one of the following prefixes, the stress usually falls on the syllable following the prefix (前缀).

e.g.

| | | | |
|---|---|---|---|
| a- | aˈrise | aˈwake | aˈsleep |
| be- | beˈside | beˈfore | beˈlieve |
| com- | comˈplain | comˈpress | comˈplete |
| con- | conˈsist | conˈsult | conˈnect |

| | | | |
|---|---|---|---|
| de- | de'tect | de'stroy | de'cide |
| dis- | dis'cuss | dis'play | dis'cover |
| em- | em'brace | em'body | em'ploy |
| en- | en'large | en'force | en'close |
| es- | es'cape | es'tablish | es'teem |
| ex- | ex'claim | ex'cite | ex'clude |
| im- | im'ply | im'prison | im'press |
| in- | in'cline | in'clude | in'form |
| mis- | mis'fortune | mis'take | mis'carriage |
| ob- | ob'serve | ob'struct | ob'tain |
| per- | per'mit | per'sist | per'form |
| pre- | pre'pare | pre'fer | pre'serve |
| pro- | pro'duce | pro'ceed | pro'claim |
| sub- | sub'mit | sub'side | sub'scribe |
| trans- | trans'fer | trans'late | trans'plant |

(2) For words with one of the following suffixes（后缀）, the stress usually falls on the preceding syllable of the suffix.

e.g.

| | | |
|---|---|---|
| -eous | er'roneous | 'courteous |
| -graphy | cal'ligraphy | bi'ography |
| -ial | prefe'rential | ˌedi'torial |
| -ian | ˌIndo'nesian | his'torian |
| -ic | ˌsyste'matic | ˌperi'odic |
| -ics | pho'netics | ˌmathe'matics |
| -ience | ex'perience | con'venience |
| -ient | suf'ficient | o'bedient |
| -ify | in'tensify | i'dentify |
| -ion | tran'sition | per'fection |
| -ious | am'bitious | re'ligious |
| -ity | ˌcuri'osity | ˌpopu'larity |
| -ive | pro'tective | pro'gressive |

(3) Words with the following suffixes do not change their stress placement.

e.g.

| | |
|---|---|
| -able | ˈreason — ˈreasonable |
| -age | ˈmarry — ˈmarriage |
| -al | proˈpose — proˈposal |
| -en | ˈdeep — ˈdeepen |
| -ful | forˈget — forˈgetful |
| -ery | maˈchine — maˈchinery |
| -hood | ˈbrother — ˈbrotherhood |
| -ing | ˈpaint — ˈpainting |
| -ish | ˈchild — ˈchildish |
| -like | ˈwolf — ˈwolflike |
| -less | ˈdoubt — ˈdoubtless |
| -ly | ˈrecent — ˈrecently |
| -ment | conˈfine — conˈfinement |
| -ness | ˈbitter — ˈbitterness |
| -ous | ˈvigour — ˈvigourous |
| -fy | ˈglory — ˈglorify |
| -wise | ˈclock — ˈclockwise |
| -y | ˈjealous — ˈjealousy |

(4) Some suffixes attract the primary stress onto themselves. In such cases there is usually a secondary stress on the first syllable if the stem word consists of more than one syllable.

e.g.

| | | |
|---|---|---|
| -ain | ˌenterˈtain | ˌascerˈtain |
| -ee | ˌpayˈee | ˌemployˈee |
| -eer | ˌpamphleˈteer | ˌprofiˈteer |
| -ese | ˌjournaˈlese | ˌCantoˈnese |

| | | |
|---|---|---|
| -ette | ˌkitcheˈnette | ˌcigaˈrette |
| -esque | ˌpictuˈresque | ˌaraˈbesque |

(5) Stress placement of compound words: Compound words are usually made up of two or more independent elements. Some are written as one word (birthday), some written with a hyphen (home-made) and some written separately like two separate words (drinking water). Here are some rules for stress placement of compound words:

a. Most compounds (esp. nouns) bear primary stress on the first element.
e.g.

| | | |
|---|---|---|
| ˈsports-ground | ˈdrugstore | ˈbathroom |
| ˈsewing machine | ˈwriting-desk | ˈteaching method |
| ˈtree-planting | ˈair-conditioning | ˈsight-seeing |
| ˈbus-driver | ˈrecord player | ˈlanguage teacher |

b. Some compounds have double stress.
e.g.

| | | |
|---|---|---|
| ˈpaper ˈtiger | ˈleather ˈshoes | ˈcotton ˈcloth |
| ˈboiling ˈwater | ˈworking ˈpeople | ˈsleeping ˈboy |
| ˈgood-ˈlooking | ˈhard-ˈworking | ˈfar ˈreaching |
| ˈwell-ˈdressed | ˈbad-ˈtempered | ˈshort-ˈsighted |

c. A very few compounds bear primary stress on the second element.
e.g.

| | | |
|---|---|---|
| withˈout | manˈkind | whatˈever |
| myˈself | forˈever | ˌeverˈlasting |

(6) Certain words of three or more syllables usually have a secondary stress besides the primary. It usually falls on the first or second syllable.
e.g. ˌautoˈmatic, ˌrecomˈmend, peˌculiˈarity

ˌuniˈversal，ˌmagaˈzine，exˌperiˈmental

## Ⅲ. Stress Influence on Meaning of Words

In English there are several pairs of two-syllable words which are identical in spelling but differ from each other in stress placement, apparently according to word class (noun, verb or adjective). If it is a verb, the stress falls on the second syllable; if it is a noun or an adjective, the stress falls on the first syllable. Some pairs possess the same or approximately the same meaning, but some pairs are semantically quite different. Here is a list of more usual words of this class.

### ■ noun / adjective

ˈabsent /ˈæbsent/ *adj.* 缺席的
ˈpresent /ˈprezent/ *adj.* 出席
ˈimport /ˈimpɔːt/ *n.* 进口，进口货
ˈexport /ˈekspɔːt/ *n.* 出口，出口货
ˈincrease /ˈinkriːs/ *n.* 增加
ˈdecrease /ˈdiːkriːs/ *n.* 减少
ˈconduct /ˈkɒndʌkt/ *n.* 行为
ˈconflict /ˈkɒnflikt/ *n.* 斗争；冲突
ˈcontest /ˈkɒntest/ *n.* 比赛，竞争
ˈcontract /ˈkɒntrækt/ *n.* 合同
ˈconvict /ˈkɒnvikt/ *n.* 罪犯
ˈextract /ˈekstrækt/ *n.* 选段
ˈobject /ˈɒbdʒikt/ *n.* 物体
ˈprogress /ˈprəʊɡres/ *n.* 进步
ˈrebel /ˈrebel/ *n.* 造反者
ˈsubject /ˈsʌbdʒikt/ *n.* 科目
ˈrecord /ˈrekɔːd/ *n.* 唱片；记录
ˈtransfer /ˈtrænsfɜː/ *n.* 调动；迁移
ˈperfect /ˈpɜːfikt/ *a.* 完美的
ˈproduce /ˈprɒdjuːs/ *n.* 产品

### ■ verb

abˈsent /əbˈsent/ *v.* 使缺席
preˈsent /priˈzent/ *v.* 赠送；提出
imˈport /imˈpɔːt/ *v.* 进口
exˈport /ikˈspɔːt/ *v.* 出口
inˈcrease /inˈkriːs/ *v.* 增加
deˈcrease /diˈkriːs/ *v.* 减少
conˈduct /kənˈdʌkt/ *v.* 指导；引导
conˈflict /kənˈflikt/ *v.* 斗争；争执
conˈtest /kənˈtest/ *v.* 争论；争夺
conˈtract /kənˈtrækt/ *v.* 签订合同
conˈvict /kənˈvikt/ *v.* 证明……有罪
exˈtract /ikˈstrækt/ *v.* 摘录
obˈject /əbˈdʒekt/ *v.* 反对
proˈgress /prəˈɡres/ *v.* 促进；进展
reˈbel /riˈbel/ *v.* 造反
subˈject /səbˈdʒekt/ *v.* 使服从
reˈcord /riˈkɔːd/ *v.* 记录
transˈfer /trænsˈfɜː/ *v.* 调职；转移
perˈfect /pəˈfekt/ *v.* 使完美
proˈduce /prəˈdjuːs/ *v.* 生产

There are also several pairs of phrases, one of which is a single-stress compound, and the other is formed by an adjective and a noun with two normal stresses. The meaning of such a pair is quite different. A few examples are:

$\begin{cases} \text{'greenhouse (a house with sides and roof of glass, kept warm for growing plants)} \\ \text{'green 'house (a house of a green colour)} \end{cases}$

$\begin{cases} \text{'blackbird (a common European singing bird)} \\ \text{'black 'bird (a bird of a black colour)} \end{cases}$

$\begin{cases} \text{'darkroom (a room cut off from all outside light, used for developing photographs)} \\ \text{'dark 'room (a room without light)} \end{cases}$

$\begin{cases} \text{'leatherjacket (larva of a crane-fly)} \\ \text{'leather 'jacket (jacket made of leather)} \end{cases}$

### Questions for Discussion

1. How many kinds of stress are there in a word? What are they?
2. What are the general rules of stress placement for simple words?
3. Please give at least 3 examples to show the general rules of stress placement for compound words.
4. Please give some examples to show stress influence on meaning of words.

### Exercise R-1

扫码听音频

 1. Stress marking: When you hear the word, repeat it, and then place a stress mark (') before the stressed syllable.

(1) carry      major      service      luggage

       innocent      attitude      political      intelligence

(2) aboard      compassion      confirm      discourage

       embark      express      objection      transform

2. Listen to the recording first, and then mark stresses on the words below (primary and secondary). Arrange them in columns so that all the words in one column have the same number of syllables and the same stress patterns.

marry, celebrate, religion, excellent, universal, condition, modern, important, automatic, nation, policy

3. Pronounce the words with the given suffixes, paying attention to the secondary stress if any.

| -ee   | stand   | appoint  | absent   |
|-------|---------|----------|----------|
| -eer  | racket  | mountain | engine   |
| -ese  | Japan   | Vietnam  | official |
| -ette | leather | novel    | statue   |

4. Read the follwing words with the given suffixes.

| love (-able)  | delight (-ful) | revive (-al)  |
| amaze (-ing)  | ripe (-en)     | snob (-bish)  |
| refine (-ery) | cow (-like)    |               |

5. Read the following words with the given suffixes.

| -eous   | courage  | advantage |
| -graphy | photo    | tele      |
| -ial    | proverb  | president |
| -ian    | music    | barbar    |
| -ic     | atom     | climate   |
| -ive    | detect   | mass      |
| -ity    | tranquil | superior  |
| -ion    | inflate  | possess   |

Unit 11  Word Stress

6. Listen and repeat the following compound words, paying attention to the word stress.

'book-case          'exercise-books      'workshop
'living-room        'carrying-pole       'swimming-pool
'time-saving        'house-keeping       'skin-grafting

7. Put stress on words of the following phrases according to the meaning given in the brackets.

(1) English teacher (a teacher who teaches English)
(2) green fly (fly of a green colour)
(3) blackboard (board used in school classrooms for writing or drawing with chalk)
(4) iron man (model made of iron)

8. Tell parts of speech and the meaning of the following words.

refuse /rɪˈfjuːz/            refuse /ˈrefjuːs/
subject /səbˈdʒekt/          subject /ˈsʌbdʒɪkt/
contrast /kənˈtrɑːst/        contrast /ˈkɒntræst/
protest /prəˈtest/           protest /ˈprəʊtest/
present /prɪˈzent/           present /ˈpreznt/
perfect /pəˈfekt/            perfect /ˈpɜːfɪkt/
record /rɪˈkɔːd/             record /ˈrekɔːd/

9. Read the following passage after the recording.

### 'One 'Man in a ˋBoat

'Fishing is my 'favourite ˋsport. I 'often 'fish for 'hours without 'catching ˋanything. But 'this does 'not ˋworry me. Some ˇfishermen are unˋlucky. Instead of 'catching ´fish, they 'catch old 'boots and ˋrubbish. I am 'even ˋless ˌlucky. I 'never 'catch ˋanything—'not even old ˋboots. 'After having ˈspent whole ˈmornings on the ˊriver, I ˈalways ˈgo home with an ˈempty ˋbag. "You must ˈgive up ˋfishing!" my ˌfriends ˌsay. "It's a ˈwaste of ˋtime." But they ˈdon't ˈrealize one imˈportant ˋthing. I'm ˈnot really ˈinterested in ˋfishing. I am ˈonly ˈinterested in ˈsitting in a ˋboat and ˈdoing ˈnothing at ˋall!

# Unit 12

## Sentence Stress

In Unit 11 we made some general observations regarding the stress in isolated words. But since speech is made up of words strung together, we must also look at these words in groups, in phrases or in sentences in order to observe what happens to the stress pattern. In natural connected speech, for various reasons, some words are stressed, others are not. The stress in a sentence is called sentence stress（句重音）. Sentence stress can be classified into three types: sense stress（表意重音）, logical stress（逻辑重音）and emotional stress（感情重音）.

## Ⅰ. Sense Stress

Sense stress is a very common phenomenon in connected speech. The distribution of such stresses is subject to the meaning that the speaker wishes to convey. In normal speech we put stress on words semantically important. Such words are called content or lexical words（实词）, such as nouns, adjectives, adverbs, notional verbs, numerals, interjections, demonstrative pronouns, interrogative pronouns and the absolute form of the possessive pronouns; the unimportant ones are called form or structural words（虚词或结构词）, which are used to join together the words that carry meaning. In unemphatic speech, such words are usually unstressed. They are articles, monosyllabic prepositions, monosyllabic conjunctions, personal pronouns, possessive pronouns, reciprocal pronouns, reflexive and relative pronouns, auxiliary and modal verbs and link verb *be*.

Examples for words with sentence stress:

### 1. Nouns

ˈ*John* is a ˈteacher from Aˋmerica.

### 2. Adjectives

What a ˈ*beautiful* ˋsight!

### 3. Adverbs

I've ˈ*seldom* ˈmet him ˋ*recently*.

### 4. Notional verbs

They would ˈ*die* ˈrather than ˋ*yield*.

### 5. Numerals

ˈ*Two* plus ˈthree ˈequals ˋ*five*.
His adˈdress is ˈforty-ˈsix ˋLinden Street.

### 6. Interjections

ˈ*Oh*, it's ˇwonderful!

### 7. Demonstrative pronouns

ˈ*This* is our ˋcollege.

### 8. Interrogative pronouns

ˈ*Who* was ˈthat on the ˋphone?

## 9. The absolute form of possessive pronouns

'This 'book is `mine.
And 'yours is over ` there.

Examples for words with no sentence stress:

## 1. Articles

He is *a* 'teacher of ` English.
'This is *the* 'book I ` want.

## 2. Monosyllabic prepositions

He was sur'prised *at* her ` attitude.

## 3. Monosyllabic conjunctions

'John, 'Henry *and* 'Robert 'all ` went *but* 'Peter ` didn't.

## 4. Personal, possessive, reciprocal, reflexive and relative pronouns

He 'taught *us* ` English.
*His* 'brother is *my* 'best ` friend.
Let's ` learn from *each other*.
They 'help *one another* in *their* ` work.
She 'thought *herself* 'better than 'anyone ` else.
'Do you 'know the 'man *who* is 'sitting ´ there?

## 5. Auxiliary and modal verbs

They *have* been in the ' countryside ` recently.
You *may* ` go ₁now.

## 6. Link verb be

He *is* a ˈgood ˋtechnician.

Special cases with no stress on content words：

(1) A content word which appears for the second time in a sentence or in a short context is not stressed.

e.g. ˈHow ˈmany ˈtimes have you been ˋthere?
ˋThree *times*.
He ˈthinks of that as a ˋchild *thinks*.

(2) If a noun is preceded by another qualifying noun，the second one is often unstressed. And these two nouns are often connected by the sense，actually they may be considered as compound words.

e.g. ˈThat is our ˋclassroom *building*.
I ˈmet her at the ˋrailway *station*.

(3) To avoid repetition we often use substitute words. These substitute words usually have no sentence stress.

e.g. — ˈWhich ˈdictionary do you ˋwant?
— That ˋsmall *one*.
— ˈWill he ˈcome to ˊmorrow?
— ˋYes，I ˋthink *so*.

(4) When demonstrative pronouns *this*, *that*, *these*, *those* indicate very weak demonstrativeness and are only the equivalent to the word "it" or the definite article "the"，they are unstressed.

e.g. I can ˈeasily ˋdo *this*.
It is ˈnecessary to ˈtake *these* preˋcautions.

(5) In phrases *this morning*, *this afternoon*, etc.，the demonstrative

pronoun *this* is not stressed.

e.g. We ar'rived *this* ` morning.

(6) In exclamatory sentences such words as *what*, *how* are usually unstressed.

e.g. *What* a 'horrible ` day!

*How* 'thoughtful she ` is!

(7) The word *street* never bears sentence stress in street names.

e.g. ` Oxford *Street*    ` High *Street*

Special cases with stress on form words:

(1) Auxiliaries, modals and link verb *be* bear sentence stress in the following cases:

  a. When they are in the initial position of a sentence, they are stressed.
   e.g. '*Do* you ✓ like it?
    '*Can* I ✓ help you?
    '*Are* you a ´ freshman?
  b. When they are in the final position, used as short answers to general questions, they are stressed.
   e.g. — 'Do you ´ like it?
    — ` Yes, I ` *do*.
    — 'Can you 'finish it in ´ time?
    — ` Yes, I ` *can*.
    — 'Are you a ✓ freshman?
    — ` Yes, I ` *am*.
  c. If they are in contracted negative forms, they are stressed.
   e.g. It '*doesn't* ` matter.
    He '*isn't* a ` doctor.
    I '*can't* ac ` cept it.

(2) Modal verbs *may*, *can*, *must*, *ought to* are usually stressed in the following cases:

    a. When *may* expresses the meaning of possibility, it bears sentence stress.

        e.g. They ˈmay ˈcome this ˋevening.

    b. When *can* expresses the meaning of astonishment, it bears sentence stress.

        e.g. ˈ*Can* it be ˈfive alˊready?

    c. When *must*, *ought to* express the meaning of strong certainty and expectation, they are stressed.

        e.g. He ˈ*must* be in the ˋroom.

            You ˈ*ought to* have ˈbeen ˋthere.

(3) Prepositions may be stressed when they are at the beginning of a sentence and followed by an unstressed syllable.

    e.g. ˈ*In* theˊ box he ˈfound a ˋletter.

(4) Subordinate conjunctions are usually stressed when they are at the beginning of a sentence and followed by an unstressed word.

    e.g. ˈ*If* you ˊwish, I'll ˋhelp you.

        ˈ*When* he ˊcomes, I'll ˈtell him aˋbout it.

(5) Reflexive pronouns in emphatic use are usually stressed.

    e.g. He ˈcouldn't ˈcome *him*ˋ*self*.

## Ⅱ. Logical Stress

Apart from sense stress there is another kind of stress which is called logical stress. The distribution of such stresses is subject to the speaker's will. The speaker may put stress on any word he wishes to emphasize. So a word logically stressed may stand at the beginning, in the middle or at the end of a sentence and it usually implies some idea of contrast. For example:

    We ˈheard ˈMary ˈsinging upˋstairs. (plain statement of fact)

We ˋheard Mary singing upstairs. (But we didn't see her.)
We heard ˋMary singing upstairs. (But we didn't hear John.)
We heard Mary ˋsinging upstairs. (But we didn't hear Mary talking.)
We heard Mary singing ˋupstairs. (But we didn't hear Mary singing downstairs.)
ˋWe heard Mary singing upstairs. (Not they heard.)
Sometimes the idea of contrast is clearly pointed out.
e.g. I bought it for ˋyou, not for ˋhim.
ˋThey can't do it, but ˋwe can.

## Ⅲ. Emotional Stress

Emotional stress is a special kind of stress. In spoken English when the speaker wants to show strong emotion, he can put strong stress on the word he wishes to emphasize. But such kind of stress doesn't imply any idea of contrast. The high-falling tone should be used in speaking or reading aloud such stressed words.

e.g. It's ˋˋwonderful!          We sucˋˋceeded!

## Questions for Discussion

1. What is sentence stress?
2. How is sentence stress classified?
3. What words are normally stressed and unstressed in a sentence?

## Exercise R-2

 扫码听音频

1. Put a stress mark (ˈ) before each syllable you would expect to be stressed in the following sentences. Listen carefully and read after the recording.

(1) I think I'll be late for class.
(2) James decided to type the letter himself.
(3) The plane was approaching the runway at high speed.
(4) In a short time the house was full of children.

(5) She saw herself in the mirror.

(6) He must have been hit on the head with a hammer.

(7) — Which is your car?

　　— The red one over there.

(8) On the whole it seemed best to cut the visit short.

(9) How hard they are working!

(10) Two heads are better than one.

**2. Listen and repeat. Notice the stress for contrast or emphasis in the following sentences.**

A ˋDialogue

— Howˋ are you?

— ˋFine，ˋthank you. And how areˋ you?

— ˈVeryˋ well. ˊThank you.

— ˈWhere are theˋ paper ˌplates?

— ˋOh，ˈdon't ˈuse theˋ paper plates. Use theˋ *china* plates，please.

— ˈWhere is the ˈappleˋ pie?

— ˈHow did you ˈget the iˈdea that it was anˋ apple pie? It is aˋ cherry pie.

A ˈTelephone Converˋsation

— ˈMay I ˈspeak to Mr. ˊAnderson，please?

— There areˋ two Mr. Andersons in this deˌpartment. They areˋ brothers. ˋWhich one do you ˌwant?

— I'm ˈnotˋ sure，| but I ˈthink I ˈwant theˋ older ˌbrother.

— That'sˋ *Jame* ˌAnderson.ˋ Just a ˊminute | and I'llˋ get him.

— ˈThank you ˈveryˋ much.

**3. Listen to the recording and then mark stresses on words which you would expect to be stressed.**

　　Watching television is a popular pastime. Both children and adults can participate. Some programmes are intellectually stimulating; others are disappointing. Many housewives watch "soap operas"（肥皂剧）during the day. Sports lovers especially enjoy football, basketball, baseball, and soccer games on television. Educational television provides an alternative to commercial programming. It also offers courses of study for college credit. However, most people watch television purely for recreation. What kind of programmes do you like?

 4. Read the following passage after the recording.

### `Am I All ´Right?

'While John 'Gilbert was in ˇhospital, | he 'asked his | 'doctor to `tell him | whether his 'operation had been suc `cessful, | but the 'doctor re `fused to ˌdo so. The 'following ´ day, | the 'patient 'asked for a 'bedside `telephone. 'When he was a ´lone, | he 'telephoned the 'hospital ex `change | and 'asked for 'Doctor `Millington. 'When the 'doctor 'answered the ´ phone, | Mr. 'Gilbert ´ said | he was in'quiring about a `patient, | a Mr. 'John `Gilbert. He `asked | if Mr. 'Gilbert's ˇoperation | had been suc `cessful | and the 'doctor ˇtold him | that it had `been. He 'then ´ asked | 'when he would be al'lowed to go `home | and the 'doctor ´told him | that he would 'have to 'stay in `hospital | for an `other two ˌweeks. Then Dr. 'Millington | asked the `caller | if he was a `relative of the ˌpatient. "`No," the ˌpatient `answered, | "'I 'am Mr. John `Gilbert."

# Unit 13

# Rhythm and Its Features

## I. Rhythm

Rhythm is the internal law of language. Rhythm in English speech is based on stress. It is, in brief, the pattern of regular arrangement and alternation of stressed and unstressed syllables.

## II. Rhythm Group and Its Division

The smallest unit of English rhythm is the rhythm group, which is called a foot (音步) in English poetry. A rhythm group is made up of only one stressed syllable plus what unstressed syllable(s) that may follow. Any unstressed syllables that precede the first rhythm group may be regarded as a silent beat.

Rhythm group division is usually marked by slashes.

e.g. 'John and his / 'brother / 'went into the / `room/.
'Would you/ 'mind / 'calling back / `later/?
Do / 'all of you / 'think we should / ´walk/?
It's[①]/ 'not / 'quite what I / `wanted /.

## III. Features of English Rhythm

English rhythm has two prominent features:

---

[①] Silent beat

## Unit 13  Rhythm and Its Features

> 1. The basic tendency of English rhythm is that the stressed syllables follow each other at roughly equal intervals of time. The correct English rhythm is natural and wave-like.

English is a stress-timed language（以重音计时的语言）, which implies that stressed syllables tend to occur at fairly regular intervals of time, i.e., the period of time from each stressed syllable to the next is approximately the same, irrespective of the number of intervening unstressed syllables.

Study the following four phrases with musical notation:

a / 'good / `man

a / 'clever / `man

a / 'wonderful / `man

an / 'educated / `man

Please pay attention to the first rhythm group of the four phrases. Though they have different numbers of unstressed syllables, they occupy the same length of time as the second rhythm group — the one stressed syllable.

Read the following two sentences and you will find that the stressed syllables occur at about the same interval, even though they are divided by different numbers of unstressed syllables.

'Have you any /'silk of this / 'colour and /'pattern/?

'Pat is / 'staying at the / 'cheap ho / `tel/.

This feature of English rhythm has great influence upon the speed of utterance（语速）and the length of sounds, especially the vowels.

(1) Influence upon the speed of utterance

The speed of utterance in connected speech is largely determined by the number of stressed syllables. The greater the number of stressed syllables, the more slowly they are read whereas the greater the number of unstressed syllables, the more rapidly they are produced.

Read and compare the following sentences:

I / ˈthink he /ˈwants to / ˋgo /. (6 syllables, 3 stressed syllables, 3 beats)

I / ˈthink he / ˈwants us to / ˈgo there on / ˋfoot/. (10 syllables, 4 stressed syllables, 4 beats)

I / ˈthink he / ˈwants us to /ˈgo there on /ˈfoot to / ˋmorrow. (13 syllables, 5 stressed syllables, 5 beats)

If two or more stressed syllables come close together, the speed of utterance is conspicuously slower. e.g.

The ˈDaniel ˈJones Proˈnouncing ˈDictionary ˈlists ˈmost ˈversions of ˈmodern ˈEnglish pronunciˋation.

Read and compare the following two sentences:

ˈBert's / ˈfriend / ˈJohn has / ˈjust / ˈsold / ˈtwo / ˈvery / ˈfine /ˈold / ˋpaintings /. (13 syllables, 10 stressed ones, 10 beats)

It would have been / ˈbetter not to have / ˈpaid for it be / ˈfore you had re / ˋceived it /. (19 syllables, 4 stressed ones, 4 beats)

It can be seen clearly that the long sentence takes less than half the time to say than the short sentence does.

The following sentences have a gradually increasing number of unstressed syllables between the stresses. As their number increases, it may be necessary to slow down the speed of stressed syllables slightly and gradually speed up the unstressed ones. e.g.

It was / ˈgood to / ˋspeak to him about it/.

It would be / ˈbetter if you had / ˋspoken to him about it /.

It would have been / ˈbetter if you had / ˋspoken to him about it /.

ˈTell her to / ˈput it / ˋdown /.

ˈTell the girl to / ˈput it / ˋdown /.

ˈTell the girl to / ˈput the book / ˋdown /.

ˈTell the girl to / ˈput the book on the / ˋtable /.

ˈTell the other girl to / ˈput the book on the / ˋtable /.

ˈTell the other girl to / ˈput all the books on the / ˋtable /.

## (2) Influence upon the length of sounds

Please compare the diphthong /əʊ/ in *no* and *notice* with the help of musical notation.

It can be seen that /əʊ/ in *no* is twice as long as that in *notice*.

Now compare the diphthong /əʊ/ in the following two sentences:

It's clear that /əʊ/ in the first sentence is much longer than that in the second one.

Here's another example:

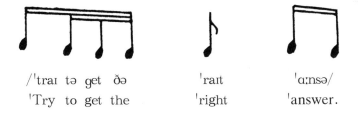

But we should make clear that we say English rhythm is detectable in the regular occurrence of stressed syllables; of course, it is not suggested that the timing is as regular as a clock—the regularity of occurrence is only relative.

e.g. He / ˈrealized that the / ˈbus / ˈwasn't going to / ˋstop for him.

When we read the above sentence, the word *bus* should be stretched out, and it is much longer than its normal length, but it's impossible for such a one-syllable rhythm group to share an exact equal duration with that of the other rhythm groups containing more than one syllable.

> **2. The other characteristic of English rhythm is the alternation of the stressed and the unstressed syllables.**

In actual speech, stressed syllables are not always evenly separated by unstressed ones. In order to maintain an evenness of the beat throughout the utterance, it is necessary for us to regulate the distribution of stresses, thus we can attain smooth rhythm in speaking or reading aloud. This peculiarity of English speech rhythm influences a lot word stress and sentence stress. We generally regulate the distribution of stresses by the following two ways:

(1) By dropping some stresses alternately

If stressed syllables succeed one another in connected speech, we usually drop some stresses. e.g.

The ˈbig brown ˈbear ate ˈten white ˈmice.

ˈMary's younger ˈbrother wanted ˈfifty chocolate ˈpeanuts.

(2) By shifting the placement of word stress

Words with two stresses (including compound words) may lose the first when closely preceded by another stressed syllable or they may lose the second when closely followed by another stressed syllable.

e.g.

a. ˈChiˈnese

ˈJohn can ˈspeak Chiˋnese.

The ˈChinese ˈpeople are ˈhardˋworkingˋpeople.

b. ˈfifˈteen

There are ˈfifteen ˈstudents in theˋroom.

He is ˈjust fifˋteen.

c. ˈsecond-ˈhand

It was ˈbought in a ˈsecond-handˋbookstore.

It was ˈbought second-ˋhand.

d. ˈupˈstairs

I ˈsaw him ˈgo upˋstairs.

She lives in an ˋupstairs room.

## Questions for Discussion

1. What is English rhythm?
2. What is the smallest unit of English rhythm?
3. How is English rhythm formed?
4. What are the features of English rhythm?

## Exercise R-3

 扫码听音频

 1. Read after the recording.

(1) You / ˈcame to / ˋsee him.

You should / ˈcome in order to / ˋmeet him.

You should have / ˈcome before it got so / ˋlate.

(2) We / ˈbought a / ˋbook.

We have / ˈbought another / ˋbook.

We could have / ˈbought another / ˋbook.

We ought to have / ˈbought ourselves another / ˋbook.

(3) I / ˈcan't / ˈcome / ˋnow.

I / ˈcouldn't / ˈcome just / ˋnow.

I / ˈcouldn't have / ˈcome be / ˋfore.

I / ˈcouldn't have / ˈcome any / ˋearlier.

I / ˈcouldn't have ap / ˈplied before / ˋyesterday.

I / ˈshouldn't have been able to ap / ˈply any earlier than / ˋyesterday.

 2. Divide the following sentences into rhythm groups and read them after the recording.

(1) They arrived in China three days ago.

(2) He asked me if I could lend him a dictionary.

(3) I think he's feeling better than he did yesterday.

(4) When we arrived at the station, we found that the train had left.

(5) Out of sight, out of mind.

(6) Spare the rod and spoil the child.

(7) He who is ashamed of asking is ashamed of learning.

(8) He that boasts of his knowledge proclaims his ignorance.

(9) The grass is always greener on the other side of the fence.

(10) Early to bed and early to rise makes a man healthy, wealthy, and wise.

**3. Double-stressed words (including compound words) are easily influenced by rhythmic variations. Listen and repeat the following pairs of sentences.**

(1) ˈChiˋnese

We are ˈboth Chiˋnese.

He ˈspecialized in ˈChineseˋ poetry.

(2) ˈarmˋchair

What a ˈnice armˋchair!

They had an ˈarmchairˋ travel.

(3) ˈfirst-ˋrate

ˈJohn is a ˈfirst-rateˋ doctor.

Her ˈacting was ˈquite first-ˋrate.

(4) ˈoff-ˋhand

He ˈgave me an ˈoff-handˋ answer.

He is ˈalways off-ˋhand.

(5) ˈupˋstairs, ˈoutˋside

He ˈlives upˋstairs; there is a ˈbell outˋside.

The ˈupstairs ˈroom has an ˈoutsideˋ staircase.

4. Listen, read and study the stress and rhythm of the following passage.

### How Many

'How many 'seconds in a `minute?
'Sixty and 'no `more in it.
'How many 'minutes in an `hour?
'Sixty for 'sun and `flower.
'How many 'hours in a `day?
'Twenty-four for 'work and `play.
'How many 'months in a `year?
'Twelve the 'calendar 'makes `clear.

 5. Read the following passage after the recording.

### My Heart Will Go On

Every night in my dreams
I see you, I feel you,
That is how I know you go on.
Far across the distance
And spaces beween us
You have come to show you go on.
Near, far, wherever you are,
I believe that the heart does go on.
Once more, you open the door,
And you're here in my heart,
And my heart will go on and on.

Love can touch us one time
And last for a lifetime,
And never let go till we're gone.

Love was when I loved you,

One true time I hold to.

In my life, we'll always go on.

You're here, there's nothing I fear,

And I know that my heart will go on.

We'll stay forever this way.

You are safe in my heart,

And my heart will go on and on.

—— Extract from the U.S. film *Titanic*

 **6. Listen to the following passage and put stress marks according to the recording.**

### The Lincoln Memorial

The Lincoln Memorial is situated in West Potomac Park, Washington, D.C. It was erected to honor Abraham Lincoln, who was president of the United States during the Civil War.

The memorial to the assassinated president looks like a Greek temple. It is surrounded by thirty-six columns, one for each state in the Union at the time of Lincoln's death. When you climb the marble steps to the memorial, you come face to face with a nineteen-foot statue of Lincoln! Two of Lincoln's speeches, the Gettysburg Address and Lincoln's second inaugural address, are carved into the monument walls.

Lincoln is considered one of the greatest of all presidents. An image of the Lincoln Memorial is reproduced on every penny and each five-dollar bill. It reminds people of his greatness.

# Unit 14

# Rhythm Patterns

In connected speech stressed syllables mostly alternate with unstressed ones. Such kind of alternation usually follows certain rhythm patterns (节奏模式). From our daily practice, we have summed up 22 typical rhythm patterns. Plenty of practice on these patterns will help us to achieve correct English rhythm, and help to guide us to use the correct pronunciation and intonation. The best way to practise English rhythm is to beat the rhythm with our hands. We find it helpful to clap our hands on each stressed syllable or to bang rhythmically on the table with a pen; at each bang comes a stressed syllable. But remember, none of the examples below has a fixed rhythm pattern or fixed intonation. They can vary in different contexts. Now, we put a "key" above each group. The sign "O" (read as da) indicates a stressed syllable, and the sign "o" (read as di) indicates an unstressed syllable.

e.g.

o O o O

(di da di da)

I ˈwant to ˋknow.

It's ˈquite all ˋright.

They've ˈgone a ˋway.

It's ˈhard to ˋsay.

## Exercise R-4

 扫码听音频

🎤 1. Read the following exercises on rhythm patterns after the recording.

(1) O O  
　　(da da)  
　　'Come ˋhere.  
　　'Work ˋhard.  
　　'Read ˋthis.  
　　'Look ˋout.  
　　'Sit ˋdown.  

　　O O  
　　(da da)  
　　'What ˋfor?  
　　'Where ˋfrom?  
　　'All ˋright.  
　　'Just ˋthen.  
　　'That's ˋtrue.  

(2) O o O  
　　(da di da)  
　　'Do it ˋnow.  
　　'Try a ˋgain.  
　　'Have a ˋtry.  
　　'Run a ˋway.  
　　'Practise ˋhard.  
　　'Put it ˋthere.  

　　O o O  
　　(da di da)  
　　'Write it ˋdown.  
　　'Half an ˋhour.  
　　'Ring me ˋup.  
　　'Just in ˋtime.  

(3) o O o  
　　(di da di)  
　　I ˋsaw him.  
　　I'm ˋsorry.  
　　I ˋthink so.  
　　I'd ˋlike to.  
　　I've ˋread it.  
　　She's ˋbusy.  

　　o O o  
　　(di da di)  
　　It's ˋeasy.  
　　as ˋwell as  
　　a ˋlot of  
　　I'd ˋrather.  

(4) o O o o  
　　(di da di di)  
　　I ˋthink it is.  

　　o O o o  
　　(di da di di)  
　　He ˋlent me one.

He ˋsaid he would.
He ˋcame with us.
I've ˋheard of it.
I've ˋpaid for it.

They ˋused to be.
Let's ˋgive him some.
He ˋtold me so.
Get ˋrid of it.

(5) O o o O
    (da di di da)
ˈSend him a ˋway.
ˈSing us a ˋsong.
ˈThrow it a ˋway.
ˈMeet him to ˋnight.
ˈWhere have you ˋbeen?

    O o o O
    (da di di da)
ˈWhat did you ˋdo?
ˈShow him the ˋway.
ˈCome for a ˋchat.
ˈLeave it a ˋlone.
ˈWhat is the ˋtime?

(6) o O o o o
    (di da di di di)
We ˋknow what it is.
I've ˋeaten them all.
a ˋlong time ago
an ˋexercise book
We ˋhad to do it.

    o O o o o
    (di da di di di)
I ˋgive it to her.
How ˋold are you then?
I've ˋwritten to him.
I ˋasked if I could.
I ˋthink it will be.

(7) o O o O
    (di da di da)
I ˈwant to ˋknow.
It's ˈhard to ˋsay.
It's ˈquite all ˋright.
a ˈyear a ˋgo

    o O o O
    (di da di da)
He ˈthought he ˋcould.
I'd ˈlove to ˋhelp.
She ˈwent a ˋway.
I ˈthink it ˋis.

(8) o O o o O
    (di da di di da)
I ˈwanted to ˋknow.
She ˈasked me to ˋgo.
the ˈman on the ˋmoon
I'm ˈglad you have ˋcome.
He ˈtold me he ˋwould.

    o O o o O
    (di da di di da)
We ˈwanted to ˋsee.
We ˈleft it be ˋhind.
I ˈthink he will ˋcome.
a ˈwalk in the ˋpark
The ˈhouse is for ˋsale.

(9) O o o o O

(da di di di da)

ˈCarry it aˋway.

ˈClean it with aˋbrush.

ˈWaiting for theˋbus.

ˈHave a cigaˋrette.

ˈCome and have aˋlook.

O o o o O

(da di di di da)

ˈDon't be such aˋfool.

ˈHalf of them haveˋleft.

ˈClimbing up theˋhill.

ˈPut it on theˋdesk.

ˈTell me all youˋknow.

(10) o O o o o O

(di da di di di da)

I ˈhope it will beˋfine.

You ˈought to go toˋbed.

He ˈwaited half anˋhour.

It ˈdoesn't make muchˋsense.

I've ˈheard of it beˋfore.

o O o o o O

(di da di di di da)

You're ˈwanted on theˋphone.

I'll ˈtry to be inˋtime.

as ˈmany as youˋlike

He ˈdidn't know theˋway.

The ˈchildren are inˋbed.

(11) o O o O o

(di da di da di)

the ˈmore theˋbetter

It ˈdoesn'tˋmatter.

a ˈcup ofˋcoffee

It's ˈtime forˋsupper.

She ˈgot aˋletter.

o O o O o

(di da di da di)

We ˈleave toˋmorrow.

I ˈwant toˋmeet him.

He ˈleft onˋMonday.

You ˈneed aˋhaircut.

I ˈcouldn'tˋhelp it.

(12) o O o o O o o

(di da di di da di di)

He ˈstarted toˋtalk to me.

She ˈwanted toˋwrite to him.

I'll ˈborrow aˋnother one.

We ˈtravelled byˋaeroplane.

He ˈcame on aˋbicycle.

It's ˈjust what Iˋthought of.

Perˈhaps you haveˋheard of it.

The ˈprice has goneˋup again.

You'll 'get it on ˋSaturday.

It's 'not the right ˋattitude.

(13) o O o o o O o o o

(di da di di di da di di di)

I 'wanted you to ˋwrite about it.

It's 'not the one I ˋborrowed from you.

I 'didn't think it ˋinteresting.

It's 'interesting to ˋread about it.

Re'member what your ˋteacher tells you.

The 'doctor didn't ˋsee the patient.

She 'bought some new py ˋjamas for him.

I 'think he did it ˋbeautifully.

This 'isn't quite the ˋmoment for it.

He 'didn't want to ˋtalk about it.

(14) O o o o o O

(da di di di di da)

'Show him up to his ˋroom.

'Throw it into the ˋfire.

'Walking along the ˋroad.

'Suffering from a ˋcold.

'Tell her not to be ˋlate.

'Sit down and have a ˋrest.

'Show me what you have ˋdone.

'What's the name of the ˋbook?

'Come and sit by the ˋfire.

'Finish it if you ˋcan.

(15) o O o O o O

(di da di da di da)

I 'think he 'wants to ˋgo.

I 'can't be'lieve it's ˋtrue.

It 'isn't 'quite the ˋsame.

It's 'not the 'one I ˋwant.

She 'has to 'stay in ˋbed.

Ex'cuse my 'being ˋlate.

It's 'time to 'light the ˋfire.

The 'roads are 'very ˋdark.

He 'hasn't 'got a ˋchance.

The 'concert 'starts at ˋeight.

(16) o O o o O o o O

(di da di di da di di da)

I 'think that he 'wants us to ˋgo.

It 'isn't the 'same as beˋfore.

Per'haps you can 'ring her toˋnight.

It 'doesn't much 'matter toˋme.

She's 'gone for a 'walk in theˋpark.

I've 'taken my 'coat to beˋcleaned.

The 'office is 'open at ˋnine.

We 'don't want to 'trouble you ˋnow.

The 'waiter will 'bring us the ˋbill.

He 'practises 'once in a ˋwhile.

(17) o O o o o O o o o O

(di da di di di da di di di da)

I 'think it was an 'excellent afˋfair.

The 'office-boy will 'show you where to ˋgo.

The 'bus is more con'venient than the ˋtrain.

He 'wanted me to 'listen to his ˋsong.

It's 'just as good as 'being in the ˋhall.

We 'finished it the 'day before he ˋcame.

I'd 'like a lump of 'sugar in my ˋtea.

We 'haven't got an 'envelope to ˋmatch.

(18) o O o O o O o

(di da di da di da di)

I 'think he 'wants to `go there.
We 'ought to 'give an `answer.
She 'married 'Mary's `brother.
I'd 'like to 'have a` nother.
We 'had to 'go on `business.
I've 'got to 'do some `shopping.
I'll 'show you 'where to `put it.
It's 'time we 'went to `dinner.
He 'studies 'every `evening.
I 'want a 'pound of `sugar.

(19) o O o o O o o O o o
(di da di di da di di da di di)
I 'think that he 'wants us to `take him there.
I 'told him to 'wait in the ` corridor.
Re'member to 'get me a ` nother one.
I 'wonder if 'David has ` heard of it.
The 'ambulance 'took him to `hospital.
You 'must have it 'ready by `Saturday.
That's 'nothing to 'do with the `argument.
I 'ought to have 'sent her a `Christmas card.
Sep'tember is 'best for a `holiday.
She 'promised to 'carry it `carefully.

(20) O o o o o o O
(da di di di di di da)
'When are you going a ` way?
'Working as hard as they `can.
'Coming back home in a `bus.
'Hurrying off to the `train.
'Giving him a ciga `rette.
'Why have they left you a `lone?
'Go to another ho `tel.

ˈWhere have you hidden the ˋkey?

ˈOpen the box by yourˋself.

ˈBuy her a pretty new ˋdress.

(21) o O o O o O o O

(di da di da di da di da)

You ˈought to ˈknow the ˈway by ˋnow.

He ˈdid his ˈbest to ˈsave the ˋchild.

That's ˈnot the ˈway to ˈfold a ˋcoat.

I ˈtold him ˈnot to ˈgo aˋway.

He ˈhas to ˈgo to ˈwork at ˋeight.

He ˈleft the ˈroom withˈout a ˋword.

They ˈused to ˈgo to ˈbed at ˋsix.

A ˈcup of ˈtea is ˈwhat I ˋneed.

I ˈcan't forˈget the ˈthing heˋsaid.

(22) o O o o O o o O o o O

(di da di di da di di da di di da)

He ˈsays that he ˈwants us to ˈtake it aˋway.

Yon ˈknow that we ˈought to disˈcuss it toˋday.

I ˈsee he's forˈgotten to ˈleave his adˋdress.

We ˈhaven't got ˈtime to arˈrange for it ˋnow.

An ˈapple a ˈday keeps the ˈdoctor aˋway.

**2. Listen and repeat the following nursery rhymes, notice their well-defined patterns of stress and rhythm.**

(1)

ˈOne, ˈtwo, ˈthree, ˊfour,

ˈMary at the ˈcottage ˋdoor,

ˈFive, ˈsix, ˈseven, ˊeight,

ˈEating ˈcherries of a ˋplate.

(2)

In 'winter 'I get 'up at ´night,
And 'dress by 'yellow 'candle `light;
In 'summer 'quite the 'other ´way,
I 'have to 'go to 'bed by `day.

(3)

I 'like to go 'out in the ´garden,
I 'like to get 'up on the `wall,
I 'like to do 'anything ´really,
But I 'hate to do 'nothing at `all.

(4)

'Twinkle, 'twinkle 'little ´star,
'How I 'wonder 'what you`are!
'Up a'bove the 'world so ´high,
'Like a 'diamond 'in the`sky.

(5)

'Work while you ´work,
'Play while you`play,
'That is the 'way
To be 'happy and `gay.

What'ever you ´do,
'Do with your`might.
'Things done by ´halves
are 'never done`right.

'One thing at a ´time,
And 'that done`well,
It's a 'very good ´rule,
As 'many can`tell.

ˈMoments are ˋuseless
When ˈtrifled aˋway;
So ˈwork while you ´work,
And ˈplay while you ˋplay.

3. Put stress marks on words you would expect to be stressed in the following passage, and then read it with a steady rhythm by beating time on the stressed syllables.

**Sports in Britain**

Britain's most popular sports are football and cricket.

There are two types of football: known locally as "soccer" and "rugby". In "soccer", players can only kick the ball, while in "rugby", players can both hold and kick the ball.

Football, particularly "soccer", has gained great popularity in Britain. "Soccer" is played in most boys' schools. There are amateur teams all over the country. Professional teams play many matches against each other every year. The game is watched by millions of people on Saturday afternoons at local stadiums and on television.

Cricket is not quite as popular as football, yet it is often called the English national sport. To many foreigners it appears a slow and rather boring game, but in fact it requires a lot of muscle and quick eye. Cricket is played in the summer. Some members of the British Commonwealth send national teams to play against each other. This is called a Test Match. These matches arouse great popular interest.

Football and cricket are not the only sports in Britain that enjoy great popularity, but they are the most widely watched outdoor games in the country.

4. Read the following poem after the recording.

### `Knowledge

*by Eleanor Farjeon*

Your 'mind is a `meadow
To 'plant for your ˎneeds;
'You are the ´farmer,
With 'knowledge for ˎseeds.

'Don't leave your `meadow
Un'planted and ˎbare,
'Sow it with ´knowledge
And 'tend it with ˎcare.

'Who'd be a 'know-`nothing
'When he might ˎgrow
The 'seed of the ´knowledge
Of 'stars and ˎsnow;

The 'science of `numbers,
The 'stories of ˎtime,
The 'magic of ´music,
The 'secrets of ˎrhyme?

'Don't be a 'know-`nothing!
'Plant in the `spring,
And 'see what a ´harvest
The 'summer will ˎbring.

# Unit 15

# Sense-groups and Pausing

## I. Sense-groups and Their Divisions

### 1. Sense-groups

Sense-groups（意群）are groups of words which are closely connected in meaning and grammar. Each sense-group comprises a number of syllables. Generally speaking, about six or seven syllables are considered appropriate. Divisions of sense-groups are marked by the single slash (/).

The following three sentences get progressively longer, and it would be convenient to cut up the longer ones into smaller groups according to their meaning and grammatical structure:

He is a professor.

The professor in the office / is a linguist.

The professor in the office / is a linguist / from America.

Sense-groups are the minimum grammatical-semantic units which bear the following implications:

(1) A sense-group is an information unit, which can show a relatively complete sense. The following sentence is divided into four groups, each of which gives us a relatively complete idea.

    e.g. The Japanese / for some reason or other / drive on the left / like the Westerners.

(2) A sense-group is a grammatical unit. It may be a complete sentence or a clause or a phrase or even a single word.

e.g. *We study English.*

*When he comes, I'll tell him about it.*

*As a rule, I get up at five every day.*

*Finally, I wish to thank all who cooperated in this important object.*

(3) A sense-group is a prosodic unit（音韵单位）:

   a. Each sense-group is a tone-group in intonation, and it indicates a particular tone pattern (for detailed information, see Part Three).

   b. Each sense-group at least consists of one rhythm group, and it shows a particular rhythm pattern.

(4) A sense-group is a breath-group（气群）or part of a breath-group — a group of words uttered conveniently in a single breath.

## 2. The Divisions of Sense-groups

The divisions of sense-groups are affected by lots of factors, so different people may divide the same sentence into different sense-groups. But some divisions are indispensable to clarity. The following sentence can be divided into two or three sense-groups according to the speaker's needs:

I'll come and sit by the fire and get warm, / and then I shall feel comfortable.

I'll come and sit by the fire / and get warm, / and then I shall feel comfortable.

When we divide sense-groups, grammatical structure is usually taken into consideration. Punctuation marks are often the important basis for us to divide such groups. In speaking or reading aloud, the limit of such a group is shown by a pause. But sometimes stress and rhythm can be decisive factors in dividing such groups.

e.g. ˈWhat are you ˋdoing, John?

It's going to ˇrain, I'm afraid.

The above two sentences contain a vocative and a parenthesis respectively, both of which are in the final position of each sentence. Though preceded by a comma, such groups of words cannot form an independent sense-group, but they should be part of the sense-group concerned. For lack of sentence stress, they cannot form a rhythm-group either. Naturally, it is impossible to have a pause before them.

## Ⅱ. Pausing

A pause (停顿) may be defined as a break, a stop, or a rest. In spoken English, this is precisely what a speaker does when he divides a sentence into two or more parts depending on the length of the sentence. Pauses are frequently made mainly for the purpose of clarity, emphasis or just taking a breath. The pause in speech is by no means of random occurrence: together with the tone-group, it tends to divide up the stream of speech into grammatically and lexically relevant sections. Pauses may be made between sense-groups. When one group is closely connected grammatically to the next, there is a slight pause; and when two groups are not so closely connected, there is a longer pause. A slight pause is usually marked by a single vertical line (│); a longer pause is marked by double vertical lines (‖).

Pauses vary in frequency and length in response to the variations of the following factors: style of writing, rate of speech, emotion and personal habits, etc. Speech is more flexible than writing, allowing us to introduce a "space" to suit speakers' or hearers' needs, but the speaker must handle pauses with skill.

Although English does not have a set of rules for pausing, here are some suggestions to help you have some idea about when and how to pause:

### 1. Do not take a pause between the following elements

(1) articles and the noun they modify (*a coat*);

(2) adjectives and the noun they modify (*new dress*);

(3) auxiliary verb and main verb (*will come*);

(4) preposition and its object (*on Saturday*);

(5) adverb and verb, adjective, or adverb they modify (*definitely going, really good, very quickly*); and

(6) subject, verb, and object (*Mary told me*).

## 2. Location and Length of Pauses

| Location of Pauses | Length of Pauses |
| --- | --- |
| between two sense-groups (without any punctuation marks) | half a beat |
| between two sense-groups (with a comma or a dash) | one beat |
| between two sense-groups (with a colon or a semi-colon) | two beats |
| between two sentences (with a full stop) | three beats |
| between two paragraphs | four beats |

## Questions for Discussion

1. Please define sense-groups.
2. How do you divide sense-groups?

## Exercise R-5

 扫码听音频

 1. Divide the following sentences into sense-groups, and then read after the recording.

(1) What we want is plenty of rain.

(2) The year before last, we spent our summer holidays in Yantai.

(3) In the living-room we will talk together, listen to music, or watch television.

(4) The Japanese, whose industry is well-known, have recently broken all export records.

(5) After returning from the work we had dinner, and then we went into the living-room.

(6) Some people, especially those living in cities, use only public transportations.

(7) "As to that," I replied, "I am not at all sure."

(8) He is a casual acquaintance whom I met occasionally on the street.

(9) I must say that shopping on Mondays instead of Sundays is a positive pleasure, so much less chaos and confusions.

(10) Certainly, Mrs. Brown, you shall have it by this time tomorrow.

2. Divide the following passage into sense-groups. Then read after the recording, paying special attention to sense-groups and pauses.

I was swimming in the Mediterranean Sea one day when I saw a large fish coming toward me at great speed. His jaws were wide open, and I was directly in his path. There was no way to avoid him. I made myself as small as possible and passed through his jaws into his stomach. The place was dark but warm. I kept thinking of how to get out of my prison, and at last I hit upon an idea. I began to hop and jump and dance around within the darkness. This movement inside of him seemed to disturb the fish, for he raised his head high up out of the water. He was seen by some men in a fishing boat who quickly harpooned him. I was congratulating myself on my good luck when I heard the sailors talking about cutting the fish up to preserve the oil. I had seen the long knives that they used, and I wondered if I, too, was going to be cut up with the fish. But my luck held. They started cutting from the tail end, and before they reached the place where I stood, I called out in a loud voice to be saved from this black hole. Imagine their great amazement when they saw me walking out of the fish! I told them the whole story, and to this day I don't think they really believed it.

3. Read the following after the recording.

(1)

'Thirty 'days 'has Sep`tember,
'April, 'June and No`vember;
'February has 'twenty-'eight a´lone;
'All the 'rest have 'thirty-`one,
Ex'cepting 'leap-year, 'that's the´time,
When 'February's 'days are 'twenty-`nine.

(2)

The 'Lion, the 'Lion, he 'dwells in the `Waste;
He 'has a big 'head and a 'very small `waist;
But his 'shoulders are 'stark and his 'jaws they are ´grim,
And a 'good little 'child will 'not play with `him.

4. Read after the recording.

### In'ventor of In`vention

It is imˇpossible | to 'measure the im'portance ofˇEdison | by 'adding up the spe'cific inˇventions | with which the 'name is as `sociated. 'Far-reaching asˇmany of them | have been in their ef'fect on 'modern civili`zation, | the 'total ef'fect of `Edison's ca´reer | sup'passes the 'sum of them `all. He did 'not 'merely 'make the incan'descent ´lamp | and the ´phonograph | and in'numerable 'other de ´vices | 'practical for 'general `use; it was `given to him to 'demonstrate the 'power of ap`plied ´science| so `concretely, | so `understandably, | so con`vincingly | that he 'altered the men`tality of man,kind. In hisˇlifetime, | 'largely be'cause of his sucˇcesses, | there 'came into 'widest ac `ceptance | the revo'lutionary con`ception | that 'man could by the 'use of his inˇtelligence | in'vent a 'new ˙mode of `living | on this `planet; the `human ´spirit, | which in 'all `ages | had re'garded the con'ditions of ´life | as es`sentially un´changing and be'yond man's con ˋtrol, | ˋconfidently, | and per'haps somewhat na ˋively, | a'dopted the con ˊviction that 'anything could be ˋchanged | and 'everything could be con ˋtrolled.

It was at the 'end of the 'nineteenth ˇcentury, | with the per'fecting of the e'lectric 'light ˊbulb, | the ˊtelephone, | the ˊphonograph, | and the ˋlike, | that the 'ordinary man be'gan to ˊfeel | that 'science could 'actually ˋbenefit him. 'Edison sup'plied the 'homely demonsˊtrations | which in'sured the 'popular ac'ceptance of ˋscience, | and 'clinched the 'popular ˇargument | which had be'gun with ˋDarwin, | about the 'place of ˋscience | in 'man's ˋoutlook on ˌlife.

— from *Interpretations* by Walter Lippmann

# Part Three

## Intonation

# Unit 16

## A Brief Introduction

In this part we will study intonation, another essential part of English phonetics. Intonation may be the most interesting and also the most difficult of the three parts. However, we'll start from the beginning.

### I. Definition

Briefly speaking, intonation means the rise and fall of the pitch of the voice during speech. Every language has its own peculiar intonation.

### II. Function

English intonation is an important means of expressing one's feelings and meanings.

Please study and observe the following:

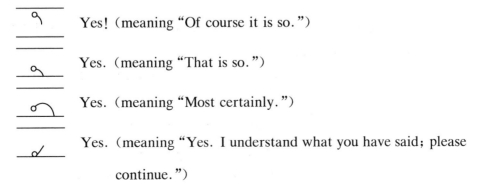

    Yes! (meaning "Of course it is so.")

    Yes. (meaning "That is so.")

    Yes. (meaning "Most certainly.")

    Yes. (meaning "Yes. I understand what you have said; please continue.")

　　　　　　Yes? (meaning "Is it really so?")

　　　　　　Yes. (meaning "That may be so.")

Take "Good morning" for example. It may convey some delicate implications and emotions when it is said with different intonations.

 Good ˋmorning.　　(High Fall—normal greeting; enthusiastic and filled with emotion.)

 Good ˎmorning.　　(Low Fall—casual greeting; cold and phlegmatic.)

 ‾Good ˊmorning.　　(High Prehead + Low Rise—glad and warm greeting.)

 ˈGood ˊmorning.　　(High Level + Low Rise—depressing, not so intimate as the above one.)

 Good ^morning.　　(Rise-fall—greeting with reproach.)

 Good ˊmorning.　　(Low Rise—perfunctory greeting.)

## Ⅲ. Illustrating Intonation

The notation systems used in this book are:

### 1. Graphic Notation(语调图解)

(1) The open dot (○) represents a stressed syllable and the small dot (·) an unstressed syllable.

(2) The space between the two parallel lines represents the normal voice range.

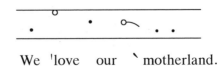

　　　　We ˈlove　our　ˋmotherland.

## 2. Tonetic Stress Marks(示调重音号)

Tonetic stress marks show not only stress, but also, by their shapes and positions, the intonation features of the relevant syllables.
Please observe the following:

| ˈM | ˈˈM | High Level | ˊM | High Rise |
| ˌM | ˌˌM | Low Level | ˏM | Low Rise |
| ˋM | ˋˋM | High Fall | ˇM | High Fall-rise |
| ˎM | ˎˎM | Low Fall | ˅M | Low Fall-rise |

e.g.
We ˈloveˋChina.
ˈAre you a ˈstudent of ˊEnglish?
Note: M stands for a syllable.

## Questions for Discussion

1. What's the definition of English intonation? And what's its function?
2. How many ways do you know can be used to illustrate intonation?

### Exercise I-1

 扫码听音频

 1. Read after the recording and observe the diagrams.

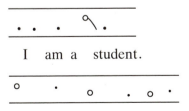

```
  o      •    •    ⌢ .
─────────────────────────
  Where  are  you  going?
```

```
  o    •   •   o    •    •   •   ⌢   •
─────────────────────────────────────────
  Are  you   a  teacher   or   a  student?
```

```
  •    •    o    ⌢
─────────────────────
  What   a   fine  day!
```

**2. Read after the recording and study the tonetic stress marks.**

He is a ˈgood ˈstudent of ˋEnglish.

ˈIs she ˈcoming to ´night?

ˈTell me ˋall about it.

What a ˋnuisance!

Would you like ´tea or ˋcoffee?

**3. Put tonetic stress marks in the following sentences and read after the recording.**

(1) Just a moment, please.

　　It's quite good, really.

(2) Do you feel tired after your walk?

(3) Can you finish the work on Saturday?

(4) I haven't the least idea about it.

(5) I thought he could do it.

(6) It looks like rain, doesn't it?

(7) We like the colour, the shape and the pattern.

(8) A: When will Tom be back?

　　B: I don't know. Why not ask Tom?

4. Read the following poem after the recording.

### 'Stopping by 'Woods on a 'Snowy ˋEvening
#### *By Robert Frost*

Whose 'woods these 'are I 'think I ˋknow.
His 'house is 'in the 'village ˋ though;
He 'will not 'see me 'stopping ´ here
To 'watch his 'woods fill 'up with ˋ snow.

My 'little 'horse must 'think it ´ queer
To 'stop with'out a 'farmhouse ˋ near
Be'tween the 'woods and 'frozen ´ lake
The 'darkest 'evening 'of the ˋ year.

He 'gives his 'harness 'bells a ´ shake
To 'ask if 'there is 'some mis ˋtake.
The 'only 'other 'sound's the ´ sweep
Of 'easy ´ wind and 'downy ˋ flake.

The 'woods are 'lovely, 'dark and ˋdeep,
But 'I have 'promis'es to ˋkeep,
And 'miles to 'go be'fore I ˋsleep,
And 'miles to 'go be'fore I ˋsleep.

# Unit 17

# Basic Tones and Their Training

## Ⅰ. Basic Tones

English tones are divided into two categories, namely, Static Tones（静调）and Kinetic Tones（动调）.

### 1. Static Tones

The tones which remain at the same height are called Static Tones. They are High Level and Low Level.

| High Level | ˈM | ˈNow |
| | ˈˈM | ˈˈNow |

| Low Level | ˌM | ˌNow |
| | ˌˌM | ˌˌNow |

| Partial Stress | • M | • Now |

### 2. Kinetic Tones

The tones which glide from one height to another are called Kinetic Tones. They are High Fall, Low Fall; High Rise, Low Rise; High Fall-rise, and Low Fall-rise.

| High Fall | ˋM | ˋNow |

# Unit 17  Basic Tones and Their Training

| | | |
|---|---|---|
| Low Fall | ˋM | ˋNow |
| | | ˎˋNow |
| High Rise | ˊM | ˊNow |
| | | ˏˊNow |
| Low Rise | ˏM | ˏNow |
| | | ˌˏNow |
| High Fall-rise (undivided) | ˅M | ˅Now |
| | | ˋ˅Now |
| Low Fall-rise (undivided) | ᵥM | ᵥNow |
| | | ˎᵥNow |
| High Fall-rise Divided | ˋM  ˊM | ˋThat's ˊright. |
| | | ˎˋThat's ˊright. |
| Low Fall-rise | ˋM  ˏM | ˋThat's ˏright. |

**N. B.** The Kinetic Tones also include Rise-fall and Rise-fall-rise. However, they are a bit too complicated and not so commonly used as those mentioned above, so they will not be dealt with in the textbook.

## II. Basic Training of Tones

Study the diagrams carefully and read the following with eight different tones.

### 1. Monosyllabic words

no, how, high, right, hard

### 2. Two-syllable words with the stress on the first syllable

| | | | | |
|---|---|---|---|---|
| H | L | | | |
| L | L | | | |
| H | F | | or | |
| L | F | | or | |
| H | R | | | |
| L | R | | | |
| H  F | R | | | |
| L  F | R | | | |

party, people, beauty, leader, rainy

### 3. Two-syllable words with the stress on the second syllable

| | | | | |
|---|---|---|---|---|
| H | L | | or | |
| L | L | | or | |
| H | F | | or | |
| L | F | | or | |

| | | | | | | |
|---|---|---|---|---|---|---|
| H | R | ___⌒___ | or | ___·⌒___ | | |
| L | R | ___·⌒___ | or | ___·⌒___ | | |
| H F | R | ___·⌒___ | or | ___⌒___ | | |
| L F | R | ___·⌒___ | or | ___·⌒___ | | |

begin, believe, again, decide, indeed

### 4. Three-syllable words with the stress on the first syllable

| | | | | |
|---|---|---|---|---|
| H | L | ___o · ·___ | | |
| L | L | ___o · ·___ | | |
| H | F | ___o · ·___ | or | ___⌒· ·___ |
| L | F | ___o · ·___ | or | ___⌒· ·___ |
| H | R | ___o · ·___ | | |
| L | R | ___o · ·___ | | |
| H F | R | ___⌒· ·___ | | |
| L F | R | ___⌒· ·___ | | |

interesting, family, library, communist, hospital

### 5. Three-syllable words with the stress on the second syllable

| | | | | |
|---|---|---|---|---|
| H | L | ___· o ·___ | | |
| L | L | ___· o ·___ | | |
| H | F | ___· ⌒ ·___ | or | ___· ⌒ ·___ |
| L | F | ___· ⌒ ·___ | or | ___· ⌒ ·___ |

| | | |
|---|---|---|
| H | R | . o . |
| L | R | . o : |
| H F | R | ˙◜◡  or  ◜◡ |
| L F | R | ˙◞◡  or  ◞◡ |

important, according, translation, conductor, impression

## Questions for Discussion

1. What are the two categories of English tones?
2. How many kinetic tones do you know?

## Exercise I-2

扫码听音频

🎙 1. Listen to the recording and read the words with different tones.

ˈcar  ˋcar  ˊcar  ˇcar    ˈgo  ˋgo  ˊgo  ˇgo
ˌheart ˋheart ˊheart ˇheart    ˋwrite  ˊwrite  ˇwrite  ˇwrite

🎙 2. Listen to the recording. Each of the flollowing is read twice.

Write the numbers (1, 2, 3) under the diagram to indicate the order they are read.

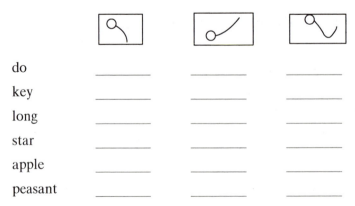

do　　　_____　　_____　　_____
key　　_____　　_____　　_____
long　　_____　　_____　　_____
star　　_____　　_____　　_____
apple　_____　　_____　　_____
peasant　_____　　_____　　_____

## Unit 17  Basic Tones and Their Training

college  _____  _____  _____
factory  _____  _____  _____

### 3. Listen and imitate the tones of the following words.

| ˌworker | worker | worker | worker |
| ˈˌhappy | happy | happy | happy |
| ˈˌsoldier | soldier | soldier | soldier |
| ˈˌcareful | careful | careful | careful |
| aˈˌgo | ago | ago | ago |
| inˈˌcrease | increase | increase | increase |
| deˈˌlight | delight | delight | delight |
| ˈˌnatural | natural | natural | natural |
| ˈˌnational | national | national | national |
| ˈˌSaturday | Saturday | Saturday | Saturday |
| ˈˌcomfortable | comfortable | comfortable | comfortable |
| toˈˌmorrow | tomorrow | tomorrow | tomorrow |
| muˈˌsician | musician | musician | musician |
| muˈˌseum | museum | museum | museum |
| perˈˌformance | performance | performance | performance |
| proˈˌnounce-ment | pronounce-ment | pronounce-ment | pronounce-ment |

### 4. Listen to the recording and practise Fall-rise Divided.

I ˋthought it ˊwas.
I'm ˋsorry to be ˊlate.
I ˋwill, if you ˊlike.
I ˋhope I'm not ˊlate.
I ˋthink he's all ˊright.
I ˋdon't want to be ˊlate.
I ˈwish I could ˋtell you all aˊbout it.

I'd ˋlike it if it's ˊblue.

I ˋdo hope you have a ˌcomfortable ˊjourney.

I ˋthought it was ˊraining.

That ˌquestion's ˋtoo hard for ˊme.

 5. Read the following poem after the recording.

### The 'Grasshopper and the ˋCricket
*by John Keats*

The 'poe'try of 'earth is 'neverˋdead:
    When 'all the 'birds are 'faint 'with the 'hotˊsun,
    And 'hide in 'coolingˋtrees, a 'voice will 'run
From 'hedge to 'hedge a'bout the 'new-mownˋmead:
That is theˋGrass'hopper's—he 'takes theˋlead
    In 'summerˋluxury,—'he has 'neverˋdone
    'With his deˊlights; for 'when tired 'out withˊfun,
He 'rests at 'ease be'neath some 'pleasantˋweed.

The 'poe'try of 'earth is 'ceasingˋnever:
    'On a 'long 'winter 'evening, when the 'frost
    'Has 'wrought aˋsilence, 'from the 'stove thereˊshrills
The ˊCricket's ˌsong, in 'warmth in'creasingˋever,
    And 'seems to 'one in 'drowsi'ness half ˊlost,
    The 'Grass'hopper's a'mong some 'grassyˋhills.

# Unit 18

# Tone-groups

## I. Tone-groups

In speech flow, the basic unit of the English intonation is a tone-group (also named "intonation group", etc.). It is comparatively complete in meaning. It contains only one focal point. The intonation of the whole tone-group is called a tune.

A phrase, a clause or a short sentence may compose a tone-group; a sentence may be said as one, two or even more tone-groups. e.g.

The sun is red.

The whole sentence is taken here as one tone-group, the tune of which is a fall. The tones of the syllables are Low Level, High Level, High Level, and High Fall.

ˈAre you a ˈworker | or a ˋpeasant?

The whole sentence contains two tunes. The first one is a Rise whereas the second is a Fall.

The ˈEnglish Deˈpartment ˈoffice | is on the ˋsecond floor.

(phrase)

ˈWhen it ˈrains | I ˈgo to ˈwork by ˋbus.

(clause)

ˇSometimes | we ˈgo to the ˈcinema in the ˋevening.

（word）

## Ⅱ. Tone-group Division

A sentence can be divided into two or more tone-groups according to the number of focal points in the mind of the speaker, which can make reading or speaking easier and convey ideas more clearly.

The chief factors that influence the division of tone-groups are meaning and grammatical structure, speed of delivery and emphasis on different parts of the sentence. cf.

ˈMost of the ˈstars are ˈbigger than the ˋsun.

ˈMost of the ˊstars | are ˈbigger than the ˋsun.

The second sentence is read more slowly and some emphasis is given to the idea "most of the stars".

Vertical bars (｜) are used between the tone-groups. e.g.

ˈMany ˈyears aˊgo, | there ˈlived an ˊemperor | who ˈcared ˈmore for ˈnew ˊclothes | than for ˈanything ˊelse | in the ˋworld.

In ˈone of his ˊbooks, | ˈMarx ˈgave some adˊvice | on ˈhow to ˈlearn a ˈforeign ˋlanguage. Heˊsaid | when a ˈperson is ˋlearning a ˈforeign ˊlanguage, | he must ˈnot ˈalways be transˈlating ˋeverything | into his ˋown language.

## Ⅲ. Structure of the Tone-group

A full tone-group (or tune) consists of five parts, i.e., prehead(调冠), head（调头）, body（调身）, nucleus（调心或调核）and tail（调尾）. Occasionally one part or more parts may be missing, but the nucleus is always essential.

Please observe the examples in the following two tables.

## Table 2

| | Prehead | Head | Body | Nucleus | Tail |
|---|---|---|---|---|---|
| 1. | | | | Stop! | |
| 2. | | | | Stop | it! |
| 3. | | Stop | | talk- | ing, please. |
| 4. | | Will | you stop | talk- | ing, comrades? |
| 5. | He was | say- | ing "Stop | talk- | ing, comrades." |

## Table 3

| | Prehead | Head | Body | Nucleus | Tail |
|---|---|---|---|---|---|
| 1. | | | | Speak. | |
| 2. | | | | Speak | about it. |
| 3. | | Don't | | speak | about it. |
| 4. | He'd | like | to | speak | about it. |
| 5. | He | asked | you not to | speak | about it. |

The following are brief explanations of each part in a tune.

**Prehead:** Any unstressed syllable or syllables preceding the first full stress of a tune.

Low Prehead is most common, but usually not shown with any mark. High Prehead is often indicated with a short horizontal stroke (ˉ).

He is a 'combat ˋhero.

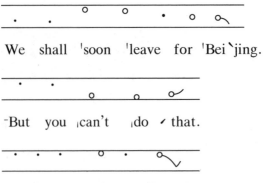

We shall 'soon 'leave for 'Bei`jing.

\-But you ˌcan't ˌdo ´that.

\-He is the queerest ˇchap.

**Head**: It is the first full stress of a tune, whether static or kinetic. There are High Head and Low Head, the former being most common. The High Head is indicated by a vertical short stroke (') placed at the top, similar to High Level, whereas the Low Head is indicated by a short vertical stroke (ˌ) placed at the bottom, similar to the Low Level.

'How do you `do?

'Are you 'coming on ´Sunday?

'Go to the `classroom, please.

Sometimes, the falling-rising tune can be preceded by a falling head.

She has a `lovely ˇvoice.

`Not ˇeveryone

ˌDon't be ˌso im`patient, ˌthen.

**Body**: It is that part of a tune lying between its head and its nucleus.

There are two types of body: High Body and Low Body, the former being very common. The main feature of the body is that it glides down gradually.

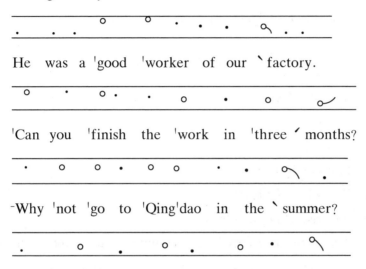

He was a 'good 'worker of our ˋfactory.

'Can you 'finish the 'work in 'three ˊmonths?

ˉWhy 'not 'go to 'Qing'dao in the ˋsummer?

You ˌmust be ˌfeeling ˌratherˋ tired.

**Nucleus**: It is the tone associated with the last fully stressed syllable of a tune. In other words, it is the stressed syllable to which the speaker wishes to give the greatest prominence by means of a pitch movement. The nucleus is essential in a tune. The pitch change takes place mainly in the nucleus or begins from it. The Fall completes itself in the nucleus. The Rise and Fall-rise, if not followed by any unstressed syllables, complete themselves in the nucleus. If followed by unstressed syllables, the pitch begins to change from the nucleus but finishes in the following syllables. e.g.

It was an un'usually 'dark ˋnight.

I could have ˋfinished it.

ˈHow did you ˈspend your ˈsummer ˋholidays?

―――――――――――――――――――――
  ο • • ο • ο • ⌒
―――――――――――――――――――――

ˈThis one is ˈnot so ˈgood as ˅that?

―――――――――――――
ᴏ  ο • ⌒
―――――――――――――

ˈIs ˈthis your ˊclass?

Types of the Nucleus:

　　1) Fall (high or low)

　　2) Rise (high or low)

　　3) Fall-rise (high or low)

The nucleus is the key part in expressing our ideas and feelings. Its direction determines the types of the tune. If the nucleus is a Fall, so is the tune.

**Tail**: It is any unstressed syllable (or syllables) following the nucleus of an utterance. e.g.

―――――――――――――――――――――
  ο • ο ⌒ • • • •
•
―――――――――――――――――――――

They ˈoften ˈread ˋnewspapers to them.

―――――――――――――――――
ο • ο ο • •
―――――――――――――――――

ˈIs the ˈplay ˊinteresting?

―――――――――――
ᴏ ⌒ ˅
―――――――――

ˈBe ˅careful!

―――――――――――――――
ᴏ ⌒ • • •
―――――――――――――――

ˈDon't ˅worry about it.

The tail may also include one or two partially stressed syllables. e.g.

ˋTell me about it.

How ˈfar is it from ˈhere?

## Ⅳ. Features of an English Tune

1. Normally a low prehead.
2. Normally a high head.
3. In the body, the stressed syllables occupy mostly level pitches and they all fall down gradually in pitch. The unstressed syllables between the stressed ones have about the same height as the stressed syllable preceding them.
4. The nucleus is usually at the end of the tune when something is uttered in isolation.
5. The changes in the tail are determined by the nucleus. In a Fall, the tail remains on a low level pitch [ˌ]; in a Rise or Fall-rise, the tail rises gradually [·].

### Questions for Discussion

1. What is the basic unit of English intonation?
2. Please explain the structure of the tone-group.
3. What is a tune? What are the features of the English tune?

### Exercise I-3

 扫码听音频

 1. Analyse the tone-groups of the following sentences and read after the recording.

(1) We must ˈlight the ˈfire to ˈwarm the ˋdining-room.
(2) ˈWill you have time to ˈtype ˊthis for me?
(3) ˈMary may be ˈgoing on ˋholiday at the ˌend of the ˌmonth.
(4) ˈCan he ˈfinish the ˈbook on ˊSaturday?
(5) We shall ˈfinish the ˈwork in ˈhalf an ˋhour.

## 2. Read the following with special attention to the prehead.

(1) You will be ˇlate.

(2) Did you ´see him?

(3) ‒ The ˋbrute.

(4) ‒ It's an ex͵traordinary ´thing.

(5) I ˈmust ˈstay at ´home | and ˈdo some ˋwork.

## 3. Read the following with special attention to the head.

(1) ˈWho ˈtold you the ˋnews?

(2) ˈDid you enˈjoy the ´play?

(3) I ͵didn't ex͵pect to ´see you here.

(4) ˈThat's ˈnot what I ˇmeant.

(5) I ˈthink it's ˈquite ˇpossible.

## 4. Read the following with special attention to the body.

(1) ˈWhy ˈdidn't you ˈtake part in ˈmaking the ˋplan?

(2) ˈCan you ˈfinish the ˈproject in ´October?

(3) ˈDidn't you ˈbring your ´raincoat?

(4) You'd ˈbetter ˈtake the umˋbrella with you.

(5) I ͵can't ͵wait for ˋJohn | to ͵finish his ´homework.

## 5. Read the following with special attention to the nucleus.

(1) He has ˈjust come ˈback from the ˋcountryside.

(2) Then ͵why did you acˋcept it?

(3) What ˈlovelyˋweather!

(4) ˈCan we ˈsmoke during the ´meeting?

(5) I ͵don't ˈthink you will sucˇceed.

(6) I ˈcan't make ˈhead or ´tail of it. Can ´you?

(7) There's ˈLondonˋAirport. ˇI used to ˋwork ´there.

(8) D'you ˈlike ˈthese ˊ flowers? ˈPut them in a ˈbeautiful ˋ vase.

(9) I ˈdon't think it's very ˋ safe, ˋ either.

(10) When ˋ can you ˌcome, may I ˌask?

(11) ˊ Mine is ˈlonger than ˋ yours.

### 6. Read the following with special attention to the tail.

(1) He is a ˈfamous ˋ scientist.

(2) ˈIs it ˊ possible?

(3) ˈDo you ˈthink it's imˊportant?

(4) It may be ˇ difficult, you know.

(5) ˋ Tell them aˌbout it.

### 7. Listen to the recording and underline the nucleus.

(1) She ˈgives me a ˋ lot of ˌhelp.

(2) ˈDo you ˈclean your ˊ classroom ˙ every day?

(3) I'm ˈgoing to the ˈtheatre to ˋnight.

(4) He was ˈwatching the ˈchildren ˋ playing.

(5) How ˋ far is it from ˌhere to the ˌstation?

### 8. Listen to the recording and supply the tonetic stress marks.

(1) The park is a long way off.

(2) Are we having a meeting this afternoon?

(3) Don't worry. He'll be well soon.

(4) Stars are giant balls of glowing gas.

(5) Shut the windows, please.

### 9. Diagrammatize the sentences.

(1) ˋ Come to me.

(2) ˇ She did.

(3) ˋCertainly I ˌwill.

(4) They ˈgo to the ˈseaside ˈeveryˋyear.

(5) ˋDon't ˌwaste so ˌmuch ˊtime.

## 10. Read the following address after the recording.

### The ˋGettysburg Adˌdress
### by ˈAbraham ˋLincoln

ˈFourscore and ˈseven ˈyears aˊgo, | our ˈfathers ˈbrought forth upon ˈthis ˊcontinent a ˈnewˋnation, | conˈceived in ˊliberty | and ˈdedicated to the propoˊsition | that ˈall men are creˈated ˋequal.

ˈNow we are enˈgaged in a ˈgreat ˈcivilˋwar, |ˋtesting |ˇwhether that nation | — orˋany ˌnation, | so conˌceived and so ˊdedicated — | can ˈlong enˋdure.

We are ˊmet | on the ˈgreatˋbattle-field of that ˌwar. | We are ˊmet | toˋdedicate | aˇportion of it | as the ˈfinalˋresting ˌplace | of ˊthose | who have ˈgiven theirˋlives | so ˈthat nation might ˋlive.

It is altoˈgether ˊfitting | andˋproper | that we shouldˋdo this.

But, in aˇlarger ˙sense, |ˇwe canˌnot ˌdedicate, | ˇwe ˌcannot ˌconsecrate, |ˋwe can˙ notˋhallow, | thisˋground. | The ˈbraveˊmen, | ˊliving andˋdead, | who ˇstruggledˊhere, | haveˊconsecrated it, | ˌfar aˈboveˇour ˙power to ˙add | or to deˋtract.

The ˈworld will ˈveryˈlittle ˊnote | or ˈlong reˋmember | what ˌwe ˌsay ˊhere; | but it can ˈnever forˋget | whatˋˋthey did ˌhere.

It is forˋus, | theˋliving, | ˌrather, to be ˌdedicated, ˊhere, | to the ˈunfinished ˊwork | that ˈthey have thus ˈfar so ˈnobly ˈcarriedˋon. | It is for ˋus to be ˋhere | ˊdedicated to the ˈgreat ˊtask | reˈmaining beˋfore us; | that from these ˈhonoredˋdead | we take inˈcreased deˋvotion | to ˈthatˋcause | for which ˊthey here ˈgave the ˈlastˋmeasure of deˌvotion; that we ˊhere | ˈhighly reˊsolve | that ˈthese ˙dead shall ˈnot have ˈdied in `vain; | that the ´ nation ˙ shall, | 'under ´ God, | have a 'new ˙birth of ˋ freedom, | and that ˋ government | ´ of the ˙ people, | ´ by the ˙ people, | ˇ for the ˙ people, | shall 'not ˙ perish from the ˋ earth.

 11. Read the following story after the recording.

## A 'Change of ˋ Idiom

An 'Englishman 'went to˙visit a ˌfriend who ˌowned a 'large ˋ fruit-growing esˌtate in Jaˋ maica. 'Greatly im˙pressed by the e'normous˙quantity of ˋ fruit he ´ saw, and 'realizing that it was 'too ˋ perishable to be exˋ ported when ´ ripe, he ex'claimed:

"¯But ´´ what do youˋˋ do with all this ˌfruit? Youˋˋ surely can't ˌeat it ˌall your ˇselves."

" ˋOh," re ˌplied his ˌfriend, ˌtaking adˌvantage of his faˌmiliˌarity with Aˌmerican ˌusage to ˌmake a ˋ pun, "we 'eat what we ´ can, and we 'can what weˋˋ can't."

This 'greatly a ˋ mused the ´ Englishman, who re'solved to reˋˇ member it for the 'benefit of his˙friends at ˋ home.

'Shortly ˙after his re'turn to ´England he at'tended a ´ dinner, at which he was 'asked to ˙ give his im'pressions of Jaˋ maica. He ˋ did so, and de'cided to ˙use his 'friends's ˙joke as a'climax to his ˋ speech; so ˌafter re'counting his ex´periences he ˙added:

"My 'friend made a 'rather˙neat ˋ pun while he was ˌshowing me ˌround his es ´ tate. I was 'struck by the 'large a˙mount of ˋ fruit he ´ had, and 'asked him˙what they ˋ did with it, to which he re ´plied: "We 'eat what we ´can, and we 'tin what we ˋˋ can't."

While his 'listeners were 'racking their˙brains 'trying to˙find the ´ pun, the ˇ speaker o'blivious of having ˌsubstituted an 'English˙usage for the o'riginal Aˇ merican one, was 'wondering why˙nobody ˋ laughed.

# Unit 19

# Functions of Tunes and Their Uses

The most commonly used tunes in English are Falling, Rising and Falling-rising. Their functions will be dealt with respectively according to the four types of sentences, i.e., the declarative sentence, interrogative sentence, imperative sentence and exclamatory sentence.

## I. Falling Tune

The Falling Tune is used basically to express **definiteness** and **completeness**. It is often used in declarative sentences, special questions, imperative sentences and exclamatory sentences.

### 1. Declarative Sentences

When used in declarative sentences, the Falling Tune expresses definiteness, completeness and subjective attitude of the speaker. Other implications it has are seriousness, confidence, stubbornness, clarity, straightforwardness, etc. The Low Fall has cool, depressed or stern coloring. e.g.

We ˈlove our ˋcountry.
It's ˈhalf past ˋtwelve.
You've ˈdone a ˈgood ˋjob.
I'll ˈcome as ˈsoon as I ˋcan.
You ˈmust be ˋpatient.

In enumerating things, the Fall is used at the end to show completeness.

You can have ´tea, or ´coffee or `milk.

We have ˈChi´nese, mathe´matics, ´English and `other ˌsubjects.

## 2. Interrogative Sentences

(1) Special Questions

Used in special questions, the Falling Tune sounds clearcut and straightforward. The High Fall is delightful and pleasant; the Low Fall may sometimes sound flat and unsympathetic, phlegmatic and agitated, quite often even hostile. Consequently it is less commonly used. e.g.

ˈWhat's the `time?

ˈWhen did you ar`rive?

ˈHow long did it ˈtake you to `get here?

Well, ˈwhen shall we `meet?

ˈWhy ˈdon't you ˈlook where you are `going?

(2) General Questions

When a Falling Tune is applied to a general question, the speaker, who has already had his own view in mind, puts the question forward as a suggestion or a subject for discussion rather than a request for immediate information. However, a Low Fall sounds phlegmatic, depressed or agitated. e.g.

ˈHave you `time this ˌafterˌnoon?

ˌShall we ˌleave it till `next week?

Could we ˈgo there to`morrow ˌthen?

Would it be ˈany `use, do you ˌthink?

ˈAre there ˈany ob`jections?

General Questions with "Will you" at the beginning have as good as the function of imperative sentences and are often read with a Fall. e.g.

'Will you be ˋquiet?

'Will you 'stop ˋtalking like that?

The negative forms of General Questions have the function of exclamatory sentences. e.g.

'Isn't it ˋwonderful?

'Haven't they 'made a ˋmess of it?

'Isn't he a 'good ˋteacher?

(3) Disjunctive Questions

The Falling Tune used in question-tags in the disjunctive questions indicates that the speaker hopes to get confirmation from the listener. e.g.

You have 'written the compoˋsition, |ˋhaven't you?

The 'film isˋinteresting, |ˋisn't it?

You 'haven't been to 'Beiˋjing, |ˋhave you?

She 'works veryˋhard, |ˋdoesn't she?

They are 'veryˋuseful, |ˋaren't they?

## 3. Imperative Sentences

The Falling Tune, often used in imperative sentences, indicates enthusiasm, firmness, and sincerity. But sometimes it has the implications of coldness and sterness. e.g.

'Tryˋthis one.

'Take aˋhandful of them.

'Don't beˋcareless.

'Come when'ever you areˋfree.

'Don't 'make so muchˋfuss about it.

## 4. Exclamatory Sentences

The Falling Tune is very common with exclamatory sentences and indicates strong moods and feelings, giving great weight and emphasis to them. e.g.

How ˋbeautiful it is!
How exˋcited I was!
What ˈwonderfulˋ news!
How riˋdiculous!
What a ˈlovely ˈday for a ˋpicnic!

## II. Rising Tune

The Rising Tune indicates basically **lack of definiteness** and **incompleteness**. It is very common with general questions. It is also used in imperative sentences in a delightful mood and declarative sentences with a question mark at the end.

### 1. Declarative Sentences

The Rising Tune used in the declarative sentence expresses doubt. The speaker has something more to say, but the listener is expected to say something so that the conversation may be carried on. The Low Rise sometimes indicates surprise, criticism or an unsatisfactory rebuttal. e.g.

You ˊlike him? ( = Do you like him?)
ˊSugar? ( = Do you take sugar?)
ˊEverybody will at˙tend the ˙meeting?
It's ˈno ˊtrouble.

### 2. Interrogative Sentences

(1) Special Questions

The Rising Tune used in special questions indicates that the speaker intends to make clear about the question; sometimes it may express an interest on the part of the speaker. If the nucleus is on the interrogative word, such feelings as surprise, dissatisfaction or opposition may be implied.

e.g.

| Verbal Context | Drill |
|---|---|
| ˋWhen is he ˏcoming? | 'When is heˊ coming?（Is that what you asked?） |
| 'How many 'English ˋ novels have you ˏread? | 'How ˊ many?（Do you wish to know how many?） |
| 'Where shall we 'hold the ˋ meeting? | ˊ Where?（Did you ask where?） |

More examples:

'What is your ˊ name?

'Where do you ˊ live?

'What did you ˊ say?

(2) General Questions

The Rising Tune is very common with General Questions; other tunes are only used in special situations. e.g.

'Are you a ˊ student?

Will you 'go to the ˊ factory?

May I ˊ borrow it?

'Have you 'answered the ˊ letter?

Would ˊ Friday suit you?

(3) Disjunctive Questions

The Rising Tune is used on the second part of the Disjunctive Question, i.e., the question-tag when the speaker expects from the listener an answer, whether positive or negative. e.g.

It's a ˋ nice ˏroom, | ˊ isn't it?（The speaker is sure that it is a nice room, hoping to get confirmation from the listener.）

We can 'start ˋ working, | ˊ can't we?

You 'didn't 'feel ˑvery ˋ well, | ˊ did you?

You 'haven't 'finished the ˋ project, | ˊ have you?

The question-tag after the imperative sentence is read with a Rising

Tune and the sentence will sound milder. e.g.

'Come and 'sit ˋ down, | ˊ won't you?

cf. 'Stand ˋ still, | ˋ will you? (The tune is rather stern.)

### 3. Imperative Sentences

The Rising Tune is sometimes used in imperative sentences. However, it may be used in speaking to children or in short imperative sentences. The Rising Tune sounds milder and more sincere than the Falling Tune. The Low Rise indicates advice and encouragement. e.g.

'Mind the ˊ door.

'Don't ˊ worry.

'Don't be ˊ long.

'Have a good ˊ time.

'Don't let me de ˊ tain you, ˙then.

### 4. Exclamatory Sentences

The Rising Tune is seldom used in exclamatory sentences. But short ones are read with a Low Rise, which sounds delightful with the implications of encouragement and casualness. e.g.

ˊ Splendid!

'Well ˊ done!

Of ˊ course.

'All ˊ right.

'O. ˊ K.!

Besides, some short sentences of greetings are spoken with a Low Rise to show friendliness, sounding lively. e.g.

¯ Good ˊ morning.

¯ Good ˊ evening.

¯ Good ˊ night.

¯ Good- ˊ bye.

⁻So ˊlong, old ˈchap.

## Ⅲ. Falling-rising Tune

The Falling-rising Tune is also widely used in English. It combines the function of the Fall and that of the Rise with a change of mind. It is used to show contrast, reservation, implication, disagreement, contradiction or warning, etc.

### 1. Declarative Sentences

The Falling-rising Tune used in declarative sentences indicates incompleteness and implications, such as concession, gratitude, regret, apology, request, reproach and rebuttal, etc.

e.g.

| Verbal Context A | Verbal Context B |
|---|---|
| What a ˈlovelyˋvoice! | ˊYes, she has a ˋlovely ˇvoice. (But that's about all that can be said for her.) |
| I ˈdon't ˈthink ˋmuch of her as an ˌactress. | She has a ˋlovely ˇvoice. (Even if her other talents are not remarkable.) |
| Is it ˈgoing to ˈkeep ˊfine? | I ˇthink ˌso. (But I'm not certain.) |
| Will you have ˊdinner with us? | I ˋwill if I ˊcan. (But I'm not sure if it's possible.) |
| ˋEveryone's ˌgone ˊhome? | ˋNot ˇeveryone. (Most have, but John's still here.) |

### 2. Interrogative Sentences

(1) Special Questions

The Falling-rising Tune used in the special question is stronger than the

Rising Tune. It expresses surprise, interest, request, sympathy, disgust and disbelief, etc.

| Verbal Context A | Verbal Context B |
|---|---|
| ˈWhat's the ˋmatter? | ˈWhat's the ˅ matter? (Everything is the matter.) |
| I ˈwon't go toˋmorrow. | ˋ What's made you change your ˊ mind? |
| ˈCan't you work it ˈout for your ˊself? | ˋ What's the ˊ answer? |
| Sorry I'm ˊ late. | Oh ˋwhy can't you ˌˌcome on ˊ time? |

(2) General Questions

The Falling-rising Tune used in the general question can express hesitation, request, agitation, exaggeration, etc. No answer is expected by the speaker. e.g.

ˋ Do you ˌthink you ˊ could?

ˋ Won't you ˌˌchange your ˊ mind?

ˋ Would you mind ˌwaiting until ˊ Friday?

(3) Disjunctive Questions

e.g.

Youˋ didn't come in the ˅ morning, | ˊ did you? (I suppose you must have come in the afternoon.)

Weˋ needn't ˅ wait for him, | ˊ need we?

I'mˋ older than ˅ you, | ˊ aren't I?

You willˋ bring it ˅back, |ˋ won't you?

Heˋ hasn't ˌbeen a˅broad, | ˊ has he?

## 3. Imperative Sentences

The Falling-rising Tune used in the imperative sentence expresses a warning or an urgent request. e.g.

˅Mind! (There's a step here.)

ˋCareful with that ˅glass! (You will drop it.)

ˋWait a ˊminute.

ˋDon't be ˊsilly.

Imperative sentences with a question-tag, e.g.

ˋFetch a ˊchair,│ˊwill you?

ˋWrite it ˊdown,│ˊwill you?

### 4. Exclamatory Sentences

The Falling-rising Tune is seldom used in exclamatory sentences. However, when used, it expresses enthusiasm, appreciation, sympathy, encouragement, regret and contempt, etc. e.g.

ˋRight you ˊare.

ˋPoor old ˊPeter!

ˋSome ˅hope!

ˋWhat a ˊpity!

## Questions for Discussion

1. What is the Falling Tune used basically to express?
2. What does the Rising Tune indicate basically?
3. What's the function of the Falling-rising Tune?

## Excercise I-4

 扫码听音频

 1. Read the following with the Falling Tune.

(1) They ˈsay they will ˈsend it by ˋpost.

(2) I ˈcan't find my ˈpencil ˋanywhere.

(3) Which ˈsubject do you preˋfer?

(4) Which ˈroad shall we ˋtake?

(5) Ring me ˈup at eˋleven.

(6) Show me your ˋticket, ˈmadam.

## Unit 19  Functions of Tunes and Their Uses

(7) What a ˋpity hê ˌcouldn't come ˌsooner!
(8) How ˋkind of you to ˌgive me ˌso much ˌhelp.
(9) You'll ˈgo to the ˈfarm toˋmorrow, | ˋwon't you?
(10) ˈAren't they ˋpretty?
(11) ˈWasn't it a ˈgood ˋfilm?
(12) ˈSend it to us as ˈsoon as you ˋcan.

### 2. Read the following with the Rising Tune.

(1) You ˌcan't do ˊthat.
(2) I ˈthink you're ˊright.
(3) (ˈ)Could you ˋtell me | if there's a ˈpost office near ˊhere?
(4) (ˈ)Do you ˈmind if I ˈopen the ˊwindow?
(5) ˈHow much do they ˊcharge?
(6) ˈWhat would you ˈlike to ˊdrink?
(7) Shall we ˈhave the ˈgame at ˊnine | or at ˋten?
(8) You're ˈtaking the eˈxam in ˋJune, | ˊaren't you?
(9) ˈMust you ˈgo now?
(10) ˈCan I ˊhelp you?
(11) ˈHave a good ˊtime.

### 3. Read the following with the Falling-rising Tune.

(1) I ˋwish | you'd ˇtold me.
(2) You are ˈnot ˇserious.
(3) ˋJust a ˊmoment.
(4) I'm ˋvery ˊsorry.
(5) I ˋwon't keep you ˊlong.
(6) ˋThat's all ˊright.
(7) ˋWhen will you be ˊback, d'you ˈthink?
(8) She's ˋbeen to the ˇfactory, | ˊhasn't she?
(9) ˋCheer ˊup.

(10) ˋJolly ˊgood.

(11) ˋWhat a disapˊpointment!

 4. Read the following after the recording.

## A ˈSelf-madeˋPresident

ˈOneˊday, |ˈLincoln ˈwent to aˋparty. At the ˇgathering, | ˈDouglas was reˈpeatedly ˈmaking reˋmarks | about ˈLincoln's ˈlowly ˈstation in ˊlife | and ˈsaying that he ˈfirst metˋLincoln | when he was a ˈshop asˋsistant of a ˌgeneral ˌstore. He ˈfinally ˈended with his reˈmarks byˊsaying, | "And Mr. ˈLincoln was a ˈvery good ˈbartender ˋtoo."

ˈPeople ˈburst into ˈlaughter imˋmediately, | but they ˈquietedˋdown | when Mr. ˈLincoln ˈsaid ˋquietly.

"ˋGentlemen, | what Mr. ˈDouglas has ˊsaid | is ˌtrue eˋnough. I ˈˈdid keep aˋgrocery, | and I ˈˈdid sellˊcotton, | ˊcandles, | and ciˋgars, | and ˇsometimesˋwhisky. But I reˈmember in ˈthoseˊdays | that Mr. ˈDouglas was one of my ˈˈbestˋcustomers. ˈMany a ˇtime have I ˈstood on ˈone side of the ˋcounter | and ˈsoldˋwhisky to Mr. ˌDouglas | on the ˋother ˌside, | but the ˇdifference between us nowˋis: I have ˊleft my ˈside of the ˋcounter, | but Mr. ˈDouglas ˈstill ˈsticks to ˋˋhis as teˈˈnaciously as ˋˋever."

# Unit 20

# Combined Tunes

In reading and speaking, a sentence may consist of one or more tunes. Some tunes are often combined. Many combined tunes are possible. The following are six common patterns.

## I. Fall + Fall

### 1. Disjunctive question (The questioner has already got his or her own views.)

It's a 'fine ˋ day, | ˋ isn't it?
The 'sentence is corˋ rect, | ˋ isn't it?

### 2. Simple sentence containing two parallel predicates

I 'went to theˋ bookstore | and 'bought a 'new dictionary.
'All the 'books were 'put into theˋ cases | and 'sent to theˋ station.
She is 'able to 'speak 'English ˋ fluently | and 'write ˙ good compoˋsitions.
They 'set off at 'ten 'p.ˋ m. | and 'got there before ˋ supper.

### 3. Main clause + adverbial clause

It's aˋ long time | since I 'saw youˋ last.
They 'aren't soˋ difficult | as theyˋ look.

He ˈdidn't ˈcome to ˋschool, | beˈcause he was ˋill.

ˈDifficulties are ˈnot ˙hard to ˋsolve | if you ˈdon't ˈlet them ˋscare you.

### 4. Main clause + non-restrictive attributive clause

We arˈrived ˋlate, | which was a ˈserious misˋtake.

The Japaˈnese ˈfascist ˈpushed us into the ˋpit, | where my ˈfather was ˈbitten to ˋdeath by a poˌlice ˌdog.

She is ˈgoing to ˈspend the ˈsummer in ˈQingˋdao, | where she has some ˈfriends and ˋrelatives.

We will ˈput off the ˈouting until ˋnext ˌweek, | when we ˈwon't be ˈso ˋbusy.

### 5. Compound sentence (coordinate clauses are not closely linked)

I ˈtried to ˈwork ˋfaster, | but I ˈjust ˈcouldn't catch ˋup with him.

ˈJohn ˈsuffered from ˈpoverty and ˋhunger, | and he had ˈvery ˙little ˋschooling.

We ˈtold him to ˋstop it, | and he ˋdid so.

He was then ˈforced to ˈleave ˋFrance, | but he ˈnever ˈstopped ˋfighting.

## II. Fall + Rise

### 1. Disjunctive question

You've ˈbeen to ˈBeiˋjing, | ´haven't you?

You ˈbought a ˈnew ˋbook, | ´didn't you?

She is ˈcoming to our ˈEnglish ˋevening, | ´isn't she?

They ˈwon't set ˈout this ˋmorning, | ´will they?

## 2. Simple sentence with an adverbial or a nominative absolute complex construction at the end

It's a ˈgood ˋbook, | on the ˊwhole.
We have ˈvery ˈlittleˋsnow here, | as a ˊrule.
We ˈdidn't see the beˋginning, | ˌbeing so ˊlate.
He ˈwasn't at theˋoffice, | inciˊdentally.

## 3. Main clause + adverbial clause

ˈCome at ˈ8 : ˋ30 | if you ˊcan.
I'll ˈgo ˈhome for theˋholidays | if it is ˊpossible.
I'll ˈcome aˋgain | if it's conˊvenient for you.
You'd ˈbetter conˈsult theˋdictionary | when you have ˊquestions.

# Ⅲ. Rise + Fall

## 1. Alternative question

Are you from theˊsouth | or from theˋnorth?
Is this a ˊdesk | or aˋchair?
ˈWhen will you ˈgo to Beiˋjing, | ˊthis week | orˋnext week?
Do preˈfer ˊtea | orˋcoffee?

## 2. Simple sentence with an adverbial at the beginning

At ˈten in the ˊmorning, | the paˈrade beˋgan.
In ˈmy oˊpinion, | it's a ˈvery ˈgood ˋbook.
At the ˈage of ˊfifteen, | he ˈjoined theˋarmy.
ˈLong long aˊgo, | there was a ˈtimid ˋrabbit.

## 3. Adverbial clause + main clause

If we ˈwork ˊharder, | we shall be ˈable to fulˈfil the ˈplan aˈhead of

ˋtime.

By the 'time we were 'half way ˊup, | I was 'almost 'out of ˋbreath.

### 4. Counting or enumerating things

ˊOne, | ˊtwo, | ˊthree, | ˊfour, | ˋfive.

'One ˊnovel, | 'two ˊpicture-books, | and 'three ˋdictionaries.

### 5. Main clause + object clause

I ˊhope | there will be some 'poems and ˋplays.

He in'sisted | that to 'save one's 'time 'means to pro'long one's ˋlife.

### 6. Main clause + restrictive attributive clause

'This is the ˊman | I 'saw ˋyesterday.

'Here is the ˊdoctor | you have been ˋlooking for.

It was a 'great his'torical eˊvent | that 'shook the 'whole ˋcountry.

### 7. Compound Sentence (Coordinate clauses are closely linked or a comparison is made.)

I must be ˊoff now, | for my 'family is exˋpecting me.

It was al'ready rather ˊlate, | so we de'cided to 'go ˋhome.

We 'love ˊpeace | but we are 'not a'fraid of ˋwar.

'Four 'times the 'government 'sent them re'lief ˊfunds, | 'four ˊtimes they deˋclined them.

## Ⅳ. Rise + Rise

### 1. Simple sentence with an appositive

Do you 'know Dr. ˊLiu, | the 'famous ˊsurgeon?

Have you 'heard about the 'kite muˊseum, | the 'well-de'signed ˊbuilding?

## 2. Simple sentence with a phrase at the beginning

In 'that ˊcase, | is it 'possible for us to 'meet next ˋweek?
'After ˊclass, | will you 'please 'clean the ˋclassroom?

## 3. Complex sentence with an adverbial clause at the beginning

If he is ˊfree, | will you 'please 'ask him to 'come to the ˊmeeting?
'When he 'comes ˊback, | would you 'tell him I ˋphoned?
'After you have 'finished your ˊhomework, | can you 'come to my ˊoffice?

## 4. Complex sentence with an attributive clause

'Have you 'met my ˊdaughter, | who has 'just re'turned from Aˊmerica?

# V. Fall + Fall-rise

## 1. Simple sentence with an adverbial or independent element at the end

I 'can't ˋdo it | just at the ˇmoment.
They 'left the ˋvillage | before ˇdawn.
It 'won't be 'raining ˋlong, | I ˇhope.
We'll 'have to be ˋgoing ₁now, | I'm aˇfraid.

## 2. Main clause + adverbial clause

I ˋwill | if you ˇlike.
She will 'try to ˋfinish it | if it is ˇpossible.
You will be ˋlate | if you 'don't ˋhurry ˋup.

ˌˌThat's ˈquite ˋ right, | as ˋ far as I ˊ know.

### 3. Compound sentence

It ˈcosts ˋ more, | but it's ˈvery ˇuseful.

It's ˈnearly ˈtime for ˋ lunch, | so you ˈmustn't ˈwalk too ˇfar.

The ˈroom is ˈquite ˋ crowded, | so you ˈcan't atˈtend the ˈlecture toˇday.

You ˈcan't ˈborrow the ˋ book, | for ˈsomebody ˈtook it aˈway this ˇmorning.

## Ⅶ. Fall-rise + Fall

### 1. Simple sentence with an adverbial or independent element at the beginning

ˈTaken as a ˇwhole, | the reˌsults ˈaren't ˋ bad.

ˈGenerally ˇspeaking, | ˈyoung ˈpeople ˈgo in for ˋ sports.

To my ˇmind, | you ought to ˈstudy anˈother ˈforeign ˋ languange.

To be ˇfrank, | I ˈdon't like the ˈbook too ˋ much.

### 2. Adverbial clause + main clasue

Proˈvided the maˈterials arˋ rive in ˊ time, | we can ˈfinish the ˈjob to ˋ day.

ˈWhile we're ˇwaiting, | we can ˈgo through our ˋ notes aˌgain.

Unˈless you ˈgo to ˋ bed ˊ early, | you ˈwon't be ˈable to get ˋˋ up ˌearly.

The ˈmore I ˋ thought aˊbout it, | the ˋ less I ˌliked it.

### 3. Compound sentence

ˈThese are ˇmine, | and ˈthose are ˋ yours.

She ˈasked me to ˇstay, | but I ˈcouldn't ˈspare the ˋ time.

The ˈmen were in ˇtime, | and ˈso was ˋˋ I.

They must 'come at ˅once, | or I 'shan't have 'time to at˴tend to them.

## Ⅷ. Fall-rise ＋ Rise

### 1. Disjunctive question

It ˴costs ˊmore, | ˊdoesn't it?
You 'haven't ˴injured the ˊothers, | ˊhave you?
He is ˴rather ˊcareless, | ˊisn't he?
It's ˴very ˊuseful, | ˊisn't it?

### 2. Main clause ＋ adverbial clause

You will 'never suc˅ceed | un'less you ˊtry 'harder.
You can 'have the ˅others | pro'vided you 'don't ˊbreak them.
I 'think you will ˅like it | when you've ˌseen what it ˊis.
You 'can't 'finish the ˅task | if you 'don't 'work with the ma ˊchines.

**Exercise I-5**

 扫码听音频

 1. **Read the following sentences with appropriate tune patterns.**

(1) Are you a student or a teacher?
(2) Are they going to cut rice or pick cotton?
(3) After breakfast they went to the classroom.
(4) In the end we arrived at the top of the mountain.
(5) Once we get over the snow mountain, you will be all right.
(6) A chair, a table, a bed and a desk.
(7) John told Paul he had lost his job again.
(8) Shanghai is a city, which has a glorious revolutionary tradition.
(9) She called at her mother's, when she met John.
(10) If you want this one, it will cost you double.

(11) The sun is much larger than the moon, and it gives a very strong light.

(12) He loved the people, and the people loved him.

## 2. Analyse the tune patterns in the following sentences and read aloud.

(1) The factory isn't far from here, is it?
(2) They set out early in the morning and arrived there before dark.
(3) The meeting had already begun when we got there.
(4) I like the film very much because it's both instructive and interesting.
(5) We must redouble our efforts, or we'll never be able to catch up with the others.
(6) They have to go there, I suppose.
(7) You can have another provided these are enough to go round.
(8) Most important of all, they have improved their English.
(9) There're two hundred and fifty students, approximately.
(10) Unless you start working early, you won't be able to finish early.
(11) If a thing is worth doing, it's worth doing well.

## 3. Enjoy listening to the following talk and try to imitate it.

### A ˈShort ˈTalk on ˈEnglish Intoˋnation

ˈLet us ˈturn for a ˈmoment to the ˈquestion of intoˋnation, and inˈstead of ˈtalking to you aˈbout it, ˈlet me ˈgive you some exˋamples. ˈHere is a ˈsentence from Proˈfessor ˈDaniel ˈJones's *Phoˈnetic ˈReadings in ˊEnglish* that I'm going to ˈread to you on ˈthree ˈdifferent intoˋnations, and I ˈleave it to ˋyou to deˈcide ˈwhich of the ˈthree is ˋEnglish. ˋListen:

(1) A ˌbad-ˌtempered ˈdog, ˌone ˈday, ˌfound his ˌway into a ˈmanger, and ˌfound it so ˌnice and ˈcomfortable that he ˌmade up his ˈmind to ˋstop there.

ˈHere's anˋother one:

(2) A ˈbad-tempered ˊdog, ˈone ˊday, ˈfound his ˊway into a ˊmanger, and

ˈfound it so ˈnice and ˈcomfortable that he ˈmade up his ˈmind to ˈstopˋthere.

ˈHere's anˈother one:

(3) A ˈbad-temperedˈdog, ˈone ˈday, ˈfound his ˈway into aˋmanger, and ˈfound it so ˈnice and ˈcomfortable that he ˈmade up his ˈmind toˋstop there.

The ˈfirst is the ˈsort of ˈthing that ˈmost of myˋGerman ₁students ₁say, the ˈsecond is the ˈsort of ˈthing that ˈmanyˋFrench ₁people ₁say. The ˇlast is a ˈ fairly ˈnormal ˈEnglish intoˈnation, and you must ˈstudy it as ˈcarefully as you ˈstudy ˈevery other ˈfeature ofˋEnglish.

Now I am going to ˈread you a ˈshortˋstory, and in it you will ˈfind exˈamples of ˈmost of the ˈusual ˈforms of ˈEnglish intoˈnation, and ˈone or ˈtwo rather ˈinteresting ˈfeatures that I will ˈcall your atˈtention toˋafterwards.ˋListen:

An ˈartist was ˈone day ˈpainting in aˋfield when aˋshepherd ˈcame aˈlong, and ˈafter ˈlooking over the ˈartist'sˋshoulder for a ˈlong time, heˈsaid:

"ˈWhat do you think you'reˋdoing?"

"ˇDoing?" ˙said the ˙artist, "ˋWhy, I'm ˈpainting aˋpicture. ₁What do ˋˋyou think I'm ₁doing?"

"Is ˈthat supˈposed to be a ˈpicture of ˈthisˈfield?"

"ˋYes."

"Iˋthought it ˈwas; it ˈisn't ˈvery muchˋlike it ₁though. Is ˈthat a ˈsheep?"

"ˋNo."

"I ₁thought itˋwas. ₁Whatˋis it?"

"ˇWell, it ˈisn'tˋfinished ˈyet, but it's ˈgoing to be aˋhayrick."

"ˋWell, why ˈdon't you ˈput aˋsheep in the ₁picture?"

"Thereˋis one."

"ˋWhere?"

"ˋHere."

"'Do you 'mean to 'say that 'that funny 'little 'thing is a ⸌ sheep?"

"⸍ Yes. ˌWhat did ⸍ you think it ˌwas?"

"⸍ I ⸌ thought it was a ⸍cow. I 'don't 'think much of your ⸍ picture."

"Hm, ⸍ you ˌseem to ˌknow more about ⸌painting than ⸍⸍ I do."

"⸍ Well, ⸍ even if I ⸌ did I 'shouldn't know ⸍ much." And with ⸌ that, he 'went on his ⸍ way.

Now, in 'that 'story you will 'find many 'types of 'English intoˊnation, and you will 'also find an exˋample of a 'very ⸍strange ˌthing that can be 'done in ⸌English by 'means of intoˋ nation. 'Use your reˋpeater and 'listen to *the* 'words, " I 'thought it ⸍ was." After " 'yes " you will 'find, _____ , but after " 'no" you will find, _____ . 'Try to trans'late these 'two ex'pressions into your 'own ⸍language, if your 'language is not ⸌English, and you will 'probably 'find it is 'not so 'easy as it ⸍ looks.

# Unit 21

# Reading of Long Sentences

## I. Tune Broken Upwards (Broken Tune or Accidental Rise)

When we read a long sentence with many stresses, if we keep our voice descending throughout, we'll certainly find it monotonous. It is usual, therefore, to relieve this monotony by making upwards breaks at suitable points; these serve to interrupt the steady downward flow of the voice and add interest to the utterance. A break is made by pronouncing an intermediate stressed syllable on a higher pitch than that occupied by the preceding level stress and then resuming the downward trend. This is what we call Tune Broken Upwards (Broken Tune or Accidental Rise). It is to be shown by the vertical arrow(↑).

Let's compare the two ways in reading the following sentences:

I 'want you to 'read the ↑'letter as 'soon as you﹨ can.

I'm 'reading a 'most 'interesting 'book by a 'new﹨ writer.

The following points ought to be observed when we have "Tune Broken Upwards":

(1) The points at which the breaks are made should be:

a. on the first stressed word of clauses, phrases or other grammatical units;

b. on the words of sufficient semantic importance which need extra prominence, irrespective of their position in the clause or phrase.

(2) The pitch of the Tune Broken Upwards cannot be higher than that of the head, i.e., the first stressed syllable in the tune.

(3) There may be one or more Tunes Broken Upwards in a sentence.

## Ⅱ. Intonation of Vocatives

The difference in intonation of vocatives is determined by their semantic importance. It is to be discussed according to their positions.

(1) The vocative at the beginning of a sentence is usually important. It is stressed and should be taken as one tone-group. It can be read with a Fall, a Rise or a Fall-rise.

'Comrade ˋLiu, | let's 'go to the ˋreading-room.
ˌNaughty ˊchild, | 'stop 'making such ˋnoises.
ˇMummy, | 'may I have an ˊapple?
ˊNora, | I'm ˋleaving ˌnow.

(2) The vocative in the middle of a sentence is usually not very important. It may be stressed or unstressed and read with either a Rise or a Fall.

I ˋsay, ˊRobert | you ˋdo look ˋclean.
But ˋreally, Mrs. ˋBrewer, | you 'needn't have 'gone to ˋso much ˇtrouble.
ˋNever ˌmind, ˊNora, | let ˋme ˌhelp you.

'Come ˋ on, ˊ Jim, | we shall 'have to 'hurry ˋ up | with this ma ˇ chine.

(3) When it is at the end of a sentence, the vocative is usually not very important. It is unstressed and treated as the tail of the preceding tone-group.

'Is the 'book on the ˊ desk, · Mary?

'That's all ˊ right, · John.

It's 'rather ˇ late, · Charlie.

Now 'don't you be ˋ rude, young ˌPeter.

## Ⅲ. Intonation of Parenthesis

The parenthesis is read in different ways determined by its semantic importance. Important parentheses are usually at the beginning or in the middle of a sentence. They are stressed and considered as separate tone-groups. They are read with either a Fall or a Rise.

Perˊhaps | you're ˋ tired | after the ˌstrain of the ˋ day.

Of ˊ course | he's a po ˋliceman.

I ˊ mean, | of ˋ course, | in the implemen'tation of the 'Party's ˋ policies.

Your sug ˊgestion, | to be ˋ sure, | will 'help us a ˋ lot.

Semantically unimportant parentheses are usually in the middle or at the end of sentences. They are normally not stressed and taken as the tail of the preceding tone-group.

'Comradeˋ Wang, for instance, | is a 'good engi ˋ neer.

'This is the ˋ only ˌthing to ˌdo, I think.

In the ˌusual ˊ place, I expect.

It 'won't be 'raining ˋ long, I hope.

# Ⅳ. Intonation of Reporting Phrases

(1) We usually read the front-position reporting phrases with a Low Rise, the rise beginning on the last stressed syllable.

He ˏsaid, | "I have ˈseen the ˈfilm alˋready."

ˈTom ˌtold his ˏfather | "ˈPeter is the ˈtallest in my ˋclass."

(2) A mid-position or end-position reporting phrase, which is considered merely as a parenthesis, is treated as the tail of the preceding tone-group.

"ˈNever ˋmind, my ˏboy, | itˋwon't ˈtake ˏlong," said Bethune.

"Letˋme do the ˌwork," ˌurged one of the ˌdoctors.

"ˋCertainly," ˌsaid the ˌold ˌman, | "I'll ˋdo it for you."

"ˇThis pattern," she ˙said, | "is ˈmuch ˈbetter than theˋother one."

However, if the preceding part is said with a Fall, the mid-position reporting phrase may sometimes be read with a Low Rise. Occasionally, if some emotion is to be expressed, the vocative may be stressed and treated as a tone-group.

"As toˋthat," I reˏplied, | "I am ˈnot at ˈall ˋsure."

"ˈLastˋnight," he ˏsaid, | "I was ˈhoping that I ˈshouldn't have to ˈwait
 muchˋlonger."

"ˈVeryˋsorry," aˌgain reˌpeated the ˏdoctor, | "but we ˈreally have ↑
 ˈonly ˈtwo vacantˋbeds | in the ˈwholeˋhospital."

"ˈThat's aˋlie!" ˌLandyˋshouted.

### Questions for Discussion

1. What is Tune Broken Upwards?
2. What ought to be observed when we have "Tune Broken Upwards"?

## Unit 21  Reading of Long Sentences

### Exercise 1-6

 扫码听音频

**1. Listen and imitate, paying attention to the Tune Broken Upwards.**

(1) And ˈso she ˈlet herself be ˈmarried to a ↑ ˈpetty ˈclerk in the ↑ ˈMinistry of Edu↘cation.

(2) ˈOne ´evening | her ˈhusband ˈcame ˈhome with a tri↑ˈumphant ˋair | ˌholding in his ˌhand a ↑ˈlarge ˋenvelope.

(3) There is ˈnothing ˈmore hu↑ˈmiliating than to ˈlook ˋpoor | among a ˈgathering of ↑ˈrich ˋladies.

(4) The aˈbove is ˈjust a ˈglimpse of ↑ ˈone ˈaspect of the ˋworkers' ˌstruggle | aˈgainst exploiˈtation in the ˋwest toˌday.

(5) My ˈbrother ˈworks in an ´office ↑ ˈall ˋday | and he ˈspends his ´evenings| ˈstudying for a deˋgree.

(6) The ˈold proˈfessor ˈlikes to ˈtake a walk  im↑ˈmediately after supper.

**2. Listen and imitate, paying attention to the intonation of vocatives.**

(1) ˅Daddy, | ˈwhere's ˋMichael?

(2) ˈOh, my ˈdearˋchap, | ˈdon't be ˅silly.

(3) ˅Mum, ˈisn't this ˈshirt ↑ tooˋbig for ´me?

(4) ˋWell, | ˈRobert, ˈhave you ˈmade up your ˋmind  ´yet?

(5) ˈHave you ˈtaken your ´medicine, ˙sister?

(6) ˈDon'tˋworry, Mrs. ˌParker.

(7) ˈDearˋSir, My ˈdear Mr.ˋJohnson, ˈLadies andˋGentlemen.

(8) Mr. ´Smith, I should ˈlike you to ˋtell me the story.

(9) John, d'you notice anything peˈculiar about this?

(10) My dear boy, you mustn't ˈplay ˈall dayˋlong.

(11) ComradeˋLiu, you ˈdon't see myˋpoint.

### 3. Listen and imitate, paying attention to the intonation of parentheses.

(1) They've 'spoilt the 'whole af ˇfair, I sup₁pose.
(2) This's 'all we have ˋgot, you ₁see.
(3) It is, therefore, 'quite ˋpossible.
(4) Itˋ isn't, howˊever, | 'soˋ difficult.
(5) He 'can't 'go aˋbroad this ₁time, I am a₁fraid.
(6) He's 'one of my 'bestˋ friends, I be₁lieve.

### 4. Listen and imitate, paying attention to the intonation of reporting phrases.

(1) 'Tomˊ asked, "'What are youˋ doing?"
(2) "You 'can'tˋ come," he ₁said ₁angrily.
(3) "We 'didn'tˋ ask him," they ex₁plained ₁briefly.
(4) "ˋSure," ₁said the ₁old ₁lady, | "I'llˋ do that for you."
(5) "'Would you 'like aˊ drink?" he ˙said with a ˙smile.
(6) "'Giveˋup, 'noˋharm!" | the ₁soldiers ₁shouted at the ₁enemy.

### 5. Read after the recording.

ˇI | who amˊ blind | can 'give one 'hint to 'those whoˋ see—one admo'nition | to 'those who would make 'full use of the 'gift ofˋ sight: ˙Use yourˋ eyes | as if toˋˋmorrow you would be ₁stricken ₁blind. And the 'same 'method can be ap'plied to theˋ other ₁senses. 'Hear the 'music ofˋ voices, | the 'song of aˋ bird, | the 'mighty 'strains of anˋ orchestra, | as if you would be 'stricken 'deaf toˋˋmorrow. 'Touch each 'object you 'want toˋ touch | as if to'morrow your 'tactile 'sense wouldˋ fail. 'Smell the 'perfume ofˋ flowers, |ˋ taste with 'relish eachˋ morsel, | as if toˋˋ morrow | you could 'never 'smell and 'taste aˋgain. ₁Make the 'most ofˋˋ every ₁sense; 'glory in

ˈall the ˈfacts of ´pleasure and ˋbeauty | which the ˈworld reˋveals to you | through the ˈseveral ˈmeans of ˋcontact | which ˈNature proˋvides. But of ˈall the ˇsenses, | ˈsight must be ˙most deˋˋlightful.

# Additional Remarks: Reading as an Exercise in Enunciation and Delivery

So far we have dealt briefly with the pronunciation, rhythm, and intonation of the English language, having laid a general foundation for spoken and communicative English. However, that is only the beginning or the first step.

Communication is the aim and purpose of our efforts at learning English. In order to enhance our communicative ability, we have to do lots of practice in reading aloud which in our consideration is the very foundation of actual speaking.

## 1. Some Basic Points

Reading is an art; reading is creative. When we read aloud a piece of writing, we are engaged in a process of re-creating with our voice, with the phonetics of the language we are using. (As a matter of fact, in the past three parts we should have included more knowledge and skills, particularly with regard to intonation. We should have given some mention of the rise-fall and rise-fall-rise intonations, etc.) There are some important techniques for us to learn and master. The few points that follow should be first taken into careful consideration.

### Breathing and Resonance in the Mouth and Nasal Cavities

In breathing we should try to use the "chest-abdomen breathing" method (胸腹式联合呼吸法). When we inhale, the diaphragm is lowered and the chest cavity extended, but when we exhale, the chest cavity is compressed

## Additional Remarks: Reading as an Exercise in Enunciation and Delivery

and the diaphragm is raised again. Try to inhale gently and deeply and exhale slowly and evenly. Correct breathing can make our voice sound melodious and pleasant to the ear, and we don't have to overstrain our vocal cords.

The next step is to practise making full use of resonance in the mouth and nasal cavities. Inhale a mouthful of air and pronounce the sound /n/, then add another sound /ɑː/, getting a prolonged /nɑː/ sound. As /n/ is a nasal sound and /ɑː/ is an oral sound, the combination of the two sounds can produce resonance in the mouth and nasal cavities. In the same way we can pronounce the following sounds /neɪ, niː; nəʊ; naɪ, nuː/. Make them high or low at different pitches. This kind of training may be dull, but it is fundamental and important.

Try to produce the following sounds in the manner illustrated:

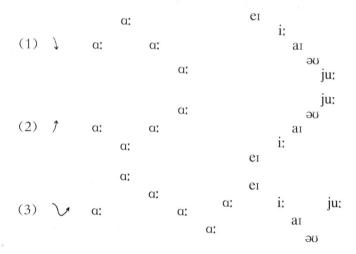

### Sense-groups and Pausing

Please refer to Part One, Rhythm. No repetition is necessary.

### Pace (or Tempo), Intensity and Pitch

By pace (or tempo) we refer to the speed of our reading aloud. We may read slowly or quickly. By intensity we refer to the strength or force of our reading. We may read forcefully or gently, loudly or in a low voice (technically we might use the term "amplitude of sound wave vibration"). In Part Two, Rhythm, we studied the various aspects of stress, including word stress, sense stress, logical stress and emotional stress, which have much to do with the "intensity" of our reading. By pitch we refer to the frequency of vibration of the vocal cords. We may make our voice high (at a higher frequency) or low (at a lower frequency) as the case requires, by tightening or relaxing the vocal cords.

## Tone and Expression

By tone (or manner of reading) we refer to the attitude of the reader. We can be friendly, gentle, delightful, happy, sad, grave, or angry, etc. as the case may be. By expression we refer to the different shades of feeling or emotion that the reader wishes to show, including love, hate, sorrow, disgust, etc. With a variety of techniques we can express all kinds of feelings and emotions. In actual speech, people do this automatically, without thinking.

## A Thorough Understanding of the Reading Material

Above everything else, a thorough and complete understanding of the piece being read is the very foundation of successful reading. It is far from enough to just understand the piece word by word. We have to know thoroughly the true meaning of the piece of reading as a whole. In particular we must be clear as to what kind of writing it is or what kind of style it belongs to. We should be able to analyse it, to comment on it and to appreciate it. We ought to read between the lines and try to find the various shades of meaning implied in every sentence, in every paragraph.

We know spoken English is necessarily different from written English. Spoken English can be further divided into formal English, informal English, colloquial English and English of familiar styles. For written English we have novels, short stories, essays, plays, films, poems, news, stories, commentaries, political articles, documents, etc.

The general principle of successful reading aloud is different ways for reading different styles of materials. Careful preparation ought to be made beforehand and various techniques should be consciously employed so as to ensure that the reading is creative.

The following is a well-known ditty read in four different ways, expressing our different emotions: excitement, disbelief, joy and sadness. Listen:

**London Bridge Is Falling Down**

London Bridge is falling down,
Falling down, falling down.
London Bridge is falling down,
My fair lady.

We have here something very special for you, some authentic listening materials of living English speech — spoken by different people in different situations. They will certainly be very good examples of communicative English for you to follow. Please listen to them and try to appreciate and enjoy them. Then you can try to imitate the reading, follow the marvelous examples vocally — they are good for your attempt at a good pronunciation. Success is bound to be yours if you believe in the motto "where there is a will, there is a way" and persist in trying, and trying again.

## 2. Models for Appreciation and Imitation

### Buying a Used Car

*Tom*: Hello. This is Tom Martino, the Troubleshooter, talking about consumer problems, questions, and complaints. Tammy, how are you doing, Tammy, and you want to talk about what?

*Tammy*: A used car that I had bought from a dealer.

*Tom*: Ah. When did you buy that used car, Tammy?

*Tammy*: About two and a half weeks ago.

*Tom*: Okay, what's the problem?

*Tammy*: We thought that there was [sic] ignition problems, because it's electrical as far as the lights and the blinkers and all. So we had taken it to an Amoco station, had a professional to [sic] look at it.

*Tom*: This is before you bought it?

*Tammy*: No, it was after we had bought it.

*Tom*: You didn't have anyone check it before you bought it? Oh, Tammy...

*Tammy*: No.

*Tom*: Okay, all right, so what happened?

*Tammy*: So when we had taken it to the Amoco station, and they had looked at it and said that there were [sic] major problems with it and it was gonna cost like a thousand dollars to have everything fixed to be able to even drive it safely.

*Tom*: So you got taken.

*Tammy*: So, yeah, we went back to the dealer, I talked to him and he...

*Tom*: You bought it "as is," didn't you, Tammy?

*Tammy*: Yeah.

*Tom*: What year is this?

*Tammy*: It's a '79.

*Tom*: '79. What kind?

*Tammy*: Ford Mustang.

*Tom*: A Ford Mustang ... and how many miles on it?

*Tammy*: I think like a 130,000.

## Can You Afford a Ford?

[*An idiomatic and conversational weather forecast. David is the talk show*

### Additional Remarks: Reading as an Exercise in Enunciation and Delivery

*host; Elliot is the meteorologist.*]

* *NHRA stands for National Hot Rod Association*

*David:* Yes, Elliot and I had a disagreement. I felt ... I just, I don't know why, I had this feeling that it was just going to be a cloudy old day today. You said, "Nope, clear as a bell." You got a bell there anywhere?

*Elliot:* I probably do. [sound effect: bell]

*David:* Yeah, and ...

*Elliot:* Meanwhile this weekend though, the NHRA* U.S. Nationals are held.

*David:* You're absolutely right. [Sound effect: car starting] Oh boy.

*Elliot:* And in the temperature department, the mercury will be hitting the brakes at night. But today and tomorrow, temperatures will be revved up from Dodge City, Kansas to Pontiac, Michigan.

*David:* Cranking up a forecast here ...

*Elliot:* And this'll afford an opportunity to enjoy sunshine.

*David:* You said "A Ford".

*Elliot:* This isn't universal, but some people are real crank cases when it gets cloudy like it was. Oh, and if that applies to you, and your name is Rod, I have one piece of news for you: It's ... well, it's not going to be hot, Rod. Actually the temperature'll be in the 80s this weekend, and it'll be quite a while before the dry air is exhausted. I don't think the temperature's going into reverse any time soon. Outdoor levels will get so much mileage out of sunshine today, tomorrow, and Sunday, but a fast moving battery of thunderstorms could race through tomorrow night or Sunday morning before the temperature downshifts. Of course, we don't know when the storms will hit, but we'll be there in the clutch.

*David:* Okay!

*Elliot:* Now behind the cold front that could cause the brief thundershowers across our area, it looks like the fan belt in the upper atmosphere will be coming through and making it a little bit cooler early next week; we may have an alternator between sunshine and thunderstorms. But here we are, home stretch of August, and you have the green light for sunshine today and tomorrow. The weekend'll be great, and it'll even be good when you go home this afternoon to crash.

*David*: Okay. I was going to take in a Chevy Chase movie, but it's too nice of weather, so ... I won't; I'll dodge that and go to a Chiefs game instead.

## Traffic Fatalities Decrease

*[A brief news report on national statistics for traffic fatalities]*

*News reporter*: Good news today on the nation's highways announced by Transportation Secretary, Andrew Card:

*Andrew Card*: The traffic fatality rate, expressed as number of deaths per 100 million miles of travel, is the commonly accepted barometer of how well we as a nation are doing in highway safety. We are now projecting, that the traffic fatality rate for 1992 will be 1.8 deaths, the lowest in history.

*News reporter*: That's 1.8 per 100 million miles traveled. That's down from 2.8 just ten years ago. The difference is about 22,000 lives a year.

## Augustus Does His Bit

### by *Bernard Shaw*

The Mayor's parlour in the Town Hall of Little Pifflington. Lord Augustus Highcastle, a distinguished member of the governing class, in the uniform of a colonel, and very well preserved at 45, is comfortably seated at a writing-table with his heels on it, reading *The Morning Post*. An elderly clerk with a short white beard and whiskers, and a very red nose, shuffles in.

*Augustus* (*hastily putting aside his paper and replacing his feet on the floor*):

    Hullo! Who are you?

*The Clerk*: The staff.

*Augustus*: You the staff! What do you mean, man?

*The Clerk*: What I say. There isn't anybody else.

*Augustus*: Tush! Where are the others?

*The Clerk*: At the front.

*Augustus*: Quite right. Most proper. Why aren't you at the front?

*The Clerk*: Over age. Fifty-seven.

*Augustus*: But you can still do your bit. Many an older man is in the G. R.'s, or volunteering for home defence.

*The Clerk*: I have volunteered.

*Augustus*: Then why are you not in uniform?

*The Clerk*: They said they wouldn't have me if I was given away with a pound of tea. Told me to go home and not be an old silly. (*A sense of unbearable wrong, till now only smouldering in him, bursts into flame.*) Young Bill Knight, that I took with me, got two and sevenpence. I got nothing. Is it justice? This country is going to the dogs, if you ask me.

*Augustus* (*rising indignantly*): I do not ask you, sir; and I will not allow you to say such things in my presence. Our statesmen are the greatest known to history. Our generals are invincible. Our army is the admiration of the world. (*Furiously*) How dare you tell me that the country is going to the dogs!

*The Clerk*: Why did they give young Bill Knight two and sevenpence, and not give me even my tram fare? Do you call that being great statesmen? As good as robbing me, I call it.

*Augustus*: That's enough. Leave the room. (*He sits down and takes up his pen, settling himself to work. The clerk shuffles to the door. Augustus adds with cold politeness.*) Send me the Secretary.

*The Clerk*: I am the Secretary. I can't leave the room and send myself to you at the same time, can I?

*Augustus*: Don't be insolent. Where is the gentleman I have been corresponding with: Mr. Horatio Floyd Beamish?

*The Clerk* (*returning and bowing*): Here. Me —

*Augustus*: You! Ridiculous! What right have you to call yourself by a pretentions name of that sort?

*The Clerk*: You may drop the Horatio Floyd. Beamish is good enough for me.

*Augustus*: Is there nobody else to take my instructions?

*The Clerk*: It's me or nobody.

*Augustus*: I addressed a meeting here last night — went straight to the platform from the train. I wrote to you that I should expect you to be present and report yourself. Why did you not do so?

*The Clerk*: The police wouldn't let me on the platform.

*Augustus*: Did you tell them who you were?

*The Clerk*: They knew who I was. That's why they wouldn't let me up.

*Augustus*: This is too silly for anything. This town wants waking up. I made the best recruiting speech I ever made in my life: and not a man joined.

*The Clerk*: What did you expect? You told them our gallant fellows are falling at the rate of a thousand a day in the big push. Dying for Little Pifflington, you say. Come and take their places, you say. That isn't the way to recruit.

*Augustus*: But I expressly told them their widows would have pensions.

*The Clerk*: I heard you. Would have been all right if it had been the widows you wanted to get round.

*Augustus* (*rising angrily*): This town is inhabited by cowards. I say it with a full sense of responsibility, cowards. They call themselves Englishmen; and they are afraid to fight. You are no patriots ... Go downstairs to your office and have that gas stove taken away and replaced by an ordinary grate. The Board of Trade has urged on me the necessity for economizing gas.

*The Clerk*: Our orders from the Minister of Munitions are to use gas instead of coal, because it saves material. Which is it to be?

*Augustus* (*bawling furiously at him*): Both! Don't criticize your orders: obey them. Yours not to reason why: yours but to do and die. That's war. (*Cooling down*) Have you anything else to say?

*The Clerk*: Yes, I want a rise.

*Augustus* (*reeling against the table in his horror*): A rise! Horatio Floyd Beamish: do you know that we are at war?

*The Clerk* (*feebly ironical*): I have noticed something about it in the papers. Heard you mention it once or twice, now I come to think of it.

*Augustus*: Our gallant fellows are dying in the trenches, and you want a rise!

*The Clerk*: What are they dying for? To keep me alive, isn't it? Well, what's the good of that if I'm dead of hunger by the time they come back?

*Augustus*: Everybody else is making sacrifices without a thought of self; and you —

*The Clerk*: Not half, they aren't. Where's the baker's sacrifice? Where's the coal merchant's? Where's the butcher's? Charging me double: that's how they sacrifice themselves. Well, I want to sacrifice myself that way too. Just double next Saturday, double and not a penny less; or no secretary for you. (*He stiffens himself shakily, and makes resolutely for the door.*)

*Augustus* (*looking after him contemptuously*): Go, miserable pro-German.

    (*The telephone rings.*)

*Augustus* (*taking up the telephone receiver*): Hallo ... Yes, who are you? Oh, Blueloo, is it? ... Yes. There's nobody in the room: fire away ... What? ... A spy ... A woman! ... Yes, I brought it down with me. Do you suppose I'm such a fool as to let it out of my hands? Why, it gives a list of all our anti-aircraft emplacements. The German would give a million for it — what? ... No. I haven't mentioned it to a soul. I mean that I haven't mentioned it to any Germans ... Pooh! Don't you be nervous, old chap. Good-bye.

*The Clerk* (*entering*): Are you engaged?

*Augustus*: What business is that of yours? However, if you will take the trouble to read the society papers for this week, you will see that I am engaged to the Honourable Lucy Popham, youngest daughter of —

*The Clerk*: That isn't what I mean. Can you see a female?

*Augustus*: Of course I can see a female as easily as a male. Do you suppose I'm blind?

*The Clerk*: You don't seem to follow me, somehow. There's a female downstairs: what you might call a lady. She wants to know can you see her if I let her up.

*Augustus*: Oh, you mean am I disengaged. Tell the lady I'm busy. (*The Clerk goes.*) Stop! Does she seem to be a person of consequence?

*The Clerk*: A regular marchioness, if you ask me.

*Augustus*: Hm! Beautiful, did you say?

*The Clerk*: A human chrysanthemum, sir, believe me.

*Augustus*: It will be extremely inconvenient for me to see her; but the country is in danger; and we must not consider our own comfort. Think how our gallant fellows are suffering in the trenches! Show her up. (*The Clerk goes out. Augustus produces a mirror and a comb from the drawer of his writing-table, and sits down before the mirror to put some touches to his toilet. The Clerk returns, showing in a very attractive lady, brilliantly dressed. Augustus hastily covers up his toilet apparatus with* The Morning Post, *and rises in an attitude of pompous condescension.*)

*The Clerk*: (*to Augustus*): Here she is. (*To the lady*) May I offer you a chair, lady? (*He places a chair at the writing-table opposite Augustus and steals out on tippoe.*)

*Augustus*: Be seated, madam.

*The Lady*: (*sitting down*): Are you Lord Augustus Highcastle?

*Augustus*: Madam, I am.

*The Lady*: (*with awe*): The great Lord Augustus?

*Augustus*: I should not dream of describing myself so, madam; but no doubt I have impressed my countrymen — and (*bowing gallantly*) may I say my countrywomen — as having some exceptional claims to their consideration.

*The Lady* (*emotionally*): What a beautiful voice you have!

*Augustus*: What you hear, madam, is the voice of my country.

*The Lady*: Ah, what we women admire in you is the man of action, the heroic warrior.

*Augustus* (*gloomily*): Madam, I beg! Please! My military exploits are not a pleasant subject.

*The Lady*: Oh, I know, I know. How shamefully you have been treated! What ingratitude! But the country is with you. The women are with you. Oh, do you think all our hearts did not throb and all our nerves thrill when we heard how you dashed at the German army single-handed and were cut off and made prisoner by the Huns?

*Augustus*: Yes, madam; and what was my reward? They said I had disobeyed orders ... I had my first taste of the ingratitude of my own country as I made my way back to our lines after the Germans let me go. A shot from our front trench struck me in the head. I still carry the flattened projectile as a trophy. Had it penetrated to the brain I might never have sat on another Royal Commission. Fortunately we have strong heads, we Highcastles. Nothing has ever penetrated to our brains.

*The Lady*: How thrilling! How simple! And how tragic! But you will forgive England? Remember: England! Forgive her!

*Augustus*: It will make no difference whatever to my services to my country. I am ever at my country's call. And now, madam, enough of my tragic personal history! You have called on business. What can I do for you?

*The Lady*: You have relatives at the Foreign Office, have you not?

*Augustus*: (*haughtily*): Madam: the Foreign Office is staffed by my relatives exclusively.

*The Lady*: Has the Foreign Office warned you that you are being pursued by a female spy who is determined to obtain possession of a certain list of gun emplacements —

*Augustus*: (*interrupting her*): All that is perfectly well known to this department, madam.

*The Lady*: Wait until you hear what I have come to tell you. Listen. This spy, this woman —

*Augustus*: (*all attention*): Yes?

*The Lady*: She is a German. A Hun ... And ... Well, she is an intimate friend of your brother at the War Office, Hungerford Highcastle: Blueloo, as you call him. Well, he has rashly let out to this woman that the list is in your possession. He forgot himself because he was in a rage at its being entrusted to you. Well ... She made a bet with him that she would come down here and obtain possession of that list and get clean away into the street with it.

*Augustus*: Good heavens! And you mean to tell me that Blueloo was such an idiot as to believe that she could succeed? Does he take me for a fool?

*The Lady*: Oh, impossible! He is jealous of your intellect. The bet is an insult to you ... And yet ... She may get the list after all. And if the German War Office gets the list — and she will copy it before she gives it back to Blueloo, you may depend on it — all is lost.

*Augustus*: (*lazily*): Well, I should not go as far as that. The German War Office is no better than any other War Office. I am not at all sure that this list of gun emplacements would receive the smallest attention. You see, there are always so many more important things to be attended to. Family matters and so on, you understand.

*The Lady*: Still, if a question were asked in the House of Commons —

*Augustus*: The great advantage of being at war, madam, is that nobody takes the slightest notice of the House of Commons.

*The Lady*: Then you think this list of gun emplacements doesn't matter!

*Augustus*: By no means, madam. It matters very much indeed. If this spy were to obtain possession of the list, Blueloo would tell the story at every dinner table in London; and —

*The Lady*: And you might lose your post. Of course.

*Augustus* (*amazed and indignant*): I lose my post! What are you dreaming about, madam? How could I possibly be spared? No; but I should be laughed at; and frankly, I don't like being laughed at.

*The Lady*: Of course not. Who does? It would never do. Oh, never.

*Augustus*: And now as a measure of security, I shall put the list in my pocket. (*He begins searching vainly from drawer to drawer in the writing-table.*) Where on earth —? That's very odd: I — (*He is interrupted by a knock at the door.*)

## A List of Available Listening Materials Recommended

1. 列辛斯基主编:《实况英语听力》,华东师范大学出版社,1996 年版。
2. 张民伦主编:《英语听力入门》(第 1—4 册),华东师范大学出版社,1999 年版。
3. Family Album, U.S.A.《走遍美国》,外语教学与研究出版社,1993 年版。
4. 何其莘主编:《英语初级听力学生用书》,外语教学与研究出版社,2002 年版。
5. 何其莘主编:《英语中级听力学生用书》,外语教学与研究出版社,2003 年版。
6. 何其莘主编:《英语高级听力学生用书》,外语教学与研究出版社,2003 年版。

# Appendix Ⅰ  Rules of Reading

## Ⅰ. Pronunciation of vowel letters in stressed syllables

### Vowel Letter A

| Types of Syllables | | Pronunciation | Sample Words |
|---|---|---|---|
| Open | Syllable | /eɪ/ | fate, wake, translate |
| Closed | Syllable | /æ/ | bag, that, pattern |
| -r | Syllable | /ɑː/ | card, large, carton |
| | | /ɔː/ | war, warn, ward |
| -re | Syllable | /eə/ | hare, stare, barehanded |

### Vowel Letter E

| Types of Syllables | | Pronunciation | Sample Words |
|---|---|---|---|
| Open | Syllable | /iː/ | me, these, metre, rebuild |
| Closed | Syllable | /e/ | bed, desk, remember |
| -r | Syllable | /ɜː/ | her, refer, jerk, certain |
| -re | Syllable | /ɪə/ | mere, here, severe |
| | | /eə/ | there, where |

Appendix I  Rules of Reading

## Vowel Letters I and Y

| Types of Syllables | | Pronunciation | Sample Words |
|---|---|---|---|
| Open | Syllable | /aɪ/ | I, nice, try, cycle |
| Closed | Syllable | /ɪ/ | ill, stick, dynasty, gym |
| -r | Syllable | /ɜː/ | bird, dirty, stir |
| -re | Syllable | /aɪə/ | fire, hire, tyre, require |

## Vowel Letter O

| Types of Syllables | | Pronunciation | Sample Words |
|---|---|---|---|
| Open | Syllable | /əʊ/ | photo, stone, total |
| Closed | Syllable | /ɒ/ | bottom, clock, spot |
| | | /ʌ/ | love, son, won |
| -r | Syllable | /ɔː/ | or, port, tortoise |
| | | /ɜː/ | word, work, world |
| -re | Syllable | /ɔː(r)/ | bore, more, before, store |

## Vowel Letter U

| Types of Syllables | | Pronunciation | Sample Words |
|---|---|---|---|
| Open | Syllable | /juː/ | mute, duty, use, music |
| | | /ɪ/ | busy |
| Closed | Syllable | /ʊ/ | put, full, butcher |
| | | /ʌ/ | cut, bud, luggage |
| -r | Syllable | /ɜː/ | nurse, fur, burden |
| -re | Syllable | /jʊə/ | cure, lure, pure |

## II. Pronunciation of vowel letters in unstressed syllables

| Vowel Letters | Pronunciation | Sample Words |
|---|---|---|
| a | /ə/ | address, appear, umbrella, human |
| a | /ɪ/ | manage, savage, village |
| a | /eɪ/ | celebrate, liberate, hibernate |
| e | /ə/ | excellent, open, student |
| e | /ɪ/ | basket, event, biggest, exam |
| i, y | /ɪ/ | important, visit, ability city, dirty, bicycle |
| i, y | /aɪ/ | exercise, paradise, pigsty, satisfy |
| o | /ə/ | polite, method, observe, pilot |
| u | /ɪ/ | minute |
| u | /ə/ | August, difficult, upon |
| u | /ju/ | particular, communist |
| u | /juː/ | attribute, execute |

## III. Pronunciation of combined letters

| Combined Letters | Pronunciation | Sample Words |
|---|---|---|
| ai, ay | /eɪ/ | main, rail, play, stay |
| ai, ay | /æ/ | plaid, plait |

续 表

| Combined Letters | Pronunciation | Sample Words |
|---|---|---|
| ai, ay | /ɪ/ | certain, mountain, holiday, portrait |
| | /e/ | said, says |
| air | /eə/ | chair, hair, pair |
| alf | /ɑːf/ | half, calf |
| all | /ɔːl/ | ball, hall, fall, small, tall |
| alm | /ɑːm/ | calm, palm |
| alk | /ɔːk/ | talk, chalk, walk |
| ance | /ɑːns/ | advance, dance, lance |
| anch | /ɑːntʃ/ | branch, stanch |
| ange | /eɪndʒ/ | change, danger, range |
| asp | /ɑːsp/ | grasp, clasp |
| ass | /ɑːs/ | class, grass, pass |
| ast | /ɑːst/ | fast, last, master, vast |
| ask | /ɑːsk/ | basket, task |
| ath | /ɑːθ/ | bath, path |
| au | /ɑː/ | aunt, draught |
| au, augh | /ɔː/ | author, audit, Austria, taught |
| aw | /ɔː/ | dawn, draw, paw, saw |
| ee | /iː/ | deed, feed, need, sleep, steel |
| ea | /iː/ | beat, leader, mean, seat |
| | /e/ | head, spread, sweat |
| | /eɪ/ | great, break |
| | /ɪə/ | idea, really, theatre |

续 表

| Combined Letters | Pronunciation | Sample Words |
|---|---|---|
| ear | /ɪə/ | fear, hear, near |
| | /eə/ | bear, pear, wear |
| | /ɜː/ | early, learn, heard |
| ear | /ɑː/ | heart, hearth |
| eer | /ɪə/ | deer, engineer, pioneer |
| ere | /ɪə/ | here, severe |
| | /eə/ | there, where |
| ei, ey | /iː/ | conceit, receive, receipt |
| | /eɪ/ | weigh, they |
| | /ɪ/ | money |
| | /aɪ/ | either, neither |
| eu, ew | /juː/ | feudal, pneumonia, few, news |
| ew | /uː/ | crew, flew, strew |
| eo | /iː/ | people |
| ia | /ə/ | special, social |
| ie | /iː/ | achieve, believe, field |
| | /aɪ/ | die, lie, tie |
| | /ɪə/ | experience, Soviet |
| ild | /aɪld/ | child, wild |
| ind | /aɪnd/ | find, kind, behind |
| io | /ɪə/ | million, period, union |
| iou | /ɪə/ | glorious, serious, furious |

续 表

| Combined Letters | Pronunciation | Sample Words |
|---|---|---|
| oa | /əʊ/ | coat, boat, float, road |
| oi, oy | /ɔɪ/ | oil, join, voice, boy, joy, voyage |
| old | /əʊld/ | bold, cold, fold, sold |
| oo | /uː/ | food, school, soon, too |
| oo | /ʊ/ | foot, book, good, stood |
| oo | /ʌ/ | blood, flood |
| oor | /ɔː/ | door, floor |
| oor | /ʊə/ | poor, moor |
| ost | /əʊst/ | post, most, host |
| ost | /ɒst/ | cost, lost, frost |
| ou | /aʊ/ | about, cloudy, shout |
| ou | /ʌ/ | country, young |
| ou | /uː/ | group, wound |
| our | /ɔː/ | course, four, pour |
| our | /ə/ | colour, labour |
| our | /aʊə/ | hour, flour |
| ough | /ɔː/ | bought, fought, thought |
| ough | /əʊ/ | though, dough |
| ous | /əs/ | dangerous, famous, infectious |
| ow | /aʊ/ | cow, down, how |
| ow | /əʊ/ | grow, show, window |
| ower | /aʊə/ | flower, powerful, tower |

| Combined Letters | Pronunciation | Sample Words |
|---|---|---|
| ui | /ɪ/ | build, biscuit |
| ure | /ə/ | figure |
| tion | /ʃən/ | liberation, nation, revolution |
| ssion | /ʃən/ | aggression, oppression, profession |
| stion | /stʃən/ | combustion, question, suggestion |
| sion | /ʒən/ | decision, invasion, revision |
| ture | /tʃə/ | culture, nature, picture |

## Ⅳ. Pronunciation of consonant letters

| Consonant Letters | Pronunciation | Sample Words |
|---|---|---|
| b | /b/ | break, rubber, job |
| | / /(= mute) | bomb, comb, tomb |
| c | /k/ | carry, clinic, subject |
| | /s/ | certain, cite, rice |
| | /ʃ/ | ocean, special, social |
| cc | /ks/ | accept, accident, success |
| | /k/ | according, account, acclaim |
| ch | /tʃ/ | beach, church, reach |
| | /k/ | character, chemistry, Christmas |
| ck | /k/ | back, cock, lock, rock |

续 表

| Combined Letters | Pronunciation | Sample Words |
|---|---|---|
| d | /d/ | did, decide, ridden |
|   | / / | handsome, Wednesday |
| dge | /dʒ/ | bridge, judge, lodge |
| f | /f/ | fly, suffer, leaf |
| g | /g/ | goat, flag, recognize |
| ge | /dʒ/ | change, large, George |
| gh | /f/ | cough, laugh, enough |
|   | / / | high, sigh, weigh |
| gn | /n/ | design, gnat, gnaw |
| gu, gue | /g/ | guard, guide, league |
| h | /h/ | harm, head, behind |
|   | / / | hour, honour, forehead |
| j | /dʒ/ | joy, journey, subject |
| k | /k/ | book, kill, kiss |
| kn | /n/ | knee, knock, knowledge |
| l | /l/, /ɫ/ | blue, roll, world |
| le | /ɫ/ | circle, apple, little |
| m | /m/ | moon, room, lamp |
| mn | /m/ | autumn, column, solemn |
| n | /n/ | naughty, niece, fan |
| ng | /ŋ/ | hang, sing, song |
|   | /ŋg/ | English |

续　表

| Combined Letters | Pronunciation | Sample Words |
|---|---|---|
| nk | /ŋk/ | bank, think, thank |
| p | /p/ | pepper, supper, map |
| | / / | cupboard, psychology |
| ph | /f/ | photo, telegraph, telephone |
| q | /k/ | Qatar, Iraq |
| qu | /kw/ | quiet, quilt, require |
| r | /r/ | rest, around, grind |
| rh | /r/ | rhyme, rhetoric |
| s | /s/ | sister, miss, transact |
| | /z/ | easy, has, husband, always |
| | /ʃ/ | Asia, Russia |
| | / / | island, isle |
| sc | /s/ | scene, science |
| sh | /ʃ/ | fresh, show, shelf |
| t | /t/ | time, butter, split |
| | / / | often, soften, whistle |
| th | /θ/ | birth, thank, width |
| | /ð/ | breathe, there, southern |
| ti | /ʃ/ | initial, patient |
| v | /v/ | advance, move, vivid |
| w | /w/ | reward, warm, with |
| | / / | answer, sword, two |

续 表

| Combined Letters | Pronunciation | Sample Words |
|---|---|---|
| wh | /w/, /hw/ | when, white, why |
| wh | /h/ | whole, who, whose |
| wr | /r/ | write, wrong, wrinkle |
| x | /ks/ | box, text, exercise |
| | /gz/ | example, examination |
| xc | /ks/ | except, excellent |
| y | /j/ | yes, yet, yield |
| z | /z/ | zoo, citizen, buzz |

# Appendix II  British English and American English[1] in Comparison

| BrE | AmE | Example | BrE | AmE |
|---|---|---|---|---|
| /ɪ/ | /ɪ/ | effect | /ɪˈfekt/ | /ɪˈfekt/ |
| /e/ | /ɛ/ | many | /ˈmeni/ | /ˈmɛni/ |
| /ɑː/ | /æ/[2] | class | /klɑːs/ | /klæs/ |
| | /ɑ(r)/ | car | /kɑː/ | /kɑr/ |
| /ɔ/ | /ɑ/ | hot | /hɔt/ | /hɑt/ |
| /ɔː/ | /ɔ/ | bought | /bɔːt/ | /bɔt/ |
| | /ɔr/ | door | /dɔː/ | /dɔr/ |
| /ʌ/ | /ʌ/ | month | /mʌnθ/ | /mʌnθ/ |
| /ɜː/ | /ər/ | fur | /fɜː/ | /fər/ |
| /ə/ | /ər/ | river | /ˈrɪvə/ | /ˈrɪvər/ |
| /eɪ/ | /e/ | late | /leɪt/ | /let/ |
| /əʊ/ | /o/ | old | /əʊld/ | /old/ |
| /ɪə/ | /ɪr/ | here | /hɪə/ | /hɪr/ |
| /ɛə/ | /ɛr/ | chair | /tʃeə/ | /tʃɛr/ |
| /ʊə/ | /ʊr/ | poor | /pʊə/ | /pʊr/ |
| /aɪə/ | /aɪr/ | fire | /ˈfaɪə/ | /faɪr/ |
| /aʊə/ | /aʊr/ | tower | /ˈtaʊə/ | /taʊr/ |
| /juː/ | /u/ | new | /njuː/ | /nu/ |
| /w/ | /hw/[3] | when | /wen/ | /hwen/ |
| /t/ | /d/[4] | city | /ˈsɪtɪ/ | /ˈsɪdɪ/ |

Notes:
  [1] K.K. symbols here as a staple.
  [2] before /s/, /f/, /n/, /l/ and /θ/.
  [3] pronunciation of the letter combination wh.
  [4] after the stressed syllabe, between one vowel and the other, or between one vowel and one voiced consonant.

# Appendix III  Glossary

| | | | |
|---|---|---|---|
| accent | 口音;重音 | body | 调身 |
| advanced RP | 先进标准发音 | broad transcription | 宽式标音 |
| affricate | 破擦音 | broken tune | 断调,句中上升 |
| air stream | 气流 | cardinal vowel | 基本元音 |
| allophone | 音位变体 | central vowel | 中元音,央元音 |
| alveolar | 齿龈音 | centring diphthong | 合口双元音, |
| alveolar fricative | 齿龈摩擦音 | | 央二合元音 |
| alveolar lateral | 齿龈边音 | "Chest-abdomen breathing" method | |
| alveolar nasal | 齿龈鼻音 | | 胸腹式联合呼吸法 |
| alveolar plosive | 齿龈爆破音 | chest cavity | 胸腔 |
| amplitude | 振幅 | clear /l/ | 清晰/l/ |
| articulation | 发音 | closed syllable | 闭音节 |
| articulator | 发音器官 | closing diphthong | 合口双元音, |
| aspirated | 送气的 | | 闭二合元音 |
| assimilation | 同化 | closing stage | 成阻阶段 |
| back of tongue | 舌后 | colloquial speech | 口语 |
| back vowel | 后元音 | complex tone-group | 复杂声调群 |
| beat | 节拍 | compound tone-group | 复合声调群 |
| bilabial | 双唇音 | connected speech | 连贯言语 |
| bilabial nasal | 双唇鼻音 | conservative RP | 保守"标准发音" |
| bilabial plosive | 双唇爆破音 | consonant | 辅音 |
| labial-velar semi-vowel | 双唇软腭半元音 | consonant cluster | 辅音连缀 |
| blade | 舌端,舌叶 | contextual assimilation | 语境同化 |

| | | | |
|---|---|---|---|
| contextual elision | 语境省音 | front of tongue | 前舌,舌前部 |
| dark /ɫ/ | 模糊/ɫ/ | front vowel | 前元音 |
| delivery | 说话方式 | full stress | 完全重音 |
| dental | 齿音 | general phonetics | 普通语音学 |
| dental fricative | 齿摩擦音 | general RP | 普通"标准发音" |
| descriptive phonetics | 描写语音学 | glide | 滑音 |
| dialect | 方言 | glottal fricative | 喉摩擦音 |
| diaphragm | 隔膜 | glottis | 声门 |
| diphthong | 双元音,二合元音 | graphic notation | 图解标示法 |
| disyllable | 双音节词 | half close vowel | 半闭元音 |
| distinctive feature | 区别性特征 | half open vowel | 半开元音 |
| ditty | 小曲 | hard palate | 硬腭 |
| double stress | 双重音 | head | 调头 |
| elision | 省音 | high fall | 高降调 |
| end stress | 词末重音 | high falling head | 高降调头 |
| enuciation | 清晰发音 | high falling nucleus | 高降调核 |
| epiglottis | 会厌 | high level tone | 高平调 |
| exhale | 呼出 | high prehead | 高调冠 |
| experimental phonetics | 实验语音学 | high rise | 高升调 |
| falling tone | 降调 | high rising head | 高升调头 |
| falling-rising tone | 降升调 | historical assimilation | 历史同化 |
| familiar colloquial style | 非正式口语体 | historical elision | 历史省音 |
| fixed stress | 固定重音 | historical phonetics | 历史语音学 |
| foot | 音步 | hold stage | 持阻阶段 |
| formal colloquial style | 正式的口语体 | incomplete plosion | 不完全爆破 |
| free variant | 自由变体 | incomplete plosive | 不完全爆破音 |
| frequency | 频率 | informal speech | 非正式口语 |
| fricative | 摩擦音 | inhale | 吸入 |
| friction | 摩擦 | initial stress | 词首重音 |

| | | | |
|---|---|---|---|
| intensity | 音强 | lower lip | 下唇 |
| International Phonetic Alphabet | 国际音标 | lower teeth | 下齿 |
| intonation | 语调 | manner of articulation | 发音方法 |
| intrusive /r/ | 外加音/r/ | melody | 旋律 |
| kinetic tone | 动调 | monophthong | 单元音 |
| labio-dental | 唇齿音 | monophthongisation | 单元音化 |
| labio-dental fricative | 唇齿摩擦音 | monosyllable | 单音节词 |
| larynx | 喉(腔) | narrow diphthong | 窄双元音, |
| lateral plosion | 边爆破,舌侧爆破 | | 窄二合元音 |
| length | 音长 | narrow transcription | 严式音标 |
| letter | 字母 | nasal | 鼻音 |
| level tone | 平调 | nasal cavity | 鼻腔 |
| liaison | 连音,连读 | nasal consonant | 鼻辅音 |
| linking of words | 词的连读 | nasal passage | 鼻通道 |
| linking /r/ | 连接音/r/ | nasal plosion | 鼻爆破 |
| lip | 唇 | nasal twang | 鼻化音 |
| lip position | 唇位 | nasalisation | 鼻化 |
| lip-rounding | 圆唇化 | nasalised | 鼻化的 |
| liquid | 流音 | nasalised vowel | 鼻化元音 |
| long vowel | 长元音 | neutral position | 中性唇位 |
| loudness | 音响,响度 | neutral vowel | 中性元音 |
| low fall | 低降调 | normal body | 正常调身,正常调体 |
| low level head | 低平调头 | normal head | 正常调头 |
| low level stress | 低平重音 | normal prehead | 正常调冠 |
| low level tone | 低平调 | normal voice range | 正常讲话音域 |
| low rise | 低升调 | notation system | 标调体系 |
| low rising head | 低升调头 | nuclear tone | 调核 |
| low rising prehead | 低升调冠 | nucleus | 调核 |
| | | nucleus placement | 调核位置 |

| | | | |
|---|---|---|---|
| nucleus-syllable | 调核音节 | plosive | 爆破音 |
| obstruction | 阻碍 | polysyllable | 多音节 |
| open rounded position | 开口圆唇位 | post-alveolar | 后齿龈音 |
| open syllable | 开音节 | prehead | 调冠 |
| open vowel | 开元音 | pretonic segment | 调核前音段 |
| oral | 口(腔)音 | primary stress | 主重音 |
| oral cavity | 口腔 | prominent syllable | 突出音节 |
| ordinary assimilation | 普通同化 | pronunciation | 发音,读音 |
| organs of speech | 发音器官 | prosodic feature | 韵律特征 |
| palatal | 腭音 | pure vowel | 单元音,纯元音 |
| palato-alveolar | 腭齿龈音 | quality | 音质 |
| palato-alveolar affricate | 硬腭齿龈破擦音 | quantity | 音长 |
| palato-alveolar fricative | 硬腭齿龈摩擦音 | rapid colloquial speech | 快速口语 |
| partial stress | 部分重音 | Received Pronunciation (RP) | "标准发音" |
| pattern | 模式 | | |
| pharynx | 咽腔 | release | 除阻 |
| phoneme | 音位 | release stage | 除阻阶段 |
| phonemic contrast | 音位对比 | resonance chamber | 共鸣腔 |
| phonemic transcription | 音位(宽式)标音 | retroflex | 卷舌的 |
| phonetic context | 语音环境 | rhythm | 节奏 |
| phonetic realization | 语音体现 | rhythm group | 节奏群 |
| phonetic symbol | (窄式)标音 | rhythm pattern | 节奏模式 |
| phonetic transcription | 语音标音 | rhythmic stress | 节奏重音 |
| phonetic unit | 语音单位 | rising tone | 升调 |
| phonetics | 语音学 | rising-falling tone | 升-降调 |
| pitch | 音调,音高 | rising-falling-rising tone | 升-降-升调 |
| place (point) of articulation | 发音部位 | root | 舌根 |
| | | rounded | 圆唇的 |
| | | rounded vowel | 圆唇元音 |

| | | | |
|---|---|---|---|
| secondary stress | 次重音 | sound | 声音, 语音 |
| semi-vowel | 半元音 | sound change | 音变 |
| sentence stress | 句重音 | sound pattern | 语音模式 |
| short vowel | 短元音 | sound system | 语音系统 |
| sibilant | 咝音 | speech | 言语 |
| silent | 不发音的 | speech communication | 言语交际 |
| simple tone-group | 简单声调群 | syllabic | 音节的 |
| soft palate | 软腭 | syllable | 音节 |
| sonorant | 响亮音 | | |

# Main References

[1] Roger Kingdon. *The Groundwork of English Intonation* [M]. London: Longmans, 1958.

[2] Roger Kingdon. *English Intonation Practice* [M]. London: Longmans, 1958.

[3] Daniel Jones. *An Outline of English Phonetics*. 9th edition [M]. Cambridge: W. Heffer & Sons Ltd., 1962.

[4] A.C. Gimson. *An Introduction to the Pronunciation of English* [M]. London: Edward Arnold Publishers Ltd., 1972.

[5] J.D. O'Connor and G.F. Arnold. *Intonation of Colloquial English* [M]. London: Longman Group Ltd., 1961.

[6] W. Stannard Allen. *Living English Speech* [M]. London: Longmans, Green & Co., 1954.

[7] Ann Baker. *Tree or Three* [M]. Cambridge: Cambridge University Press, 1982.

[8] Ann Baker. *Ship or Sheep* [M]. Cambridge: Cambridge University Press, 1977.

[9] Daniel Jones, A. C. Gimson. *Everyman's English Pronouncing Dictionary*. 13th edition ed [M]. London: Dent & Sons, 1981.

[10] 许天福等.现代英语语音学[M].西安:陕西人民出版社出版,1985.

[11] 周考成.英语语音学引论[M].上海:上海外语教育出版社,1984.

[12] 桂灿昆.美国英语应用语音学[M].上海:上海外语教育出版社,1986.

[13] 陈文达.英语语调的结构与功能[M].上海:上海外语教育出版社,1987.

[14] 张凤桐.英国英语语音学和音系学[M].成都:四川大学出版社,1996.

[15] 刘明霞、王勇等.英语听力与口语教程[M].济南:山东友谊社,1995.

[16] 张凤桐.英国英语语音学和音系学(第三版)[M].成都:四川大学出版社,2002.

[17] Alan Cruttenden. *Gimson's Pronunciation of English*:吉姆森英语语音教程, sixth edition [M]. 北京:外语教学与研究出版社;London: Edward Arnold

Publishers Ltd.,2001年.

[18] General Received Pronunciation of British English:现代英语标准发音[M].成都:四川大学出版社,2004.